INSPIRE / PLAN / DISCOVER / EXPERIENCE

VENICE
AND THE VENETO

VENICE
AND THE VENETO

CONTENTS

DISCOVER 6

EXPERIENCE 70

NEED TO KNOW 250

Left: Colourful buildings of Burano
Previous page: Church of Santa Maria della Salute
Front cover: Canal Grande with gondolas and Rialto
Bridge at sunset, Venice

DISCOVER

WELCOME TO
VENICE AND
THE VENETO

Incredible architecture and astounding collections of priceless art. Charming *campi* (squares) and a magical maze of canals. Rolling hills, medieval towns and meandering wine routes. Whatever your dream trip entails, this DK Eyewitness travel guide is the perfect travel companion.

① Squero di San Trovaso, a gondola boatyard in Venice.

② Sunset in the Dolomites.

③ Colourful houses line the canal on the island of Burano.

④ An outdoor restaurant on the Grand Canal.

Venice is a labyrinthine, dreamlike city. It is also an extremely fragile one, with rising waters and mass tourism endangering its fragile microcosm. Yet you can still enjoy its many wonders without leaving a trace: so put down your selfie stick and respect the city and its inhabitants. Sure, Venice is home to myriad must-see sights: its ostentatious basilica, opulent palazzos and acclaimed art galleries such as the Accademia and Peggy Guggenheim Collection. But this tiny city also squeezes an immense store of heritage into its hidden corners and quieter *sestieri* (neighbourhoods), where you'll find yourself far from the bustle of San Marco.

Beyond Venice, the Veneto mainland is a mix of bucolic valleys and medieval towns. Verona offers archaeological history and a generous dose of romance, while fun-loving Padua is home to an ancient university and a chapel full of Giotto's frescoes. Beyond, vine-yards stripe the hillsides, and the picturesque pastel-hued towns that hug the shores of Lake Garda offer relaxation and endless watery pursuits, while to the north stand the precipitous peaks of the Dolomites.

Although a relatively small area, Venice and the Veneto can be overwhelming. We've broken the region down into easily navigable chapters, with detailed itineraries, expert local knowledge and comprehensive maps to help plan your perfect trip. Whether you're staying for a weekend, a week or longer, this DK Eyewitness travel guide will ensure that you see the very best the area has to offer. Enjoy the book, and enjoy Venice and the Veneto.

REASONS TO LOVE
VENICE AND THE VENETO

Superb Roman ruins, romantic towns, lakeside adventures and delectable cuisine, all washed down with a glass of one of the region's sublime wines; the reasons to love this corner of Italy go far beyond the sights of Venice.

1 CARNEVALE

Let your imagination run riot at this world-famous event. Here, you can join revellers taking to the streets of Venice dressed in costumes ranging from the Baroque to the bizarre.

PADUA 2

Roman ruins and magnificent squares: the city of Padua has plenty to offer. Head to the Cappella degli Scrovegni *(p205)* to see Giotto's sublime frescoes dance across the interior walls.

3 ART OLD AND NEW IN DORSODURO

From the Accademia *(p140)* to the Punta della Dogana *(p146)*, Venice is home to art of all ages. Feeling inspired? Find a shady spot, sharpen your pencil and get sketching.

VALPOLICELLA VINES 4

Explore lush Valpolicella vineyards *(p238)* and indulge in some of Italy's finest wines. If red is not to your taste, nearby Soave *(p234)* is on hand with refreshing white, amber or rosé varieties.

CRUISING DOWN VENICE'S GRAND CANAL 5

One of the world's greatest waterways. Take the slow boat, vaporetto No. 1, and stand on deck for views of lacy façades and life in a city in which everything happens by water.

LOCAL CUISINE 6

Venetian cuisine is centred around the sea. Head to the Rialto Market *(p107)* to admire the day's catch before feasting on seafood at one of the city's many fine restaurants.

THE DOLOMITES 7

These majestic mountains are the ideal setting for getting back to nature. Paraglide from their precipitous peaks or ramble through ancient alpine forest while inhaling that fresh mountain air.

CYCLING AROUND LAKE GARDA 8

Miles of dramatic shoreline, a "floating" bike route and pretty stop-off points like Sirmione make Lake Garda (p230) an ideal spot for an adventure on two wheels.

9 FAIR VERONA

See a breathtaking show at the world's third-largest Roman Arena (p223) or embrace the romance as you peer over the balcony of Juliet's House (p225) in search of your Romeo.

10 HIDDEN VENICE

In Venice, hidden treasures, quiet *campi* and green spaces reward those who dare leave the tourist bubble. Go further still to discover the humble charm of Venice's lagoon islands.

PIAZZA SAN MARCO 11

Venice's must-see square contains so many incredible sights that it takes time to let its beauty sink in. Grab a coffee and let San Marco's colonnaded grandeur wash over you.

ARCHITECTURAL WONDERS 12

Balanced on thousands of tree trunks, Venice is a marvel. Within it, intricate façades line canals, gilded domes glitter in the sun, and the spires of grand basilicas pierce the heavens.

0 metres 500
0 yards 500
N ↑

Canale delle Sacche

Canale delle

Canale delle

Madonna dell'Orto

Campo del Ghetto Nuovo

CANNAREGIO
p154

Gesuiti

Campo San Geremia

TRONCHETTO

Ca' d'Oro

SAN POLO AND SANTA CROCE
p98

Campo della Peschiera

Ponte di Rialto

Santa Maria Gloriosa dei Frari

Campo San Polo

Canal Grande

SAN MARCO
p72

SANTA MARTA

Campo Santa Margherita

Campo Sant' Angelo

La Fenice

Piazza San Marco

Campo Santo Stefano

DORSODURO
p136

Accademia

Santa Maria della Salute

Canal della Giudecca

GIUDECCA

EXPLORE
VENICE AND
THE VENETO

This guide divides the six *sestieri* of Venice and the surrounding Veneto region into nine colour-coded sightseeing areas, as shown on this map. Find out more about each area on the following pages.

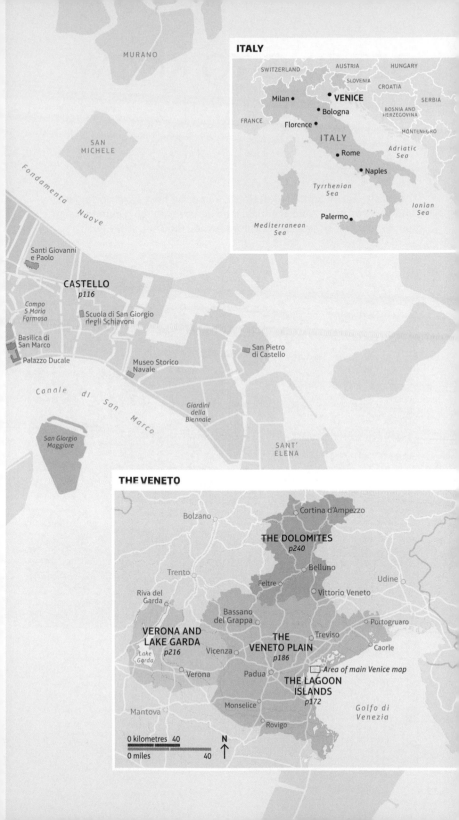

MURANO

SWITZERLAND   AUSTRIA   HUNGARY

SLOVENIA

Milan ●   ● **VENICE**

CROATIA

● Bologna   SERBIA

FRANCE   Florence ●   BOSNIA AND
HERZEGOVINA

ITALY   MONTENEGRO

*Adriatic
Sea*

● Rome

*Tyrrhenian
Sea*   ● Naples

*Ionian
Sea*

Palermo ●

*Mediterranean
Sea*

SAN
MICHELE

Fondamenta Nuove

Santi Giovanni
e Paolo

CASTELLO
p116

*Campo
S Maria
Formosa*

Scuola di San Giorgio
degli Schiavoni

Basilica di
San Marco

Palazzo Ducale

Museo Storico
Navale

San Pietro
di Castello

Canale di San Marco

*Giardini
della
Biennale*

*San Giorgio
Maggiore*

SANT'
ELENA

THE VENETO

Bolzano   ○ Cortina d'Ampezzo

THE DOLOMITES
p240

Trento ○   ● Belluno

Riva del
Garda ○   Feltre ○   ○ Vittorio Veneto   Udine ○

Bassano
del Grappa ○   ○ Portogruaro

**VERONA AND
LAKE GARDA**
p216   Vicenza ○   **THE
VENETO PLAIN**
p186   Treviso ○

*Lake
Garda*   Caorle ○

○ Verona   Padua ○   □ *Area of main Venice map*

Monselice ○   **THE LAGOON
ISLANDS**
p172   *Golfo di
Venezia*

Mantova ○

○ Rovigo

0 kilometres   40
0 miles   40

N
↑

GETTING TO KNOW
VENICE AND
THE VENETO

The focal point of Venice is San Marco, home to a host of world-famous landmarks in one square alone. Beyond Venice's lagoon, wondrous sights, spectacular landscapes and world-renowned food and wine await.

PAGE 72

SAN MARCO

This *sestiere* is considered the hub of Venice, and its eponymously named Piazza sees tourists and the district's wealthy residents sipping coffee side by side surrounded by some of the city's most famous monuments. Designer shops and jewellery stores line the grand streets of Via XXII Marzo, while towards Rialto the establishments become a little less exclusive.

Best for
Sightseeing and shopping

Home to
Basilica di San Marco, Palazzo Ducale, Museo Correr

Experience
Climbing the campanile (bell tower) at San Giorgio for sweeping views of the city

PAGE 98

SAN POLO AND SANTA CROCE

Home to artisan workshops and traditional taverns, these two districts retain a local feel. Thanks to the Architecture Institute, it's also a popular haunt for students, particularly in the bustling Tolentini area. During the day charming squares teem with gleeful children after the school day is done. At night the area becomes a natural meeting spot and local bars and trattorias spill on to the streets that surround the Rialto Market.

Best for
Gastronomy and art

Home to
Rialto Market, Basilica dei Frari, Scuola Grande di San Rocco

Experience
A post-market cichetto and aperitivo at a market bar

PAGE 116

CASTELLO

Once home to the workers of the Arsenale shipyard, Castello retains a grittier ambience than much of Venice. It is also quieter the further east you go and contains plenty of peaceful squares and green spaces – increasingly rare in the busy San Marco area. Via Garibaldi is a popular local shopping street by day and a lively watering hole in the evening, and the neighbourhood is home to some of the best restaurants in town. In May, Castello springs to life with the Biennale art and architecture international exhibitions.

Best for
Exploring quiet squares with a local feel

Home to
San Zaccaria, Arsenale, Santi Giovanni e Paolo

Experience
Get off the beaten track and discover seldom-visited spots like San Francesco della Vigna and San Pietro di Castello

→

PAGE 136

DORSODURO

Occupying a prime piece of Grand Canal real estate, arty Dorsoduro is home to the city's best galleries, contemporary art hubs and the venerable Ca' Foscari University. As a result, there's a lively social scene here that centres around Campo Santa Margherita in the evening. The sunny, south-facing Zattere promenade is also a popular drinking spot for Venetians and offers peaceful walks in the winter.

Best for
Art galleries, student haunts and late-night bars

Home to
The Accademia, Peggy Guggenheim Collection, Ca' Rezzonico

Experience
Watching the sunset from the Zattere

PAGE 154

CANNAREGIO

Cannaregio is something of a paradox, being both a residential neighbourhood and a major tourist thoroughfare, due to the Strada Nuova (the long street that leads from the train station to the Rialto Bridge). Settled in the Renaissance, it is less of a maze than the medieval Rialto and is characterized by a series of long, straight canals which are lined with bars and restaurants – the greatest concentration in the city. It's also the location of the Ghetto, a tiny island which was once the home of Venice's Jewish community.

Best for
Restaurants, bars and quiet green areas

Home to
The Ghetto, Santa Maria dei Miracoli, Ca' d'Oro

Experience
A guided tour of the Ghetto's historic synagogues

PAGE 172

THE LAGOON ISLANDS

Quieter than the city centre, the lagoon islands offer respite from the crowds. Each island has its own distinctive charm. Artsy Murano is known for its artisan glass-making, while Burano is famed for its candy-coloured houses. Then there's the isolated reverance of Torcello and the meditative atmosphere of San Francesco del Deserto, both of which feel a world away from fun-loving Lido, where Venetians flock in the summer months. With beaches in no short supply here, it's the perfect spot to enjoy an aperitivo accompanied by sunset views of Venice.

Best for
Beaches, early Venetian settlements and Palladian churches

Home to
Redentore Church, Torcello, Murano, San Lazzaro degli Armeni

Experience
A tour of Murano's Museo del Vetro and see glass-blowers at work

→

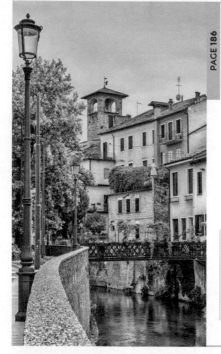

PAGE 186

THE VENETO PLAIN

Far from the hustle and bustle of Venice, the towns and cities of the Veneto plain are often overlooked by tourists. But they hide some under-appreciated examples of art and architecture, including Giotto's stunning Cappella degli Scrovegni and Palladio's Teatro Olimpico. From the rough and ready streets of Mestre, Venice's mainland offshoot, to the lush, rolling hills of Conegliano on the Strada del Prosecco Route, via historic Roman spa towns, this is a fascinating area worthy of an extended visit.

Best for
Archaeological sites, thermal spas and superlative art

Home to
Cappella degli Scrovegni, Teatro Olimpico, Villa Rotonda, Basilica di Sant'Antonio

Experience
A boat trip down the Brenta Canal

PAGE 216

VERONA AND LAKE GARDA

Set astride the Adige river, Verona has long been an important crossroads and preserves more ruins (including its own arena) than anywhere outside Rome. To the north, hills rise up into the wine country of Soave and Valpolicella before dropping down to the sunny shores of Garda, Italy's largest lake. Here you'll find pretty lakeside towns and plenty of outdoor pursuits.

Best for
Roman ruins, world-class wines and outdoor pursuits

Home to
Verona Arena, San Zeno Maggiore, Sirmione

Experience
Circumnavigating the perimeter of Lake Garda by bicycle

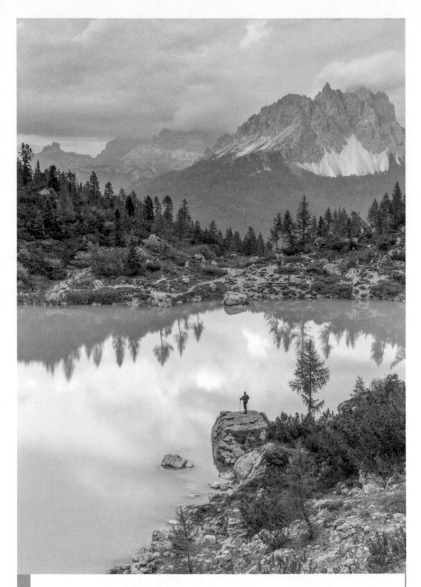

THE DOLOMITES

Just two hours from Venice, the Dolomites offer a respite from city life and the chance to reconnect with nature. The sculpted pink peaks and wildflower-filled valleys of this mountain range form a unique ecosystem – making it a designated UNESCO World Heritage Site. Opportunities for adventurous sporting activities abound, but easy walks along gentle trails mean that this region can be enjoyed by visitors of all abilities. And of course, even here among the wood-panelled mountain chalets, it is possible to find wonderful architecture and works of art.

Best for
Breathtaking views, natural wonders, historical sites

Home to
Cortina d'Ampezzo, Titian's Birthplace, Belluno

Experience
Taking a chair lift to reach some of Italy's highest points

←

① San Marco Campanile.

② Colourful Burano.

③ The view from the San Giorgio Maggiore bell tower.

④ Visitors exploring the Accademia galleries.

3 DAYS
in Venice

Day 1

Morning Get up bright and early to reach Piazza San Marco *(p76)* before the crowds descend. Take a moment to enjoy the grand surroundings before entering the Basilica di San Marco *(p78)*, then head straight next door to the Palazzo Ducale *(p82)* to admire its magnificent combination of Byzantine, Gothic and Renaissance architecture and explore its dingy dungeons. Refuel with a coffee at the historic Caffè Florian *(p89)*. From here, a short stroll through the busy streets will lead you to the Rialto Bridge *(p107)*. Cross over to get to the famous Rialto Pescheria, also an excellent lunch spot.

Afternoon Make for the San Polo district and the Scuola Grande di San Rocco *(p104)* with its remarkable cycle of Tintorettos. For a further dose of unforgettable art, head straight to the towering church of Santa Maria Gloriosa dei Frari *(p102)*, which includes two works by Titian and a beautiful triptych by Giovanni Bellini.

Evening Sip on tasty cocktails at Il Mercante *(www.ilmercantevenezia.com)*, overlooking the Frari, before sampling some delicious Venetian cuisine at one of San Polo's local restaurants *(p113)*.

Day 2

Morning Start the day in the serene *sestiere* of Cannaregio at the magnificent Ca' d'Oro *(p158)*, one of the city's most atmospheric Gothic palaces. It's a short walk to the Ghetto *(p160)* for a tour of the area's synagogues and fascinating museum. There are plenty of great low-key restaurants for lunch *(p165)*.

Afternoon Heading north will take you to the Fondamente Nuove *(p166)*, where you can catch a boat to the islands of the northern lagoon. First stop is Murano *(p179)* for a glass tour, while not forgetting to visit the 12th-century Basilica dei Santi Maria e Donato. Hop back on the vaporetto to the picture-perfect island of Burano. Buy some famous S-shaped biscuits to munch on as you walk around the brightly painted houses. From here, another boat ride will bring you to the verdant hush of Torcello *(p176)*, the peaceful location of Venice's first basilica clad with shimmering golden mosaics.

Evening Enjoy a delightful dinner at Torcello's family-run Locanda Cipriani *(www.locandacipriani.com)* before catching the last boat back to the city.

Day 3

Morning Dorsoduro is all about art. Start with the Accademia *(p140)* and walk among the works of acclaimed Venetian artists before a short walk east to the Peggy Guggenheim Collection *(p144)* for some modern greats. Stop here for lunch on the terrace overlooking the pretty garden.

Afternoon Take the water bus from Zattere to the island of San Giorgio Maggiore *(p94)*. The climb up the bell tower is rewarded with stunning views of the city. From here take a boat to Riva degli Schiavoni *(p124)* and walk along the waterfront to the imposing entrance of the Arsenale *(p130)*.

Evening Treat yourself to a drink on Danieli's rooftop terrace *(p122)* followed by dinner in one of Castello's charming neighbourhood restaurants *(p125)*.

$\rightarrow$

1 Turquoise waters
surround Sirmione.

2 Statue of Juliet in Verona.

3 Taking in the view from Col
Druscie, Cortina d'Ampezzo.

4 Strolling through the
picturesque Via del Municipio.

5 DAYS
in Veneto

Day 1

Morning Starting in Padua *(p198)*, marvel at Giotto's lapis-blue frescoes in the Cappella degli Scrovegni *(p205)* before exploring the ancient university grounds Refuel at the famous Caffè Pedrocchi.

Afternoon Chug down the Brenta Canal *(p202)* on a half-day cruise, and admire the Palladian villas that line the banks.

Evening Back in Padua, rub shoulders with the locals at one of the city's many excellent drinking holes.

Day 2

Morning From Padua, wind your way along the Valpolicella Wine Route *(p238)*, stopping for lunch at one of the many hilltop *cantine* (tasting rooms).

Afternoon Visit picturesque Peschiera on the shores of Lake Garda *(p230)*, and hire a bike to explore at your own pace.

Evening Head to neighbouring Sirmione for fabulous views before embarking on a sunset dinner cruise.

Day 3

Morning Next stop Verona *(p220)*, where you can experience ancient Rome at one of the oldest Roman amphitheatres in the world – the Arena. Grab lunch at one of the many restaurants offering local fare.

Afternoon Walk to Casa di Giulietta and channel your inner Shakespeare as you pen your own love letter with the letter-writing Juliet Club *(p225)*.

Evening Keep the romance alive with a pre-dinner stroll around the lush grounds of Giardino Giusti, then crack open a bottle of Valpolicella while sampling the region's famous *bollito misto*, which consists of mixed boiled meats. Ristorante Greppia serves the best in town *(www. ristorantegreppia.it)*.

Day 4

Morning This morning is all about Andrea Palladio in nearby Vicenza *(p190)*. Visit the illusionary Teatro Olimpico and fall for its trompe-l'œil trickery. After a morning of theatrics, lunch on traditional dishes in the heart of town.

Afternoon Head north to the glamorous mountain resort of Cortina d'Ampezzo *(p246)*, set against the dramatic backdrop of the Dolomites. Hike or take a cable car up the Tofana for breathtaking views.

Evening Bunk down at one of the *rifugios* (refuges) on Col Gallina or Averau and watch the mountains turn pink at sunset before searching for constellations in the crystalline night sky.

Day 5

Morning Explore the winding streets of Belluno *(p247)* and admire its magnificent Duomo and Palazzo dei Rettori.

Afternoon Continuing south, stop off at the medieval town of Treviso *(p210)*. Stroll along its willow-lined canals and ancient city walls before visiting the church and chapterhouse of San Nicolò to admire their 14th-century frescoes.

Evening Treat yourself to a reservation at Toni del Spin *(Via Inferiore 7)* and delight in local dishes such as *faraona alla peverada*, guinea fowl served with pomegranate sauce. Spend the night in the luxury Hotel Relais Monaco *(www. relaismonaco.it)* to end your trip in style.

Foundations of a Floating City

Venice is home to a dizzying array of architectural styles and influences, but don't lose sight of the bigger picture. Venetian builders made the impossible a reality by creating structures that appear to float on water. The secret lies beneath the surface: layers of Istrian stone laid on top of closely packed wooden piles plunged deep into the ground. As you stroll through the city's ancient streets and navigate its intricate web of canals, be sure to take the time to appreciate this sheer feat of medieval engineering.

$\longrightarrow$

Laying the foundations for the new Campanile on Piazza San Marco, 1905

VENICE AND THE VENETO FOR
ASTOUNDING ARCHITECTURE

Featuring architectural styles from Medieval to Neo-Classical, Venice's ostentatious palaces and opulent churches are testament to the Republic's powerful reign. Also amid these Renaissance and Baroque beauties are some surprising contemporary additions.

Building Bridges

This extraordinary city is made up of dozens of islets, crisscrossed by 391 bridges. Most visitors make a beeline for the Bridge of Sighs or the Rialto Bridge, which legend says was only finished after a deal with the Devil in 1592. But Venice's other bridges are also worth seeking out: turf wars were fought on the aptly named Ponte dei Pugni (Bridge of Fists), while the impressive Ponte della Libertà was built to connect the city to the mainland.

$\longrightarrow$

A gondolier passing under the Rialto Bridge at sunset

Palazzos and Palladio

Admire the many palazzos that line Venice's Grand Canal *(p54)* for the price of a vaporetto ticket. Among them is the Venetian Gothic-style Ca' d'Oro *(p158)*, named for its once shimmering, now faded, gold-leaf exterior. But lavish façades and ostentatious design are prevalent across the Veneto. Tread the boards at Andrea Palladio's Teatro Olimpico *(p194)* in Vicenza, a city defined by his signature style, or admire the many fine Palladian villas that line the Brenta Canal *(p202)*.

→

Ornate façade of Ca' d'Oro overlooking the Grand Canal

The World in One City

For centuries, Venice linked the Adriatic and the Mediterranean seas to Constantinople, Egypt and Syria, and the influence of these lands can be clearly seen in the city's architecture. Take a tour of the Eastern Med as you explore the ground-floor arcades and open galleries of the Fondaco dei Turchi *(p112)*; gaze upon the crenellations of the Palazzo Ducale *(p82)* and the domes of the Basilica di San Marco *(p78)* that were modelled on Constantinople's Church of the Holy Apostles; and admire the unmistakably Islamic tilework of many a canalside palazzo.

←

One of the magnificent colonnades that surround the Palazzo Ducale in Venice

Modern Marvels

Contemporary structures abound in Venice. Architects such as Tadao Ando, who designed the Teatrino di Palazzo Grassi *(p93)*, Santiago Calatrava, designer of metallic Ponte della Costituzione, and Carlo Scarpa who realized many of the Veneto's most iconic buildings, all left their mark on this ancient city. The Architecture Biennale showcases cutting-edge architectural works from around the globe. For anyone with a penchant for contemporary design and the latest architectural innovations, it's well worth a visit.

→

Bamboo Stalactite by VTN Architects at the Venice Architecture Biennale 2018

THE BUILDING OF VENICE

Venice is built on a patchwork of 117 low-lying islands in the middle of a lagoon. To overcome these extremely challenging conditions, early Venetian builders developed a unique construction technique, building with impermeable stone supported by larchwood rafts and timber piles. This method proved effective and most Venetian buildings are remarkably robust, many having stood for at least 400 years. By 1500 the city had taken on much of its present shape.

THE CAMPO

The fabric of Venice is made up of scores of self-contained island communities, linked by bridges to their neighbouring islands. Each has its own well, church and bell tower, centred on a *campo* (square), once the main focus of commercial life. Palazzos, with shops and warehouses at ground-floor level, border the *campo* which is connected to workshops and more humble houses by a maze of side alleys.

↑ Campo San Boldo with its central water well in San Polo

This square, with its central wellhead and businesslike landward façades, is typical of Medieval Venetian construction. Ornate decoration on buildings was usually reserved for the canalfront façades.

Campaniles often lean because of slight movement in the subsoil.

Water grilles

Rainwater was channelled through grilles into a clay-lined cistern filled with sand.

Istrian stone, a type of marble, was used to create damp-proof foundations.

Closely packed piles do not rot in the waterlogged subsoil because there is no free oxygen, vital for microbes that cause decay.

THE CAMPANILE FOUNDATIONS

When the Campanile *(p86)* collapsed in 1902, the ancient pilings underpinning the landmark were found to be in excellent condition, after 1,000 years in the ground. All buildings in Venice are supported on oak and pine piles, harvested in the forests of the northern Veneto and shipped downriver to the Venetian Lagoon. Once driven through the lagoon subsoil, they create an immensely strong yet flexible foundation. Even so, there is a limit to how much weight they can carry. The Campanile, its height having been increased several times, simply grew too tall and collapsed. When the tower was rebuilt, larger timber foundations were used.

Campo Santa Maria Mater Domini, a typical medieval square

Did You Know?

Despite wooden piles supporting the city for centuries, Venice is sinking by 2mm every year.

Palazzo roofs, laid with light, glazed tiles, had gutters to channel rainwater to the well.

Façades were built of lightweight rose-coloured bricks, sometimes left bare, sometimes weatherproofed with plaster.

Bridges were often privately owned and tolls were charged for their use. Originally, none had railings, creating a night-time hazard for the unwary in the dark streets.

Oak or pine piles were driven into the ground before building work began. They rest on the solid caranto ((compressed clay and sand) layer at the bottom of the lagoon.

Caranto is compacted clay and sand in alternate layers, which provides a stable base for building.

Rowing Around

Set your own pace by taking a stand-up rowing lesson, Venetian style. Explore the city's labyrinthine canals and waterways in the historic centre and beyond with a qualified rower from Row Venice (*www.rowvenice.org*). There's even a *cichetto* tour, during which you row to two bars for sustenance, but watch out for low-hanging bridges.

←

Rowing on one of the city's quiet side canals with Row Venice

VENICE AND THE VENETO
ON THE WATER

Whether delivering goods, moving house or simply going to work, much of Venetian life takes place on the water. A gondola or vaporetto ride is a must, but rowing and sailing on the lagoon are also popular pursuits, while the Brenta Canal and Lake Garda offer watery adventures in the heart of the Veneto.

Vaporetto Adventures

Vaporettos, or water buses, chug up and down the Grand Canal and around Venice's lagoon. For tourists, a single ride is €7.50, but there are plenty of travelcard options that make it a convenient and inexpensive way to see the city. Boats fill up fast, especially during Carnevale, but nothing beats cruising along the Grand Canal *(p54)* after a hard day's sightseeing.

> **ACQUA ALTA**
>
> *Acqua alta* (high water) affects the city from October to March, and is caused by a combination of low atmospheric pressure, strong sirocco winds from the south and high tides. As warning sirens fill the air people head for higher ground, shopkeepers rush to put up protective barriers and street sweepers lay out duckboards. Piazza San Marco is among the most vulnerable spots.

Gondolas Galore

In their heyday gondolas numbered over 10,000. Now around 400 survive. Pick-up points are dotted around the city, with prices set by a consortium. A 40-minute ride for up to six passengers costs €80 (€120 after 7pm). On a tight budget? Take a *traghetto*, a gondola ferry that crosses the Grand Canal, a bargain at just €2. If you still haven't had your fill, head over to the Squero di San Trovaso *(p150)* to see where gondolas are made and repaired.

→

A *traghetto* transporting people across the Grand Canal

Setting Sail

Have an experienced sailor take you out on the lagoon in a traditional *bragozzo (www.il bragozzo.it)*, or set sail on the wind-ruffled waters of Lake Garda *(p230)*. Check out Sailing Du Lac Multisports Centre in Riva del Garda *(www.sailingdulac.com)*.

←

Sailing around the lagoon on a traditional Venetian *bragozzo*

Boating Beyond the City

Venice's patrician families escaped to country estates on the Brenta Canal *(p202)* in summer. Why not do the same? The Il Burchiello cruise *(www.ilburchiello.it)* includes lunch, villa visits and a night in Padua. Lake Garda *(p230)* offers boat trips to Isola Del Garda and around Sirmione *(www.gardatours.com)*.

↑ Neo-Gothic villa on Isola del Garda, Lake Garda's only island

↑ An early morning vaporetto cruise down the Grand Canal

Market Fresh

The Rialto's stalls teem with fresh fish and local produce, but markets and *fruttivendolo* (greengrocers) can be found all over Venice. Santa Marta has a weekly market every Monday, Lido has one on Tuesdays, and Sacca Fisola on Fridays. Floating fruit and veg vendors are moored in Campo San Barnaba and on Via Garibaldi.

> **INSIDER TIP**
> **Cheap Eats**
>
> *Cichetti*, Venetian small plates, can be a satisfying meal without breaking the bank. Head to a local bar before lunch or early evening for the best selection.

Tempting displays brim with fresh produce at Rialto Market ↑

VENICE AND THE VENETO FOR
FOOD LOVERS

While not as renowned for its cuisine as other regions, the Veneto has some delicious local dishes and, with the Adriatic on its doorstep, seafood takes pride of place. In Venice, Michelin-starred restaurants beckon, but even a humble *cichetto* washed down with local wine is a culinary treat.

Fine Dining

Tourist traps aside, Venice is home to some exemplary fine dining restaurants, some with a Michelin star. The charming Osteria Da Fiore *(www.ristorantedafiore.com)* has long been serving classic Venetian dishes with a twist, while at Il Ridotto *(www.ilridotto.com)*, behind Piazza San Marco, fish plays a big part on the menu. Don't miss bucolic Venissa *(www.venissa.it)* – it has a thriving kitchen garden and produces Venice's only white wine, the rare Dorona.

←

Delicately spiced poached pears with gelato at Da Fiore

TOP 5 **VENETIAN DELICACIES**

Seppie in Nero
Cuttlefish cooked perfectly in its own ink.

Sarde in Saor
Fried sardines marinated with onions and currants.

Pasta e Fagioli
A humble dish of pasta and borlotti beans.

Fegato alla Veneziana
Calf's liver, sautéed onions and polenta.

Bigoli in Salsa
Buckwheat pasta served with anchovies.

Cooking Courses

At the Acquolina cooking school *(www. acquolina.com)*, Marika Contaldo offers classes in her wonderful Lido home. Courses include trips to Rialto Market and half-day taster sessions. Further afield, at Villa Quaranta *(www.villaquaranta.com)* in Verona, master the art of making fresh pasta while sipping on a glass of Valpolicella.

↑ Learn how to make fresh pasta from scratch

THE HISTORY OF VENETIAN CUISINE

Venice made its fortune on trade and one of its most important goods was locally produced salt. Used to preserve fish and other food, salt was essential for sailors going on long journeys. Rice was introduced by the Arabs via Spain and has been grown in the Veneto for centuries, while spices such as nutmeg and cloves entered Venetian cuisine via its trade links with the East.

↑ Gelato, the perfect accompaniment to a canalside stroll

Something Sweet

Tiramisù is one of the Veneto's most famous creations: literally meaning "pick me up", you can find this calorific mix of coffee, mascarpone and sponge in most restaurants. Be sure to swing by Gelateria Alaska *(Calle Larga dei Bari)* where they serve unusual flavours like ginger, rose, or orange and rocket; plus, their chocolate ice cream is the best in town.

La Strada del Prosecco

Linking Conegliano and the rolling hills of Valdobbiadene, the Prosecco wine route *(p213)* will take you to some of the best prosecco *cantine* (tasting rooms) in Italy. Start in pretty Follina *(p210)* and head to Cantine Gregoletto *(www.gregoletto.it)* for a wine tasting. It's well worth staying over night so you can indulge in the fizz.

→

Sunset over the vine-striped hills of Valdobbiadene

VENICE AND THE VENETO
BY THE GLASS

Aperitivo time. As the day slides into evening, outdoor tables become packed with both locals and tourists, and a palpable energy fills the air. Of course, spritz is the traditional tipple, though cocktails are becoming more popular, but in a region heaving with vineyards, wine will always be the drink of choice.

Did You Know?

The word "spritz" comes from the Austro-Hungarian practice of adding a splash of soda water to Italian wines.

Venetian Spirit

While classic cocktails are popular in many a Venetian bar, the spritz is ubiquitous all over Italy, and nowhere more so than in the Veneto, where it originated in the 1800s. The three most popular versions are made with Select, Aperol or Campari. A spritz is made by mixing the bitter of your choice with prosecco and soda water (or sparkling water) and is usually served with an olive and an orange slice. After a hard day's sightseeing, sit back and enjoy a glass before dinner as you watch the sun set in a pretty piazza.

Wine Tasting on the Valpolicella Route

Heading west from Verona to Lake Garda is the famous Valpolicella Wine Route *(p238)*. Many winemakers also run B&Bs, so you can spend more than a day in the bucolic hills. The Valpolicella Consortium *(www.consorziovalpoli cella.it)* has a handy app to guide you around the many producers. Veronality *(www. veronality.com)* offers an Amarone tour, or for a fully immersive experience, stay on the wine-producing farm Agriturismo San Mattia *(www.agriturismo sanmattia)* just outside Verona.

← Enjoying the elegant and aromatic flavours of Amarone Classico in a Valpolicella vineyard

Distinctively orange Aperol spritz and *cichetti* by the canal
↓

Venetian City Vines

Venice was once full of vineyards, but few exist today. Venissa *(www.venissa.it)*, on Mazzorbo, produces rare and pricey wines from the local Dorona di Venezia grape. The Laguna nel Bicchiere association *(www. lagunanelbicchiere.it)* teaches the history of viticulture in Venice and promotes wines from the city's few remaining vineyards.

↑ Sampling local wines at Venissa on the island of Mazzorbo, Venice

Get Creative

The Scuola Internazionale di Grafica *(www.scuolagrafica. it)* hosts workshops in everything from printing to calligraphy. Create your own Renaissance masterpiece at the Bottega del Tintoretto *(www.tintorettovenezia.it)* next door to the master's home. Or try out etching, woodcutting and silk-screen printing at DoppioFondo *(www.doppiofondo.org)*.

←

Typesetting and printing at the Scuola Internazionale di Grafica

VENICE AND THE VENETO FOR
ART LOVERS

Venice contains incredible artworks in its galleries, churches and museums. Gothic sculpture, Renaissance painters or conceptual art, you'll find them here in spades. Yet the city itself is described as a work of art, so if museums aren't your thing, simply enjoy the colour and beauty to be found on every street.

BEHIND THE MASK

Today, Venetian masks are synonymous with Carnevale, but in the past the city's denizens could spend much of the year in disguise. The simple white *bauta* was the most popular choice. The Plague Doctor mask with its distinctive hooked beak was once worn as protection against the plague, its beak tightly packed with herbs. Other masks stem from *commedia dell'arte*, with Harlequin a perennial favourite.

Make Your Own Mask

Fancy having a go at making your own Venetian mask? It's great fun and gives you an insight into the complex techniques behind the finished product. One of the best mask shops in town is Ca' Macana *(www.camacana.com)*, which runs classes for large groups and individuals. Over two hours, learn the history of mask-making before decorating your own.

→

An artisan decorating a mask with vibrant colours in his Venice workshop

↑ Piet Mondrian's *Composition No. 1*, at the Peggy Guggenheim

Museums and Galleries

Venice's Accademia *(p140)* houses masterpieces by artists like Bellini, Carpaccio and Titian, while the Museo Correr *(p88)* in Procuratie Nuove presents the city's history and its greatest artists. For a modern twist, explore Palazzo Grassi *(p93)* and Punta della Dogana *(p146)*, hosting temporary exhibitions of contemporary artists, while the Peggy Guggenheim Collection *(p144)* is a treasure trove of modern art. In Padua, appreciate Giotto's frescoes in the Cappella degli Scrovegni *(p205)*, and in Verona, savour Italian modernists at the Galleria d'Arte Moderna Achille Forti *(p225)*.

🔍 HIDDEN GEM
Palazzo Cini

Between the Accademia and the Peggy Guggenheim Collection, the often overlooked Palazzo Cini is packed with artistic treasures by the likes of Botticelli, Giotti and Piero della Francesca.

Immersive Experiences

Who said art should be enjoyed from a distance? Next to the main building, the Teatrino Palazzo Grassi *(p93)* hosts all manner of weird and wonderful performances, from live concerts and experimental soundscapes to video screenings and lectures. During the Art Bienniale *(p48)* Venice comes alive with art showcases and exciting interactive exhibits in venues across town.

↑ Music performance at Palazzo Grassi, and *(inset)* Set Up music and dance at Punta della Dogana

Beloved Bookshops

Libreria Marco Polo *(www.libreriamarcopolo. com)* is Venice's most beloved independent bookshop. Its flagship store is on Campo Santa Margherita but it has also opened the first bookstore on the Giudecca *(p180)*. Both branches contain books in English and host literary evenings. Quirky Libreria Acqua Alta *(p127)* has a staircase made of books and cats sleeping in boats piled high with well-thumbed volumes. If it's art books you are after, Libreria Bertoni *(www.bertonilibri.com)* has an excellent range of exhibition catalogues, monographs and discount coffee-table tomes.

→

Colourful chaos in Venice's quirky Libreria Acqua Alta

VENICE AND THE VENETO FOR
BOOKWORMS

The Serenissima was a 15th-century printing powerhouse, producing more books than anywhere else. As such, Venice has spawned more than its fair share of stellar writers, and inspired many more. With a famous literary festival and bookshops galore, the region is a literary paradise.

TOP 4 NOVELS SET IN VENICE

The Aspern Papers (1888)
Henry James's novella is based on the letters between P B Shelley and his wife's stepsister.

Death in Venice (1912)
Thomas Mann's story of obsession was made into a film in 1971.

Don't Look Now (1973)
Daphne du Maurier's chilling short story will make you wary of children in red coats.

The Comfort of Strangers (1981)
Unnamed Venice is the setting for this twisted novel by Ian McEwan.

Literary Luminaries

Carlo Goldoni greatly impacted Italian theatre. His Casa di Goldoni *(p109)* allows fans to witness his living space. A Venetian womanizer, Casanova's memoir, *Story of My Life*, provided a glimpse into 18th-century life. Explore further at the Casanova Museum *(www.casanovamuseum.com)*. Venice's obscure 16th-17th-century female writers, Veronica Franco, Sara Coppia Sullam and Barbara Strozzi, penned proto-feminist texts and music.

Tiepolo's *Minuet* (1756), inspired by Goldoni's *Commedia dell'arte* ↑

Lovely Libraries

As you'd expect of a city famous for printing, Venice has some impressive libraries, none more so than the Biblioteca Nazionale Marciana *(p87)*. Founded in 1537 and housing over 750,000 volumes, it also contains Fra Mauro's famous map of the world and works by Titian and Veronese. Ca' Foscari University's Cultural Flow Zone *(www.unive.it)* hosts exhibitions, workshops and events. The Fondazione Querini Stampalia *(p125)* has one of the best-stocked libraries in town. Take a guided tour of its sumptuous rooms, or you can apply for your own card to enter independently.

←

Fra Mauro's 1450 map of the world is housed in the Biblioteca Nazionale Marciana

CONTEMPORARY AUTHORS

Besides writers from around the world, including American author Donna Leon who attained global recognition for her Commissario Brunetti detective series based in the city, Venice has produced plenty of home-grown talent of its own. Perhaps the most famous Venetian contemporary author is Tiziano Scarpa, thanks to his hugely successful *Venice is a Fish*. He also won the prestigious Premio Strega in 2009 for his novel *Stabat Mater*, which tells the story of an orphaned girl who learns the violin under Antonio Vivaldi. Enrico Palandri, renowned for novels like *Ages Apart* and *The Other Evening*, resided in London before coming back to his hometown.

Literary Festivals

Incroci di Civiltà *(www.unive.it)* is organized by Venice's Ca' Foscari University and brings together high-calibre authors from around the world. Past participants have included Jonathan Coe and Ian McEwan. Meanwhile, Verona celebrates all things Shakespeare every April, with talks, guided walks and performances *(www.casashakespeare.it)*.

↑ Celebrated Chinese writer Su Tong speaking at the Incroci di Civiltà book festival 2019

Classical Concerts

Opportunities to attend live classical concerts abound in Venice, where many deconsecrated churches house orchestras. The Venice Music Project *(www.venicemusic project.it)* performs in St George's Anglican Church, San Vidal hosts the Interpreti Veneziani and La Pietà *(p123)* is home to the talented Virtuosi Italiani.

←

Venice Music Project performing at St George's Anglican Church

VENICE AND THE VENETO FOR
MUSIC LOVERS

Birthplace of Vivaldi and Luigi Nono and much loved by both Wagner and Stravinsky, Venice is where opera began. Classical music and opera are still performed all over town, and intimate venues offer a contemporary line-up. Meanwhile, Padua and Verona host big-name artists in super-size venues.

A Night at the Opera

The resplendent Teatro La Fenice *(p92)* offers a variety of opera and classical performances. Teatro Malibran *(p169)* – a 900-seat theatre built in 1677 by the Grimani brothers – works alongside La Fenice and hosts events throughout the year. Once the site of gladiatorial combat, Verona Arena *(p223)* is a magnificent venue for open-air opera. Performances take place from June to September with world-class performers.

> **INSIDER TIP**
> ### Fenice Tickets
>
> Tickets can be pricey. For a discount, ask at the Fenice ticket office for seats with restricted views. The experience is just as breathtaking.

Music Festivals

The Venezia Jazz Festival (*www.venetojazz.com*) is held in venues around the city throughout July, while the Biennale hosts a contemporary music festival every autumn (*www.labiennale.org*). Also in autumn, Veneto Concertante is a series of classical concerts held in historic locations throughout the Veneto.

→

Jack Savoretti performing at the Venezia Jazz Festival

Live and Loud!

Verona's Arena *(p223)* is a spectacular place to see big-name performers. But smaller venues are championing live music in Venice too. Charming Paradiso Perduto *(Fondamenta della Misericordia)*, Osteria Da Filo *(Santacroce 1539)* and the Venice Jazz Club *(Dorsoduro 3102)* keep contemporary music alive in the city.

←

Famous Italian singer Zucchero wows fans at Verona Arena

Musical Greats

Born in Castello, Vivaldi's baptism records take pride of place in the church of San Giovanni in Bragora *(p129)*. Mozart and Wagner were frequent visitors to the city; visit the Wagner Museum in Venice Casino *(www.casinovenezia.it)*. Other big names include Stravinsky and Venetian avant-garde composer Luigi Nono.

↑ Performance of *Turandot* in Venice's most famous opera house, La Fenice

→

Painting of composer and violinist Antonio Vivaldi dated 1723

Pedal Power

The Veneto is cycling-obsessed, producing many a world-class cyclist. Due for completion in 2026, Lake Garda's new floating cycle path hugs 140 km (86 miles) of shoreline. With the option to substitute tougher sections with a boat ride, even less energetic cyclists can participate. For something a tad more energetic, why not try some Giro d'Italia climbs *(www.dolomitemountains.com)*.

←

Taking in spectacular scenery by bike, near Cortina d'Ampezzo

VENICE AND THE VENETO FOR
THE GREAT OUTDOORS

With miles of sandy beaches on the Adriatic, dramatic mountain ranges to the north and rolling countryside in between – not to mention the largest lake in Italy – Venice and the Veneto offer ample opportunities for outdoor activities that will get your heart racing and your adrenaline pumping.

Hiking in the Veneto

Whether it's rolling hills, flat wetland or dramatic peaks, the Veneto is ideal hiking territory. Walk from the centre of Vicenza up Monte Berico on part of the 80-km (50-mile) Montegalda-Tonezzo del Cimone route *(www. camminiveneti.it)*. Malcesine *(p232)*, nestled between Lake Garda and the surrounding mountains, is an excellent base from which to explore the area's many scenic trails.

Take to the Skies

For a bird's-eye view of the Dolomites, take to the skies with a trained paraglider *(www.iflytandem.net)*. These tandem flights run in summer and winter, and offer jaw-dropping vistas of knife-edge peaks and plummetting valleys. If that sounds like too much work, hop aboard a hot-air balloon *(www.mongolfiera.net)* and be swept up and away over the undulating Veneto hills and plains.

↑ Hot-air balloons over the little church of St Johann in Ranui

Majestic Mountains

In summer, hiking and climbing are popular activities in the dramatic Dolomites. The more adventurous can try the *vie ferrate* – routes equipped with cables and fixed anchors to help climbers reach lofty peaks. In winter, take to the pistes: all the major slopes have skiing and snowboarding schools.

← A climber on an exposed *via ferrata* in the Dolomites

City Activities

Venice's Lido might have a leisurely vibe, but it is actually action packed. There's a gorgeous golf club *(www.circologolfvenezia.it)* on its southern tip, while just steps from the beach lies Tennis Club Del Moro *(www.tennisclubcadelmoro. com)* with both clay and synthetic grass courts.

→ Sunseekers escape the city in favour of relaxing on sandy Lido beach

↑ Hikers rest up at Rifugio Vicenza in the Dolomites

Green Spaces

Sant'Elena, Giardini and the Giardinetti Reali are the best-known public parks in Venice, but there are many more. Parco Savorgnan is a green oasis just off Campo San Geremia. It has a children's playground and plenty of quiet spots for a picnic or a snooze. Further north is Parco Groggia, which has its own theatre. Giardini Papadopoli is a verdant haven next to Piazzale Roma where kids can let off steam. On the Lido's southern tip is the Alberoni "oasis", with wooded walks and a cycle path.

←

Giardinetti Reali on
Riva degli Schiavoni, just
off Piazza San Marco

VENICE AND THE VENETO FOR
PEACE AND QUIET

Around 20 million people flock to Venice annually, and the crowds can be overwhelming. Veer off the main drag and venture beyond the centre to find plenty of quiet corners, idyllic villas, green spaces and hidden gems that offer welcome respite from the bustling tourist hot spots.

Island Escapes

Venice's lagoon islands feel a world away from the packed city centre. Sample the local flavours of Sant'Erasmo, known as Venice's kitchen island, or wander the cloistered monastery and serene grounds of tiny San Francesco del Deserto *(p180)* for a contemplative visit.

→

An aerial view of the
island of San Francesco
del Deserto

HIDDEN GEM
Be Amazed
The Borges Labyrinth is a stunning maze made from boxwood plants. Tours are led by the Giorgio Cini Foundation *(www.visitcini.com)*.

Seeking Inspiration

Many renowned writers, poets and thinkers have found inspiration in Venice's quiet places. English poet Lord Byron spent several years on San Lazzaro degli Armeni *(p183)*, where he sought inspiration and learned Armenian. Petrarch, a poet and scholar, settled in Arquà *(www.arquapetrarca.com)*, which he described as "rich of green vegetation and full of peace".

→

Colourful bulidings reflect the sun in Gardone Riviera

Venice's Serene Sestieri

In quiet Castello and Cannaregio, treasures await those who venture off the beaten track. Independent boutiques and quirky shops line quiet streets and family-run *osterie* serve delicious dishes at, believe it or not, reasonable prices. Here you will find the real Venice.

←

Tree-lined Viale IV Novembre next to Parco delle Rimembranza in Castello

Rural Retreats

Idyllic villas and tranquil escapes abound in the Veneto. In Follina, the gorgeous 14th-century Hotel Villa Abbazia *(www.hotelabbazia.it)* offers elegant luxury in the foothills of the Italian Alps, and Parco Giardino Sigurtà *(p226)* in Valeggio sul Mincio, is a gardener's paradise.

→

Leafy Parco Giardino Sigurtà, a peaceful haven just outside Verona

Go Locavore

Support local business by shopping at local greengrocers, fishmongers and markets. The I & S stall at Santa Marta market (on Monday mornings) sells organic fruit and vegetables from Sant'Erasmo and has a delightful farm shop in Cannaregio *(www.iesfarm.it)*. The Natura Sì healthfood store *(www.naturasi.it)* satisfies all your eco-friendly desires, while Osteria Zanze XVI *(www.zanze.it)* meticulously sources local produce to create zero-kilometre cuisine.

$\rightarrow$

Lemon trees and fresh produce for sale at a Venetian street market

SAVE VENICE!

Mass tourism, pollution, rising water levels and wave-induced erosion are just some of the issues that Venice has to contend with. A number of charities, grassroots movements and environmental scientists are searching for solutions to safeguard this most precious of cities. Here's how you can help.

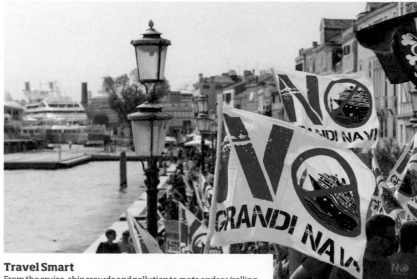

Travel Smart

From the cruise-ship crowds and pollution to *moto ondoso* (rolling seas) and the destructive wave action caused by motorboats, the city is under strain. Consider your transport options carefully to limit your impact, and opt for public transport whenever possible. Cruise ships are a particularly contentious issue. Deemed a threat to the lagoon ecosystem, large cruise ships (weighing over 25,000 tonnes) were banned from entering the Giudecca Canal in 2021.

↑ No Grandi Navi campaign for a ban on cruise ships entering the lagoon

Shop Local

Whether you want to pick up some Murano glassware, a Venetian mask for Carnevale or some quirky souvenirs to take home, always try to buy the genuine article from a local vendor rather than an imported fake. Check out Gilberto Penzo's model boats *(www.veniceboats.com)*, try on Gondola-shaped shoes at Giovanna Zanella's workshop *(www. giovannazanella.com)*, or venture under the Rialto arches, where Daniele and Stefano Attombri *(www. attombri.com)* fashion antique Murano beads into stunning necklaces.

←

An artisan carefully moulding molten glass into the shape of a horse at a Murano factory

TOP 6 EASY WAYS TO REDUCE YOUR IMPACT

Bring Your Own Bottle
Tap water is drinkable; top up at fountains.

Picnic Politely
Choose your spot wisely; don't sit on bridges or doorsteps.

Respect Local Life
Allow Venetians to go about their business and respect their space.

Follow Rubbish Rules
Be sure to put litter in the correct bins and recycle responsibly.

Avoid Rush Hour
Steer clear of public transport at busy times.

Say No to Plastic
Carry a shopper and avoid plastic bags.

PRESERVING THE CITY

There are multiple organizations working to protect Venetian heritage as well as its fauna and flora. The largest is Save Venice, whose dedicated team restores architecture and artworks, funded by the generosity of wealthy benefactors.

Get Your Hands Dirty

There are plenty of ways to get involved during your stay. Venice Calls *(www. venicecalls.com)* runs regular graffiti elimination days, as well as canal dredging and beach cleaning. The WWF *(www.wwf.it)* runs fun workshops, nature walks and rubbish collecting parties around the Alberoni dunes on the Lido. Further afield, dust off your binoculars and head to the Po Delta Park *(www. parcodeltapo.org)* to help count birds in one of the area's largest wetlands.

↑ A volunteer painting over unsightly graffiti on a city wall

A YEAR IN
VENICE AND THE VENETO

JANUARY

New Year's Day, Venice Lido (1 Jan). Hardy bathers plunge into the Venetian Lagoon to mark the beginning of a new year.

△ **La Regata delle Befane** (6 Jan). Coinciding with Epiphany, competitors dress as witches, and give children stockings full of presents.

FEBRUARY

△ **Carnevale** (10 days up to Lent). This festival is celebrated across the region, with the most extravagant pageants, concerts and balls.

Verona in Love Festival (week of 14 Feb). A week of romancing, poetry and love-themed festivity in the city of Shakespeare's star-crossed lovers, Romeo and Juliet.

MAY

Primavera del Prosecco (May–Jun). The Prosecco Spring Festival features wine tastings and vineyard tours along the Strade del Prosecco from Conegliano to Valdobbiadene.

△ **La Sensa** (1st Sun after Ascension). A symbolic marriage ceremony between Venice and the sea, with boat races and street celebrations.

JUNE

△ **Venice Biennale** (Jun–Nov). The world's biggest contemporary art show takes place in odd-numbered years. In even-numbered years, the city hosts the Biennale d'Architettura.

Vogalonga (2nd Sun after Ascension). Hundreds of boats partake in the 32-km (20-mile) "Long Row" from Palazzo Ducale to Burano and back.

SEPTEMBER

Regata Storica (1st Sunday). Venice's favourite regatta recalls the arrival of the Queen of Cyprus in 1489, with a costumed pageant on the Grand Canal.

△ **Venice Glass Week** (2nd week). Displays, demonstrations and celebrations of all things glass in Venice, Murano and Mestre.

OCTOBER

Feast of the Must (1st Sunday). Parties celebrate the completion of the harvest in Sant'Erasmo, with barefoot dancers pressing grapes the traditional way.

△ **Venice Marathon** (last Sun). Eight thousand runners take to the streets for the city's annual international marathon.

MARCH

△ **Benedizione del Fuoco**
(Maundy Thursday). The start of Easter is
marked with the "Blessing of the Fire" in the
Basilica di San Marco.
Arte Laguna Prize *(all month)*. A renowned
international contemporary art competition
showcasing works in the Arsenale.

APRIL

△ **Su e Zo per i Ponti** *(1st Sunday)*. A 12-km
(7.5-mile) charity fun run through streets of
Venice and up and down the city's 45 bridges.
Festa di San Marco *(25 Apr)*. Venice's patron saint
is honoured with a gondola regatta. Men cross
Piazza San Marco with a rose for their sweetheart.

JULY

Opera Festival *(Jul–Sep)*. A renowned festival
of opera staged in Verona's breathtaking
Roman Arena.
△ **Festa del Redentore** *(3rd weekend)*. A boat
race, fair and fireworks commemorate
Venice's deliverance from the plague in 1576.
Sardellata al Pal del Vo *(last weekend)*.
Moonlit sardine-fishing displays take place
at Pal de Vo, Lake Garda, then the catch is
enjoyed on the lakeshore, accompanied
by celebratory fireworks.

AUGUST

Ferragosto *(15 Aug)*. The Feast of the
Assumption is celebrated with many towns and
villages hosting food festivals and fireworks.
△ **Venice Film Festival** *(late Aug–1st week Sep)*.
One of the world's most important celebrations
of cinema, drawing film stars to Venice's Lido.

NOVEMBER

Festa di San Martino *(11 Nov)*. Children in
Venice celebrate the feast of St Martin and
seek sweet treats from local bakeries.
△ **Festa della Salute** *(21 Nov)*. People cross
the Grand Canal to extol La Madonna della
Salute for deliverance from the 1631 plague.

DECEMBER

Mercatini di Natale, Venice *(early–24 Dec)*. The
city's Christmas lights are illuminated, Campo
San Polo becomes an ice rink and squares and
palazzos host Christmas markets.
△ **Regata dei Babbi Natali** *(Sun mid-month)*.
Rowers dress as Santa Clauses and compete on
the Grand Canal before taking part in a water
parade featuring Santa and his elves.

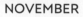

A BRIEF
HISTORY

From its origins in Roman Venetia to its prosperity during the Renaissance, the history of this slowly sinking city never ceases to fascinate. More than 20 million visitors a year succumb to the magic of this improbable place, where the streets are filled with water and the past is evident at every turn.

Roman Domination

The Veneto took its name from the Veneti, an Indo-European tribe who settled in northeastern Italy around 600 BCE. They are also known as Paleoveneti so as not to be confused with modern-day inhabitants of the Veneto. However, by the 3rd century BCE, the region had been taken over by the Romans, and the Veneti citizens of Verona, Vicenza, Este and Treviso granted Roman citizenship. Verona was built as a pivotal base for the Roman armies as they pushed their empire northwards. Roman Venetia, and its capital Padua, thrived for centuries until attacks from Barbarian tribes brought about the fall of Rome in the 5th century CE.

1 Ancient map of Venice. ↑

2 An 18th-century depiction of Verona's Roman amphitheatre.

3 Byzantine art in the Basilica di San Marco.

4 A manuscript details Venetian ships partaking in the Crusades.

Timeline of events

3rd century BCE
Veneto is annexed by the Romans; Verona, Aquileia, Padua and Latinum founded.

401
Goths invade; the people of Veneto migrate to the lagoon.

421
Refugees build on the islets of Rivo Alto (Rialto) and establish the city of Venice.

697
Paolo Lucio Anafesto becomes the first Doge of Venice.

828
Venice steals the relics of St Mark; his winged lion is the symbol of the republic.

The Founding of Venice

The imperial administration began to crumble. Venice emerged when the Goths invaded and the people of Veneto fled to the lagoon. Legend claims the city was founded in 421 CE on 25 April, St Mark's Day. Trade links with Byzantium were forged, and the city prospered on its salt trade. The first doge, elected in 697, was a Byzantine magistrate. In 828, the Venetians brazenly stole the relics of St Mark the Evangelist from Alexandria for their basilica. This signalled their ambition to become the foremost city in Christendom. Shortly after, they proclaimed the religious and political independence of the islands – the Venetian Republic.

La Serenissima and The Crusades

The Venetian Republic (697-1797), traditionally known as *La Serenissima*, was a maritime republic. Before long, Venice dominated trade in the Mediterranean and Adriatic seas, as well as commerce between Europe, North Africa and Asia. It provided supplies and shipped Crusaders to fight the Saracens in the Holy Land; in the Fourth Crusade, which culminated, in 1204, with the conquest of the Byzantine capital, Constantinople.

> ### WHERE TO SEE ROMAN VENETO
>
> Verona has a higher concentration of ancient Roman sites than anywhere outside of Rome; its Archaeological Museum is full of fine mosaics and sculptures, while Castelvecchio has rare early Christian glass and silver. Museums can be found at Este, Adria, Treviso and Portogruaro, situated near Concordia.

1000
Venice controls the Adriatic coast. The "Marriage of Venice to the Sea" ceremony is inaugurated.

1096–1204
Venice and the cities of the Veneto join the Crusades.

1260–95
Famed Venetian merchant, explorer and writer, Marco Polo, sets off to explore Asia.

1453
Constantinople falls to the Turks, leading to the first Ottoman-Venetian War.

1348–9
The plague, the Black Death, kills half of Venice's population.

1

2

Age of Art and Music

The Venetian empire reached its zenith in the 15th century, and by the 16th century, Venice had a monopoly on Mediterranean trade and had colonized all of northeastern Italy. As well as great wealth, the region enjoyed an inspired era of art and music – dominated by such innovative painters as Bellini, Tintoretto, Titian, Tiepolo, Veronese and Canaletto; composers Monteverdi, Gabrieli and Vivaldi; the architect Palladio; and the astronomer Galileo. It was to endure through the Renaissance until the fall of the Venetian Republic.

The Fall of the Venetian Republic

In 1797, Napoleon Bonaparte invaded Venice and brought about the end of the 1,000-year-old City State. Venice and its territories were given to Austria in exchange for Lombardy. Swapped for decades between France and Austria, many disgruntled Venetians joined the vanguard of the revolutionary Risorgimento fighting to unify Italy, and eventually freed themselves from Austrian rule in 1866. The Veneto became part of the Kingdom of Italy four years later.

THE LEAGUE OF CAMBRAI

Keeping hold of such a vast empire meant that Venice was in a near-constant state of war. The League of Cambrai, formed in 1508 by Pope Julius II and the Holy Roman Emperor Maximilian, sacked the cities of the Veneto, but the region remained loyal to Venice's benign rule. The city continued to dominate the Eastern Mediterranean for another 200 years.

Timeline of events

1530
Luigi da Porto of Vicenza writes the original story of Romeo and Juliet.

1703
Composer Vivaldi becomes musical director of La Pietà.

1797
Napoleon Bonaparte invades the Veneto; the doge abdicates and the Venetian Republic ends.

1472
The King of Cyprus is poisoned after marrying Venetian noble Catherine Cornaro.

1639
Plague strikes Venice again, reducing the population to 102,200.

Tourism and the 20th Century

With the advent of the Biennale art exhibition in 1895, Venice remained the vanguard of art and architecture. The Lido became a stylish resort, with grand hotel developments along its sandy shoreline, and the Venice Film Festival started in 1932.

During both World Wars, Venice was surprisingly unscathed, but fighting took place in the Veneto's mountain passes. In 1966, the city was hit by the worst floods in its history. UNESCO launched its Save Venice Appeal, sparking worldwide concern.

Venice and the Veneto Today

Today, Venice treads a fragile line between living city and floating museum. The flood defences inaugurated in 2020 have proved key in protecting the city. In 2017, however, UNESCO threatened to place the city on its "in danger" list, due to concerns over cruise ships, mass tourism and damage to the lagoon ecosystem. There has also been a 70 per cent drop in the city's population since 1950, with residents departing for the mainland due to a lack of affordable housing and a decline in local businesses. Responsible tourism is, therefore, vital to the city's future.

1 Galileo Galilei.

2 1007 print of Napoleon in Venice.

3 Entrance to the Venice Biennale, 1895.

4 Tourists in the flooded St Mark's Square during high season.

Did You Know?

Elena Cornaro Piscopia was the first woman to gain a degree. It was from Padua University in 1678.

1846

A causeway connects the city to the mainland and the Italian rail network.

1861

Vittorio Emanuele becomes King of Italy; Venice and the Veneto are freed from Austrian rule five years later.

1966

The worst flood in Venetian history. Save Venice Appeal launched; plans for flood gates begin.

2017

The #EnjoyRespect Venezia campaign calls for responsible tourism in the city.

GRAND CANAL

Known to the Venetians as the Canalazzo, the Grand Canal sweeps through the heart of Venice, following the course of an ancient riverbed. Since the founding days of the empire it has served as the city's main thoroughfare. Once used by great galleys or trading vessels making their stately way to the Rialto, it now teems with vaporetto, launches, barges and gondolas. Glimpses of its glorious past, however, are never far away. The annual re-enactment of historic pageants, showcasing the traditions of the Venetian Republic, brings a blaze of colour to the canal. The most spectacular is the Regata Storica held in September, a huge procession of historic craft packed with crews in traditional costumes, followed by boat and gondola races down the Grand Canal.

The series of palaces bordering the winding waterway, built over a span of around 500 years, presents some of the finest architecture of the Republic. A roll call of the old Venetian aristocracy, almost every palazzo bears the name of a grand family. Bright frescoes may have faded, precious marbles worn and foundations frayed with the tides, but the Grand Canal is still, to quote Charles VIII of France's ambassador in 1495, "the most beautiful street in the world".

THE GRAND CANAL
SANTA LUCIA TO PALAZZO FLANGINI

The Grand Canal is best admired from a gondola or a vaporetto. Several lines travel the length of the canal, but only the No. 1 goes slowly enough for you to take in the many spectacular buildings and magnificent palazzos that line this waterway.

The journey from Santa Lucia station to the terminus at San Zaccaria takes about 40 minutes. Nearly 4 km (2 miles) long, the canal is spanned by four bridges, the Scalzi, the Rialto, the Accademia and the Constituzione – known by locals as the Ponte di Calatrava after its designer, Santiago Calatrava. The modern bridge, controversial due to its structural flaws, expensive repair needs and slippery glass surface, links Piazzale Roma and Santa Lucia station.

INSIDER TIP
Vaporetto Tickets

A one-way ticket costs €9.50 and it is valid for 60 minutes. Save money by purchasing a 1-, 2-, 3- or 7-day pass for public transport (*www.venezia unica.it/en*); passes cover vaporetto and bus travel. Always validate tickets at the machines at the vaporetto stop.

Santa Lucia railway station, *built in the mid-19th century and remodelled in the 1950s, links the city with the mainland.*

La Direzione Compartimentale, *the administration offices for the railway, was built on the site of the church of Santa Lucia and other ancient buildings.*

| 0 metres | 50 |
| 0 yards | 50 |

N

The Ponte degli Scalzi straddling the Grand Canal

Santa Lucia to Palazzo Flangini

GRAND CANAL

Locator Map

THE SCALZI

The Roman Catholic church of Santa Maria di Nazareth is known today as the Scalzi, meaning barefoot after the supposedly "shoeless" Carmelites who found it. Inside is the tomb of Ludovico Manin, last doge of Venice, who was forced to abdicate by Napoleon Bonaparte in 1797 when French troops marched on the city.

Palazzo Flangini *was designed by Giuseppe Sardi, a leading 17th-century architect.*

Palazzo Calbo Crotta *is now the four-star Hotel Principe. Fine antiques that once decorated the palace are in Ca' Rezzonico (p147).*

Santa Maria di Nazareth *is known today as the Scalzi.*

Ponte degli Scalzi

↑ The Grand Canal from Santa Lucia to Palazzo Flangini

Campo San Simeone Grande, *named after the nearby church, overlooks the canal.*

Casa Adoldo *and* **Palazzo Foscari-Contarini**

San Simeone Piccolo, *built in 1738, was based on the Pantheon in Rome. It is open for worship only.*

Palazzo Diedo, *also known as Palazzo Emo, is believed to be the birthplace of Angelo Emo (1731–92), the last admiral of the Venetian fleet.*

↑ Sunrise over the turquoise dome of San Simeone Piccolo

THE GRAND CANAL
SAN GEREMIA TO SAN STAE

San Geremia
to San Stae

GRAND CANAL

Locator Map

This stretch of the canal sees the beginning of a series of impressive palaces, their opulent façades facing out on to the water for all to see.

Many remarkable buildings line this section of the Grand Canal, but perhaps one of the most breathtaking is Ca' Vendramin Calergi; its opulence and ostentatious design became a model on which other Venetian palazzos were designed.

Palazzo Labia, *frescoed with Tiepolo's* Story of Cleopatra, *is intermittently open to the public (p169).*

San Geremia *houses the relics of St Lucy, formerly preserved in Santa Lucia, where the station now stands.*

Ca' dei Cuori *(House of Hearts) was named after the hearts in the family coat of arms.*

→

The Grand Canal from San Geremia to San Stae

Palazzo Giovanelli *was acquired by the Giovanellis in 1755. They were admitted into the Great Council in 1668 for a fee of 100,000 ducats.*

Palazzo Donà Balbi

CA' VENDRAMIN CALERGI

This early Renaissance palace, designed by Mauro Coducci, now houses the Casino di Venezi, Venice's oldest casino. The opulent building was once home to numerous doges and prominent people through history. The Wagner Museum is also housed in this building, and it celebrates the life and works of the famous composer who died here in 1883.

Canal-front palazzos and the ↑
church of San Geremia at sunrise

170

The number of
buildings that line the
canal – many of them
grand palazzos.

San Marcuola, *dedicated to St Ermagora and
St Fortunatus, was built in 1728–36 by Giorgio
Massari, but the façade was never completed.*

Ca' Vendramin Calergi

Palazzo Marcello,
*was the birthplace of
composer Benedetto
Marcello in 1686.*

**Fondaco dei
Turchi** *was once a
splendid Veneto-
Byzantine building.
It now houses the
Museo di Storia
Naturale (p112).*

**Palazzo
Tron**

Palazzo Belloni Battagia
*was built by Longhena in
the mid-17th century for the
wealthy Belloni family, who
bought their way into
Venetian aristocracy.*

San Stae *is striking for
its Baroque façade, graced
by marble statues. It was
funded by a legacy left
by Doge Alvise Mocenigo
in 1709 (p113).*

Deposito del Megio,
*a crenellated building
with a reconstructed Lion
of St Mark, was a granary
in the 15th century.*

0 metres   50   N
0 yards   50   ↑

THE GRAND CANAL
PALAZZO BARBARIGO TO THE MARKETS

Here the canal is flanked on both sides by stately palaces, built over a period of five centuries. Look out for the spectacular Ca' d'Oro, whose Gothic façade once glittered with gold.

As you cruise down this section of Venice's main waterway, the opulence of the canalside palazzos continues. With its stalls of fresh produce and local delicacies, the Rialto Market (p107) is a perfect stopping point for hungry travellers to disembark and sample some of the finest local flavours before continuing their exploration of the canal.

Palazzo Barbarigo *retains its 16th-century frescoed façade.*

Ca' **Foscarini***, a Gothic building of the 15th century, belonged to the Foscari family before it became the residence of the Duke of Mantua in 1520.*

Ca' **Pesaro***, a huge and stately Baroque palace designed by Longhena, houses the Galleria Internazionale d'Arte Moderna and the Museo d'Arte Orientale (p113).*

Ca' Corner della Regina *is owned by the Fondazione Prada. It houses the Prada contemporary art collection.*

A palazzo's ornate interior and courtyard, overlooking (inset) the Grand Canal of the Ca' d'Oro

CANALETTO

Antonio Canale (1697–1768), known more commonly as Canaletto, is best known for his *vedute* or views of Venice, in which he portrayed the daily life of his beloved city. He studied in Rome, but lived in Venice for most of his life. One of his patrons was Joseph Smith (1682–1770) who became the English consul in Venice. Sadly, there are very few of his paintings left on view in the city.

The façade of **Palazzo Gussoni-Grimani** *once had frescoes by Tintoretto. It was home to the English ambassador in 1614–18.*

Palazzo Fontana Rezzonico *was the birthplace of Count Rezzonico (1693), the fifth Venetian pope.*

Ca' d'Oro, *the most famous of Venetian Gothic palaces (p158), houses paintings, frescoes and sculpture from the collection of Baron Giorgio Franchetti.*

Palazzo Sagredo *passed from the Morosini to the Sagredo family in the early 18th century and exemplifies Veneto-Byzantine and Gothic styles.*

Palazzo Foscarini *was the home of Marco Foscarini, a diplomat who rose to the position of doge in 1762.*

		N
0 metres	50	↑
0 yards	50	

Palazzo Morosini Brandolin

The **Pescheria** *has been the site of a busy fish market for six centuries.*

The Grand Canal ↑
from Barbarigo
to the Markets

Tribunale Fabbriche Nuove, *Sansovino's market building, is now the seat of the Assize Court.*

THE GRAND CANAL
THE RIALTO QUARTER

As you chug along, the canal meanders back on itself, bringing into view the famous Rialto Bridge, one of the most recognizable in the city. This marks your arrival in the Rialto Quarter.

The area around the Rialto Bridge is the oldest and busiest quarter of the city. Traditionally it was a centre of trade, and crowded quaysides and colourful food markets still border the canal south of the bridge. Gaze upon the action from the top deck as locals and tourists alike jostle for space and bargains.

THE DANDOLO FAMILY

The illustrious Dandolo family, based in medieval Venice, produced four doges, 12 procurators of San Marco, a patriarch of Grado and a queen of Serbia. The first of these doges was Enrico Dandolo (d 1205), who, despite being old and blind, was the principal driving force in the Crusade to sack Constantinople in 1204. The other remarkable doge in the family was the humanist and historian Andrea Dandolo (d 1354).

Palazzo Papadopoli *is now the luxury Aman Canal Grande Venice Hotel, but its splendid hall of mirrors has been preserved.*

Palazzo Barzizza, *rebuilt in the 17th century, still preserves its early 13th-century façade.*

Palazzo Grimani *was built in 1556 by Michele Sanmicheli for the Procurator, Girolamo Grimani. It is now the city's Court of Appeal.*

↑ The iconic Rialto
Bridge linking the
two sides of the Rialto

Fondaco dei Tedeschi,
*originally used as a warehouse
and lodgings for German
traders, has been refurbished
as a luxury department store.*

Palazzo Camerlenghi,
*built in 1528, was once the
offices of the camerlenghi
(city treasurers). The ground
floor was the state prison.*

The Rialto Bridge (p107) *was
built to span the Grand Canal in
the city's commercial quarter.*

0 metres   50   N
0 yards   50   ↑

Riva del Ferro *is
the quayside where
German barges off-
loaded ferro (iron).*

Palazzo Manin-Dolfin *was built
by Sansovino, but only his Classical
stone façade survives. The interior
was completely transformed for
Ludovico Manin, last doge of Venice.*

Palazzo Bembo, *a 15th-century
Gothic palace, was the birthplace of
the Renaissance cardinal and scholar
Pietro Bembo, who wrote one of the
earliest Italian grammars.*

Casetta Dandolo *was the
birthplace of Doge Enrico
Dandolo (ruled 1192–1205).*

Palazzo Farsetti and **Palazzo
Loredan** *are both occupied by the
City Council. Palazzo Farsetti became
an academy for young artists, one of
whom was Canova.*

**Palazzo
Farsetti**

↑ The Grand Canal cuts
through the bustling
Rialto Quarter

THE GRAND CANAL
LA VOLTA DEL CANALE

This section of the tour encompasses yet more grand palazzos, some of which now form part of the Ca' Foscari University, founded in 1868.

The point where the canal doubles back sharply on itself is known as La Volta – the bend. This splendid curve was long ago established as the finishing stretch for the highly anticipated Regata Storica (p48), which still takes place on the first Sunday in September every year.

0 metres   50   N
0 yards   50

Palazzo Marcello, which belonged to an old Venetian family, is also called "dei Leoni" because of the lions either side of the doorway.

Palazzo Balbi, seat of the regional government, was built for Nicolò Balbi. From here, Napoleon viewed the 1807 regatta, held in his honour.

Ca' Foscari was built for Doge Francesco Foscari in 1437. It is now part of the University of Venice.

Palazzo Giustinian was the residence of Wagner in 1858–9, when he was composing the second act of Tristan and Isolde.

Ca' Rezzonico, now the museum of 18th-century Venice (p147), became the home of the poet Robert Browning and his son, Pen, in 1888.

Palazzo Mocenigo

Palazzo Moro Lin

Palazzo Grassi (p93)

Palazzo Cappello Malipiero

Palazzo Barbarigo della Terrazza, built in the 1560s, was known for its roof terrace. It now houses the German Institute.

Palazzo Cappello-Layard was the home of English archaeologist Sir Austen Henry Layard.

← La Volta del Canale as it turns a sharp bend

Palazzo Corner Spinelli, *Mauro Coducci's outstanding Renaissance palace, became a prototype for other mansions in Venice.*

Palazzo Garzoni *is now part of the university. The traghetto linking Calle Garzoni to San Tomà is one of the oldest in Venice.*

Palazzo Balbi at Ca' Foscari University, and *(inset)* the ballroom at Ca'Rezzonico ↓

THE GRAND CANAL
CA' REZZONICO TO THE GUGGENHEIM

The southern stretch of the canal widens somewhat, and as buildings become increasingly spaced out, the epic parade of palaces is interspersed with open spaces and leafy gardens.

This section of the Grand Canal takes in some of the most prestigious art galleries in the world. Hop off at the Accademia to see works by Venetian artists such as Titian, Bellini and Giorgione at the Accademia galleries, or visit the marvellously modern Peggy Guggenheim collection just downstream. Here you will find works by more than 200 contemporary artists representing powerful avant-garde movements such as Cubism, Futurism and Surrealism. Then hop back on board to head to Venice's crown jewel, Piazza San Marco.

Palazzo Franchetti Cavalli *belonged to Archduke Frederick of Austria, who died here in 1836.*

Palazzo Falier *was said to have been home to Doge Marin Falier, who was beheaded for treason in 1355.*

The **Accademia** *galleries, within the former church, monastery and Scuola della Carità, house the world's greatest collection of Venetian paintings (p140).*

GRAND CANAL

Ca'Rezzonico to the Guggenheim

Locator Map

The wooden **Accademia Bridge** *was built in 1932 as a temporary structure to replace a 19th-century iron bridge. By popular demand it has been retained.*

Palazzo Contarini del Zaffo, *a magnificent Renaissance palace of the late 1400s, was built for a branch of the ubiquitous Contarini family. It is now owned by the Polignac family.*

Looking down the canal from *(inset)* the wooden Accademia Bridge ↑

Palazzo Barbaro *comprises two palaces, one of which was bought by the Curtis family in 1885. Monet and Whistler painted here and Henry James wrote* The Aspern Papers *here.*

Casetta delle Rose *was the home of Italian poet Gabriele d'Annunzio during World War I.*

Ca' Grande, *a huge Classical palace, was designed In 1545 by Sansovino for Giacomo Cornaro, nephew of the Queen of Cyprus. The family was one of the richest in Venice.*

0 metres	50	N
0 yards	50	↑

Ca' Dario, *built in 1487, is a charming but strangely ill-fated palace.*

↑ Ca' Rezzonico to the Peggy Guggenheim Collection

Peggy Guggenheim *established her collection of modern art in Venice in 1951 (p144). She chose as her venue the unfinished Palazzo Venier dei Leoni.*

↑ The Basilica Santa Maria della Salute on the Grand Canal in Venice

The Palazzo Gritti-Pisani, *where John Ruskin stayed in 1851, is better known today as the five-star Hotel Gritti Palace.*

Palazzo Contarini Fasan *is known as the House of Desdemona from Shakespeare's Othello.*

Palazzo Salviati, *the former headquarters of the Salviati glass company.*

GRAND CANAL

To La Salute and San Marco

Locator Map

The deconsecrated Gothic brick church of **Abbazia San Gregorio**.

Santa Maria della Salute, *a Baroque church of monumental proportions (p145), is supported by over a million timber piles.*

THE GRAND CANAL
TO LA SALUTE AND SAN MARCO

The view along the final stretch of the canal is one of the finest and most familiar in Venice. At the mouth rises the magnificent church of La Salute with the busy San Marco Basin beyond.

Time your vaporetto trip to arrive at the church of Santa Maria della Salute at sunset to see this iconic area of the city at its most spectacular. Disembark at Salute and stroll along Fondamenta Salute to the Punta della Dogana. The view from here, taking in the Palazzo Ducale, the towering Campanile of San Marco and the Zecca, is easily one of the most memorable in Venice.

Palazzo Giustinian
is the headquarters of the Venice Biennale.

← Santa Maria del Gilgio to La Salute and San Marco

Giardinetti Reali, *the Royal Gardens, were created by Napoleon to improve his view from the Procuratie Nuove.*

0 metres 50
0 yards 50
N ↑

The **Punta della Dogana** (p146)

→ Giardinetti Reali, a tranquil green space just off Piazza San Marco

EXPERIENCE

Cycling in Piazza delle Erbe, Padua

SAN MARCO

The political and judicial nerve centre of Venice, the *sestiere* of San Marco has been at the heart of Venetian life since the early days of the Republic. It was here, in around the 9th century, that early settlers, migrating to the inner lagoon from nearby coastal towns, made their homes and built their most important places of worship. It was also here that the first Chapel of the Doge was constructed, not far from the present site of the basilica. It was dedicated to San Theodore, the first patron saint of Venice. However, he was later ousted by San Marco, whose relics were plundered from Alexandria in 828 – it was a bold move in Venice's pursuit to become a global power free from Byzantine rule.

The greatest showpiece of the Republic of Venice was the Piazza San Marco, home to the rulers of the longest enduring republic in Europe, and the Basilica di San Marco, one of the most ostentatious churches in the Christian world. Much of the architecture here has changed little from the era of the Republic, making it a highlight of any visit to Venice – and consequently, one of the busiest areas of the city.

SAN MARCO

Must Sees

1. Piazza San Marco
2. Basilica di San Marco
3. Palazzo Ducale
4. Campanile

Experience More

5. Torre dell'Orologio
6. Biblioteca Nazionale Marciana
7. Museo Correr
8. Museo Archeologico
9. Harry's Bar
10. Columns of San Marco and San Teodoro
11. San Moisè
12. Ridotto
13. Palazzo Contarini del Bovolo
14. Santa Maria Zobenigo
15. Campo San Bartolomeo
16. La Fenice
17. Campo Santo Stefano
18. Palazzo Grassi
19. San Salvatore
20. Museo Fortuny
21. San Giorgio Maggiore
22. Stanze del Vetro
23. San Zulian
24. Mercerie

Eat

1. Bar All'Angolo
2. Le Café
3. Acqua Pazza
4. Al Bacareto
5. Bacaro Da Fiore
6. Trattoria Vini da Arturo

Drink

7. Caffè Florian
8. Gran Caffè Lavena
9. Museo Correr Coffee Shop

Stay

10. Hotel Novecento
11. Hotel Santo Stefano
12. Corte di Gabriela

Shop

13. Bevilacqua
14. Chiarastella Cattana
15. Rubelli

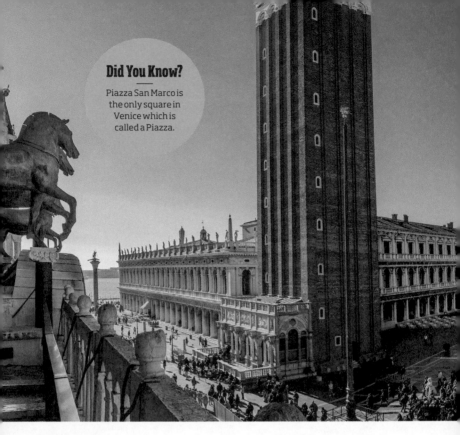

PIAZZA SAN MARCO

H7 **San Marco**

Long the political and religious heart of Venice, Piazza San Marco was once just a monastery garden crossed by a stream. The glittering Basilica di San Marco and Palazzo Ducale command the east side of the square, while the stately Procuratie Vecchie and Nuove that flank its sides have, for centuries, been the backdrop for magnificent processions. Today the piazza continues to bustle, with a museum complex, cafés and costumed revellers during Carnival.

Throughout its long history Piazza San Marco has witnessed pageants, processions, political activities and countless Carnival festivities. Tourists flock here in their thousands to see two of the city's most impressive and important sights – the Basilica di San Marco (p78) and the Palazzo Ducale (p82). However, there is much else to entertain here besides the basilica, with three historic cafés, open-air orchestras and smart glass and jewellery boutiques beneath the arcades of the Procuratie. So close to the waters of the lagoon, the Piazza is one of the first points in the city to suffer at *acqua alta* (high tide).

Tourists and Venetians alike can then be seen picking their way across the duckboards that crisscross the flooded square. The best time to appreciate the beauty of the Piazza is in the early hours, when only the city sweepers and pigeons are here.

> There is much else to entertain here besides the basilica, with three historic cafés, open-air orchestras and smart glass and jewellery boutiques.

↑ The grand Piazza San Marco, overlooked by *The Horses of San Marco*

Timeline

814 CE
Foundations of Doge's Palace laid.

1720
▲ Caffè Florian is thought to be the oldest café in Europe. It was opened on 29 December, by Floriano Francesconi as "Alla Venezia Trionfante" (to the Triumphant Venice).

1810
Napoleon demolishes San Geminiano church to make way for Ala Napoleonica.

1902
▽ Campanile collapses and is rebuilt in 1908.

1966
Record floods hit the Piazza, with water levels 1.94 m (6.4 ft) above sea level.

1989
▽ Pink Floyd concert, on a floating stage, attracts over 100,000 people.

② ⌖ Ⓜ ⌂

BASILICA DI SAN MARCO

⑨ H7 🏛 Piazza San Marco 🚏 San Marco 🕐 9:30am–5:15pm Mon–Sat, 2–5:15pm Sun
Ⓦ basilicasanmarco.it

Venice's spectacular basilica blends the architectural and decorative styles of East and West to create one of Europe's greatest buildings. Inside, this Byzantine extravaganza is embellished with golden mosaics, icons and ornate marble carvings.

Exterior of San Marco

Built on a Greek cross plan and crowned with five huge domes, San Marco owes its splendour to countless treasures from the Republic's overseas empire. Among these are copies of the famous bronze horses brought from Constantinople in 1204, and a wealth of columns, bas-reliefs and coloured marbles studded across the main façade. Mosaics from different epochs adorn the five doorways, while the main portal is framed by some of Italy's loveliest Romanesque carving (1240–65). Initially built in the 9th century, this is the third church to stand on the site.

↑ Romanesque carvings surrounding the arches of the main portal

> **San Marco owes its splendour to countless treasures from the Republic's overseas empire.**

←

Façade and campanile of the basilica, seen from Piazza San Marco

Timeline

828–978
▲ A church is built to house relics of St Mark, stolen from Alexandria. It burns down in 976 and is rebuilt in 978.

978–1117
▲ The church is replaced by a grand basilica, "the House of St Mark", reflecting Venice's growing power.

1117–c1300
▲ 4,240 sq m (45,622 sq ft) of gleaming golden mosaics are added to the domes, walls and floors of the basilica.

1807
▲ The doge's private chapel until 1807, San Marco succeeds San Pietro di Castello as the cathedral of Venice.

↑ Ornate coloured marble panels on the exterior of the basilica

Inside the Basilica

San Marco's magnificent interior is clad with dazzling mosaics, which begin in the narthex, or atrium, of the basilica and culminate in the glittering panels of the Pentecost and Ascension domes. The Genesis Cupola in the atrium has a stunning scene of the Creation of the World described in concentric circles. The *pavimento*, or floor, is also patterned with mosaics in marble and glass. Steps from the atrium lead to the Museo Marciano, which houses the basilica's famous horses. Other treasures include the jewel-encrusted Pala d'Oro, the Nicopeia icon and the precious hoards of silver, gold and glassware in the Treasury.

Statues of St Mark and angels, which crown the central arch, are additions from the early 15th century.

The Pentecost Dome was probably the first dome to be decorated with mosaics.

The four horses of St Mark are replicas of the gilded bronze originals now protected inside the basilica's museum.

> San Marco's magnificent interior is clad with dazzling mosaics, which culminate in the glittering panels of the Pentecost and Ascension domes.

The imposing San Marco Basilica with its majestic architecture. ↑

→ Stunning mosaic of Christ in Glory in the vast Ascension Dome

The Ascension Dome features a magnificent 13th-century mosaic of Christ surrounded by angels, the 12 Apostles and the Virgin Mary.

The alabaster columns of the altar canopy, or baldacchino, are adorned with New Testament scenes.

St Mark's body, believed lost in the fire of 976 CE, reappeared when the new church was consecrated in 1094. The remains are housed in the altar.

The mosaic pavement shows beautiful pictures of birds and beasts.

The Treasury is a repository of precious artifacts from both Italy and Constantinople.

PALA D'ORO

Beyond the Cappella di San Clemente lies the entrance to San Marco's most valuable treasure: the Pala d'Oro. This bejewelled altarpiece consists of 250 enamel paintings on gold, enclosed within a gilded silver frame. Napoleon stole some of the precious stones in 1797, but the screen still gleams with rubies, pearls and sapphires

Mosaics

The earliest of the basilica's gleaming mosaics date from the 12th century, and were the work of skilled mosaicists from the East. Their delicate techniques were soon adopted by Venetian crafters who gradually took over the basilica's decoration, combining Byzantine inspiration with Western influences. During the 16th century, many works by Tintoretto, Titian, Veronese and other leading artists were reproduced in mosaic.

Museo Marciano

Look out for signposts to the Loggia dei Cavalli which lead you up to the museum. Here, the gallery offers a splendid view into the basilica. The star exhibits are gilded bronze horses, stolen from the top of the Hippodrome (ancient racecourse) in Constantinople in 1204.

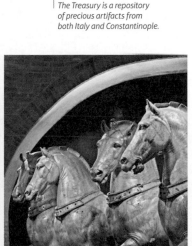

←

Gilded bronze horses housed in the Museo Marciano

3 ✍️ 🎵 💻 🛍️

PALAZZO DUCALE

📍 J7 🚪 Piazza San Marco 1 🚏 San Marco 🕐 10am–7pm daily; last adm: 30 mins before closing 📅 1 Jan, 25 Dec 🌐 palazzoducale.visitmuve.it

A magnificent combination of Byzantine, Gothic and Renaissance architecture, the Palazzo Ducale (Doge's Palace) was the official residence of the 120 doges who ruled Venice from 697 to 1797. Artists such as Titian, Tintoretto and Bellini vied with each other to embellish the palace with painting and sculpture, not to mention architects Antonio Rizzo and Pietro Lombardo, the latter responsible for the ornate western façade.

The Palazzo Ducale was founded in the 9th century, when a fortress-like structure stood on this spot. The present palace owes its external appearance to the building work of the 14th and early 15th centuries, despite a string of fires in the 1500s. The designers broke with tradition by perching the bulk of the pink Verona marble palace on lace-like Istrian stone arcades, with a portico supported by columns below. The result is a light and airy masterpiece of Gothic architecture.

Sala del Senato

Sala delle Quattro Porte

Sala del Collegio

Anticollegio

The walls of the Sala dello Scudo, once part of the doge's private apartments, are covered with maps of the world. In the centre are two giant 18th-century globes.

The Porta della Carta was the main entrance to the palace.

Did You Know?

The Sala del Maggior Consiglio is one of the largest rooms in Europe. It could seat up to 2,000 council members.

New doges were crowned on the Giant's Staircase with the glittering zogia or dogal cap.

The exterior of the palace, ↑ bathed in early morning sunlight

Sala del Consiglio dei Dieci

Interrogations took place in the Torture Chamber. Suspects were hung by their wrists from a cord in the centre of the room.

Sala della Bussola

The Bridge of Sighs

↑ The *Drunkenness of Noah* sculpture, symbolic of the frailty of man

An early 15th-century sculpture of the Drunkenness of Noah is set on the corner of the palace.

The Ponte della Paglia, built of Istrian stone, has a pretty balustrade of columns and sculpted pine cones.

Tintoretto's huge Paradise (1590) fills the end wall of the Sala del Maggior Consiglio.

The Loggia commands fine views of the lagoon.

← The grand Palazzo Ducale, seen from Piazza San Marco

Exploring the Palazzo Ducale

A tour of the Palazzo Ducale takes visitors through a succession of richly decorated chambers and halls, arranged over four floors, culminating with the Bridge of Sighs, which links the palace to the prisons. The Secret Itineraries tour gives access to parts of the palace normally out of bounds, including the prison cell from which Casanova escaped.

State Apartments and Council Chambers

The doge's private State Apartments on the second floor were built after the fire of 1483. Looted under the orders of Napoleon, they are bare of furnishings, but the lavish ceilings and colossal carved chimneypieces in some of the rooms give an idea of the doges' lifestyle. The Sala dello Scudo, or map room, contains maps and charts, while the picture gallery features some incongruous wooden demoniac panels by Hieronymus Bosch.

The Scala d'Oro (golden staircase) leads to the third floor and its Council Chambers. In the Sala del Consiglio dei Dieci, the awesomely powerful Council of Ten, set up in 1310, would meet to investigate and prosecute crimes concerning the security of the state. Napoleon pilfered some of the Veroneses from the ceiling

←

Veronese's *Rape of Europa* in the Anticollegio chamber

→

The magnificent Sala del Maggior Consiglio, featuring Tintoretto's *Paradise*

WHO COULD JOIN THE GREAT COUNCIL?

By the mid-16th century Venice's influential Great Council had around 2,000 members. Any Venetian of high birth over the age of 25 was automatically entitled to a seat - with the exception of those married to someone of non-noble birth. From 1646, those from merchant or professional classes with 100,000 ducats to spare could buy their way in.

but two of the finest found their way back here in 1920: *Age and Youth* and *Juno Offering the Ducal Crown to Venice* (both 1553–4).

The magnificent Anticollegio chamber was the waiting room for those meeting with the Council. The end walls are decorated with mythological scenes by Tintoretto: *Vulcan's Forge*, *Mercury and the Graces*, *Bacchus and Ariadne* and *Minerva Dismissing Mars*, all

↑ Dank corridor leading to cells in the palace prisons

painted in 1578. Veronese's famous *Rape of Europa* (1580), opposite the window, is one of the most eye-catching works in the palace.

In the Sala della Bussola were lions' heads, letterboxes where citizens could post anonymous bills denouncing others for their crimes, real or imaginary. The wooden door in this room leads to the rooms of the Heads of the Ten, the State Inquisitors' Room and thence to the torture chamber and prisons.

The star attraction of the palace is the monumental Sala del Maggior Consiglio. It was here that the Great Council convened to vote on constitutional questions, to pass laws and elect the top officials of the Serene Republic. Tintoretto's huge *Paradise* (1587–90) occupies the eastern wall. Measuring 7.45 by 24.65 m (25 by 81 ft), it is one of the largest oil paintings in the world. A frieze along the walls illustrates 76 doges by Tintoretto's pupils. The portrait covered by a curtain is Marin Falier, who was beheaded for treason in 1355.

Prisons

The Bridge of Sighs links the palace to what were known as the New Prisons, built between 1556 and 1595. Situated at the top of the palace, just below the leaded roof, are the *piombi* cells (*piombo* means "lead"). These cells are hardly inviting, but prisoners here were far more comfortable than the criminals left to fester in the *pozzi* – the dark dank dungeons at ground level. The windowless cells of these ancient prisons are still covered with the graffiti of the convicts.

Did You Know?

Notorious womanizer Casanova escaped from the palace prisons through a hole in the roof of his cell.

→

The Campanile,
illuminated in
evening sunlight

4

CAMPANILE

📍 H7 🏛 Piazza San Marco � San Marco 🕐 9:30am–9:15pm daily
🚫 In bad weather 🌐 basilicasanmarco.it

From the top of San Marco's campanile, towering high above the Piazza, visitors can enjoy sublime views across the city, the lagoon and, visibility permitting, the peaks of the Italian Alpine range on the horizon.

The first tower, completed in 1173, was built as a lighthouse to assist navigators in the lagoon. In the Middle Ages, it took on a less benevolent – and far more gruesome – role as the support for a torture cage where offenders were imprisoned and in some cases left to die. The tower's present appearance dates from the early 16th century, when it was restored after an earthquake. The campanile survived the vicissitudes of time until 14 July 1902, when its foundations gave way and it collapsed. The only casualties were the Loggetta at the foot of the tower and the custodian's cat. The following year, with the help of many donations, the foundation stone was laid for a campanile "dov'era e com'era" (where it was and how it was). The new tower – built to resemble the 16th-century version – was opened on 25 April (St Mark's Day) 1912. Due to small structural shifts, work has begun in order to reinforce the foundations. There is no known end date for the work.

THE BELLS OF THE CAMPANILE

Ringing through the city, the five bells in the Campanile have been employed to mark Venice's city rhythms for centuries. The Maleficio bell was sounded to announce an execution, the Nona rang at midday, the Trottiera spurred on the nobles' horses for assemblies in the Palazzo Ducale, and the Mezza Terza was used to indicate that the Senate was in session. The Marangona bell is still sounded to mark midnight.

EXPERIENCE MORE

Torre dell'Orologio

H7 ⌂ Piazza San Marco ⛴ San Marco ◷ For guided tours only; times vary, check website (book ahead) 🖥 visitmuve.it

This richly decorated Renaissance clock tower stands on the north side of the Piazza, over the archway leading to the Mercerie (p95). Built in the late 15th century, its central section is thought to have been designed by Mauro Coducci. Displaying the phases of the moon and the zodiac, the gilt and blue enamel clock was designed with seafarers in mind. A story spread that the two inventors of the complex clock mechanism subsequently had their eyes gouged out to prevent them from ever creating a replica.

During Ascension week and Epiphany, the clock draws many visitors, who watch the figures of the *Magi* emerge from side doors to pay their respects to the Virgin and Child, whose figures are set above the clock. At the very top, two bronze *Mori* (Moors) strike the bell on the hour.

Guided tours are available throughout the year in English, French and Italian They depart from the Museo Correr ticket office.

Biblioteca Nazionale Marciana

H7 ⌂ Piazzetta (entrance from Museo Correr) ⛴ San Marco ◷ 8:30am-6:30pm Mon-Fri, 8:30am-12:30pm 24 & 31 Dec 🔒 Public hols 🖥 bibliotecanazional emarciana.cultura.gov.it

Praised by Andrea Palladio as the finest building since antiquity, the library was designed by the architect Jacopo Sansovino. During construction the vaulting collapsed; Sansovino was blamed and imprisoned. Freed only after an appeal, he had to reconstruct the building at his own expense.

At the top of the stairway is a rare example of Jacopo de' Barbari's bird's-eye view map of Venice dating to 1500 (p88). The salon features two ceiling paintings by Paolo Veronese.

The spire, 98.5 m (323 ft) high, is topped with a golden weather vane.

The five bells in the tower each had their role during the Republic.

An internal lift, installed in 1962, provides easy access to the top of the tower.

The Loggetta was built in the 16th century by Jacopo Sansovino.

Allegorical reliefs from Verona were carefully rebuilt after 1902.

↑ The towering Campanile dominates the Venetian skyline

↑ Manuscripts displayed beneath the gilded ceiling in the Biblioteca Nazionale Marciana

Museo Correr

📍 **H7** 🏛 **Procuratie Nuove; entrance Ala Napoleonica** 🚏 **San Marco** 🕐 **10am–6pm daily; last adm: 5pm** 🌐 **correr.visitmuve.it**

With the 19th-century Royal Palace serving as backdrop, a collection of marble statues by Italian Neo-Classical sculptor Antonio Canova (1757–1822) is the first exhibit at the Museo Correr. This is followed by the bathroom and boudoir of Sissi, the Empress Elizabeth, along with other sumptuous rooms laid out in the 1830s and 1850s that make up the restored Imperial Apartments. The next section, titled Venetian Culture, is found in the older, but confusingly named, Procuratie Nuove. This collection captures the history of the Venetian Republic, from daily life to its peculiar public institutions, through maps, armour and a host of doge-related exhibits.

On the second floor is the *Wunderkammer* (Collection of Wonders), which draws from the legacy of the wealthy abbot and art collector Teodoro Correr, founder of the museum. The collection includes coins, a narwhal tooth and the famous *Map of Venice* by Italian

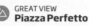

📷 GREAT VIEW
Piazza Perfetto

For stunning views of St Mark's Square, the first-floor windows of the Museo Correr offer a birds-eye view and directly face the basilica; in late afternoon, the sun bounces off the gold mosaics of its façade.

painter and printmaker Jacopo de' Barbari. This spectacular woodcut, completed in 1500, depicts a bird's-eye view of Venice, intricately carved from six wooden blocks to create a mural-size print with every building, canal and *campo* accounted for. The Pinacoteca (picture gallery) is also located on this floor. Images are displayed chronologically so that the evolution of Venetian painting is evident. The most famous works in the gallery are the Carpaccios: *A Portrait of a Young Man in a Red Hat* (around 1490) and *Two Venetian Ladies* (around 1507).

---

⑧ 🚶 🥾
Museo Archeologico

📍 **H7** 🏛 **Piazzetta; entrance from Museo Correr** 🚏 **San Marco** 🕐 **Apr–Oct: 10am–6pm daily; Nov–Mar: 10am–5pm daily** 🌐 **archeologico-venezia.cultura.gov.it**

Housed in both the Biblioteca Nazionale Marciana and the Procuratie Nuove, the museum provides a quiet retreat from the bustle of San Marco. The collection owes its existence to the generosity of Domenico Grimani, son of Doge Antonio Grimani, who bequeathed all of his Greek,

←

Daedalus ties wings to his son Icarus in this Canova sculpture, Museo Correr

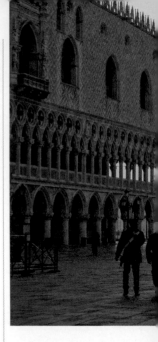

Roman and earlier sculpture, together with his library, to the state in 1523.

---

⑨
Harry's Bar

📍 **H7** 🏛 **Calle Vallaresso 1323** 🚏 **San Marco**

Celebrated for cocktails, *carpaccio* and its American clientele, Harry's Bar is famous throughout Venice. Founded in 1931 by the late Giuseppe Cipriani, it was financed by a Bostonian called Harry who thought Venice had a dearth of decent bars. They chose a storeroom at the Grand Canal end of the Calle Vallaresso as their location, conveniently close to Piazza San Marco. Since then, the bar has seen a steady stream of American visitors, among them Ernest Hemingway, who used to come here after shooting in the lagoon. The bar became the most popular venue in Venice, patronized by royalty, film stars and heads of state. These days, there are far more American tourists than famous figures, often there

↑ The winged lion of St Mark overlooking the Piazza from its column

to sample the Bellini cocktail, a mix of sparkling prosecco and white peach purée, which Giuseppe Cipriani invented. Aesthetically, the place is unremarkable and there is no terrace for meals alfresco.

⑩

Columns of San Marco and San Teodoro

◘ H7 ◭ Piazzetta ▤ San Marco

Along with all the bounty from Constantinople came the two huge granite columns which now tower above the Piazzetta. These were said to have been erected in 1172 by the engineer Nicolò Barattieri, architect of the very first Rialto Bridge. For

> **Venetians are a superstitious lot; you'll never catch them walking between the two columns of San Marco and Teodoro.**

his efforts he was granted the right to set up gambling tables between the columns. A more gruesome spectacle on the same spot was the execution of criminals, which took place here until the mid-18th century. Venetians are a superstitious lot; you'll never catch them walking between the two columns.

The western column is crowned by a marble statue of St Theodore, who was the patron saint of Venice before St Mark's relics were smuggled from Alexandria in 828 CE. The statue is a modern copy – the original is kept for safety in the Palazzo Ducale (p82).

The second column is surmounted by a huge bronze of the Lion of St Mark. Its origin remains a mystery, though it is thought to be a Chinese chimera with wings added to make it look like a Venetian lion. In September 1990 the 3,000-kg (3-tonne) beast made the journey to the British Museum in London for extensive restoration, and was returned with great ceremony and skill to the top of the column.

DRINK

Caffè Florian
This is the oldest coffeehouse in Europe – and probably one of the most expensive. Order a classic coffee or try the famous hot chocolate.

◘ H7 ◭ Piazza San Marco 57 ⊠ caffe florian.com

Gran Caffè Lavena
Richard Wagner's old haunt has Florian's glamour but with a smaller bar bill.

◘ H7 ◭ Piazza San Marco 133/4 ⊠ lavena.it

Museo Correr Coffee Shop
Enjoy one of the best views in town with your coffee – you don't need a museum ticket.

◘ H7 ◭ Procuratie Nuove ⊠ correr. visitmuve.it

⑪
San Moisè

📍G7 🏛Campo San Moisè
📞04152858 40 🚉San Marco
🕐9:30am-12:30pm Mon-Sat

Completed in 1668, this church has a Baroque façade and many statues, swags and busts. Its architecture was disliked by some, with John Ruskin, author of *The Stones of Venice*, calling it (in characteristic anti-Baroque outrage) the clumsiest church in Venice.

The interior has a collection of art and sculpture from the 17th and 18th centuries. In the nave is the tombstone of John Law, a Scottish financier who founded the Compagnie d'Occident to develop the Mississippi Valley. His shares collapsed in 1770 in the notorious South Sea Bubble, and he fled to Venice, surviving on his winnings at the Ridotto.

→

The photogenic spiral staircase at Palazzo Contarini del Bovolo

⑫
Ridotto

📍G7 🏛San Marco, 1332
🚉San Marco 🕐To hotel guests and on request
🌐hotelmonaco.it

In an effort to control the gambling mania that swept Venice in the 1600s, the state allowed Marco Dandolo to use a wing of his palace as the first public gaming house in Europe. In 1638 the Ridotto was opened, with the proviso that players came disguised in a mask. In 1774 the Great Council closed the casino's doors on account of the number of Venetians ruined at its tables, the stated aim

being "to preserve the piety, sound discipline and moderate behaviour" of the city's people.

In 1947, the old Palazzo Dandolo was converted into a theatre. Now restored, it is part of the Monaco and Grand Canal hotel.

⑬
Palazzo Contarini del Bovolo

📍G7 🏛Corte Contarini del Bovolo, 4303 San Marco
🚉Rialto or Sant'Angelo
🕐10am-6pm daily 🌐scala contarinidelbovolo.com

Tucked away in a maze of alleys (follow the signs

 PICTURE PERFECT
Double Vision
The Bovolo staircase offers two great photo ops: capture a graphic, architectural image looking up from below (you'll need to crouch), then a wonderful view of the Basilica di San Marco from the top.

←

The much-maligned Baroque façade of the church of San Moisè

from Campo Manin), this palazzo is best known for the graceful external stairway that leads to the top of its tower. In Venetian dialect *bovolo* means "snail shell"– appropriate for describing the spiral shape of the stairway. Built in 1499, the tower is open to the public. The ticket for the palazzo also admits you to the Tintoretto room located on the second floor, which houses a collection of art from the 16th and 17th centuries.

14

Santa Maria Zobenigo

📍F7 🏛️Campo Santa Maria del Giglio 🚏Santa Maria del Giglio ⏰10:30am–5pm Mon–Sat 🌐chorus venezia.org

Named after the Jubanico family, who are said to have founded it during the 9th century, this beautiful church is also referred to as Santa Maria "del Giglio" ("of the lily"). The exuberant Baroque façade, completed in 1681, was financed by the affluent Barbaro family and was designed to glorify their naval and diplomatic achievements. Instead of the traditional biblical imagery,

EAT

Bar All'Angolo
Friendly bar selling scrumptuous sandwiches, light meals and salads. Great if you're on the go.

📍F7 🏛️Campo Santo Stefano 3464 📞041 522 07 10

€€€

Le Café
Great coffee, light meals and cakes galore.

📍F7 🏛️Campo Santo Stefano 2797 🌐lecafe venezia.com

€€€

Acqua Pazza
The Amalfi Coast comes to Venice, with delectable coastal dishes and outdoor seating in the square.

📍F7 🏛️Campo Sant' Angelo 3808 🌐venice acquapazza.com

€€€

Al Bacareto
A family-run restaurant serving local specialities.

📍E7 🏛️San Samuele 3447 🌐bacareto.it

€€€

Bacaro Da Fiore
A wide array of *cichetti* and wines, and restaurant service for a formal meal.

📍F7 🏛️Calle de le Botteghe 3461 🌐ristorantedafiore.com

€€€

Trattoria Vini da Arturo
A Venetian staple and one of the few to focus on hearty meat dishes. Small menu, superb wines.

📍F7 🏛️Calle dei Assassini 3656 📞041 528 69 74

€€€

the centre of the façade is occupied by a statue of Admiral Antonio Barbaro (who died in 1679), surrounded by representations of various heroic virtues and marble relief maps of locations, such as Corfu and Split, where the admiral served the Republic. Other statues are of his brothers, and at the top is the Barbaro coat of arms.

Inside, the furnishings are more conventional. There's also a tiny museum showcasing church ornaments and statues depicting the Annunciation. Paintings include *The Sacred Family*, attributed to Rubens (if so, it is the only work by the Flemish painter in Venice) and two works by Tintoretto.

15

Campo San Bartolomeo

📍G5 🚏Rialto

Close to the Rialto on its eastern side, the square of San Bartolomeo, named for the apostle Bartholemew, bustles with life, particularly in the early evening, when young Venetians rendezvous here. They meet at the cafés and bars that line the square or by the bronze statue of Carlo Goldoni (1707–93), Venice's prolific and most celebrated playwright. His statue, in a fitting spot for a writer who drew his inspiration from daily social intercourse, was created by Italian sculptor Antonio del Zotto in 1883.

SHOP

Venice's most exclusive neighbourhood, San Marco is home to several sumptuous furnishing stores, some of which have been producing textiles for centuries. Whether you are looking for velvet damask or the finest linen, these stores are sure to have it.

Bevilacqua
📍 F7/8 🏛 Campo Santa Maria del Giglio 2520 🌐 bevilacqua tessuti.com

Chiarastella Cattana
📍 E7 🏛 Salizada San Samuele 3216 🌐 chiara stellacattana.com

Rubelli
📍 F7 🏛 Ca' Pisani Rubelli 3395 🌐 rubelli.com

16 M3

La Fenice

📍 F7 🏛 Campo San Fantin 🚉 San Marco 🌐 teatrolafenice.it

Theatre houses were enormously popular in the 18th century, and La Fenice, the city's oldest theatre, was no exception. Built in 1792 in Classical style, it was one of several privately owned theatres showing plays and operas to audiences from all strata of society. In December 1836, a fire destroyed the interior but a year later it was resurrected, just like the mythical bird, the *fenice* (phoenix), which is said to have arisen from its ashes.

Another fire in early 1996 again destroyed the theatre, except for its façade. Now beautifully rebuilt, La Fenice shares the concert and opera season with the Malibran Theatre near Rialto.

Throughout the 19th century the name of La Fenice was linked with great Italian composers. Verdi's *La Traviata* (1853) and Rossini's *Tancredi* (1813) and *Semiramide* (1823)

→
Statue of the Dalmation scholar Nicolò Tommaseo in Campo Santo Stefano

all premiered here. During the Austrian Occupation *(p52)*, red, white and green flowers, symbolizing the Italian flag, were thrown on stage to shouts of "Viva Verdi" – the letters of the composer's name standing for "Vittorio Emanuele Re d'Italia". More recently, the theatre saw premieres of Stravinsky's *The Rake's Progress* (1951) and Britten's *The Turn of the Screw* (1954).

17

Campo Santo Stefano

📍 F7 🚉 Accademia or Sant'Angelo

Also known as Campo Francesco Morosini after the 17th-century doge who once lived here, this *campo* is one of the most spacious in the city. Bullfights were staged until 1802, when a stand fell and killed some of the spectators. It was also a venue for balls

Contemporary stage set amid restored Rococo opera boxes at La Fenice ↑

and Carnival festivities. Today it is a pleasantly informal square. The central statue is Nicolò Tommaseo (1802–74), a key figure in the 1848 rebellion against the Austrians.

Deconsecrated six times on account of the violence that took place within its walls, the 14th-century church of Santo Stefano today is remarkably serene. It houses notable works of art, including some paintings by Tintoretto.

At the southern end, the austere-looking Palazzo Pisani, overlooking the Campiello Pisani, has been the Conservatory of Music since the 19th century. Music wafts from its open windows all through the year.

18
Palazzo Grassi

⊙ E7 ⊟ Campo San Samuele, San Marco 3231 ⊟ San Samuele ⊙ 10am–7pm Wed-Mon ⊠ pinault collection.com

Set on the Grand Canal, this landmark gallery dates back to 1740, when a merchant family commissioned Giorgio Massari to design the building. It is now home to the François Pinault collection, housing contemporary masterpieces by Jeff Koons, Damien Hirst and Michelangelo Pistoletto. Its inspirational sister gallery is Punta della Dogana (p146).

19
San Salvatore

⊙ G6 ⊟ Campo San Salvatore ☎ 041 241 38 17 (for private tours) ⊟ Rialto ⊙ 9am–noon & 3–6pm Mon–Sat, 3–7pm Sun

The interior of this church is an excellent example of Venetian Renaissance architecture. If the main door is closed, visitors can enter by the side entrance, which is squeezed between shops on the Mercerie (p95). The present church was designed by Giorgio Spavento in the early 16th century, and continued by Tullio Lombardo and Jacopo Sansovino. The pictorial highlight is Titian's *Annunciation* (1566) over the third altar on the right.

20
Museo Fortuny

⊙ F6 ⊟ Palazzo Pesaro degli Orfei, Campo San Beneto ⊟ Sant'Angelo ⊙ Exhibitions only ⊠ fortuny.visitmuve.it

Mariano Fortuny y Madrazo was born in 1871 in Granada and moved to Venice in 1889. In the early 20th century he purchased the Palazzo Pesaro, a late Gothic palazzo that was owned by the influential Pesaro family. The large rooms make a splendid setting for the precious Fortuny fabrics. Woven with gold and silver threads, they were created using Renaissance techniques and ancient dyes. The collection also includes paintings by Fortuny, deco-rative panels and a few of the finely pleated silk dresses considered a milestone in early 20th-century women's fashion. Today, the rooms are open during visiting design and photo exhibitions.

FORTUNY FACTORY

Mariano Fortuny was an entrepreneurial grafter and Renaissance man, interested in science as much as art. He opened the Fortuny factory on Giudecca island in 1921. It was here that his workers created Fortuny's trademark fabrics. Still in operation today, the factory is shrouded in secrecy and out of bounds, although it is possible to visit the showroom, strictly by appointment only.

STAY

Hotel Novecento
Enjoy stylish
rooms at this calm
Venetian retreat.

📍F8 🏠Calle del
Dose 2683-4
🌐novecento.biz

€€€

Hotel Santo Stefano
Elegant rooms in a 15th-
century watchtower.

📍F7 🏠Campo Santo
Stefano 2957
🌐hotelsantostefano
venezia.com

€€€

Corte di Gabriela
Contemporary
design and high-spec
gadgets in a frescoed
19th-century palazzo.

📍F6/7 🏠Calle dei
Avvocati 3836
🌐cortedigabriela.com

€€€

21

San Giorgio Maggiore

📍J8 📞041 522 78 27
🚤San Giorgio 🕐Apr-Oct:
9am-7pm daily; Nov-Mar:
8:30am-6pm daily

Appearing like a stage set
across the water from the
Piazzetta, the little island
of San Giorgio Maggiore has
been captured on canvas
countless times. The church
and monastery, built between
1559 and 1580, are among
Andrea Palladio's greatest
architectural achievements.
The church's temple front and
spacious, serene interior, with
its perfect proportions and
cool beauty, are typically
Palladian in that they are
modelled on the Classical
style of ancient Rome. Within
the church, the major works
of art are the two Tintorettos
on the chancel walls: *The Last
Supper* and *Gathering of the
Manna* (both 1594). In the
Chapel of the Dead is his last
work, *The Deposition* (1592–4),
finished by his son Domenico.
The top of the tall campanile,
reached by a lift, affords
a panorama of St Marco's
palaces across the lagoon.

Centuries ago, Benedictine
monks occupied the original
monastery. It later became
a centre of learning and a
residence for eminent foreign
visitors. Following the fall of
the Republic in 1797 (*p52*) the
monastery was suppressed
and its treasures plundered.

In 1829 the island became
a free port, and in 1851 the
headquarters of the artillery.
By this time it had completely
changed out of all recognition.
The complex regained its
role as an active cultural
centre when the monastery,
embracing Palladio's cloisters,
refectory and library, was
purchased in 1951 by Count
Vittorio Cini. Today it is a
thriving Venetian cultural
foundation, hosting concerts,
international events and
fascinating exhibitions.

Did You Know?

San Giorgio Maggiore's
original buildings were
destroyed in an
earthquake in the
13th century.

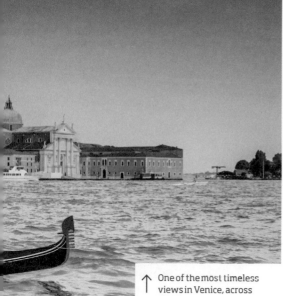

One of the most timeless views in Venice, across the lagoon to San Giorgio

In the middle of the park on the island is an evocative open-air amphitheatre, the Teatro Verde, constructed of white Vicenza stone.

22

Stanze del Vetro

◉ J8 ◘ Isola di San Giorgio Maggiore 8 ➰ San Giorgio ◷ 10am-7pm daily ⊕ lestanzedelvetro.org

Standing behind the Church of San Giorgio Maggiore is the Stanze del Vetro (the Glass Rooms). A joint project between the Cini Foundation and Pentagram Stiftung, the aim is to celebrate and study the art of glass-making from the 19th century until today. The modern exhibition space is housed in part of the erstwhile boarding school that once stood on the island. Temporary exhibitions of major artists run throughout the year, even spilling out into the garden for larger installations. The gift shop has an excellent range of books about glass art, as well as delightful glass souvenirs.

23

San Zulian

◉ H6 ◘ Campo San Zulian (Giuliano) ➰ San Marco ◷ 9am-7pm daily

On the bustling Mercerie, the church of San Zulian (or Giuliano) provides a refuge from the busy alleys. Its interior features gilded woodwork, 16th- and 17th-century paintings, and sculpture. The central panel of the frescoed ceiling portrays *The Apotheosis of St Julian*, painted in 1585 by Palma il Giovane. The 16th-century church façade was designed by Sansovino and paid for by the rich physician Tommaso Rangone.

→ Statue of Tommaso Rangone atop the entrance to San Zulian

His bronze statue stands out against the white Istrian stone walls.

24

Mercerie

◉ H6 ➰ San Marco or Rialto

Divided into the Merceria dell'Orologio, Merceria di San Zulian and Merceria di San Salvatore, this is a principal shopping area. Linking Piazza San Marco with the Rialto, it is made from a string of narrow alleys, lined by small shops and boutiques. The 17th-century English author John Evelyn described it as "the most delicious streete in the World for the sweetnesse of it". He wrote of perfumers, apothecary shops and nightingales. Today all this has been replaced with fashion, footwear and glass.

At the southern end, the relief over the first archway on the left portrays the woman who in 1310 accidentally stopped a revolt. She dropped her pestle out of the window, killing the standard-bearer of a rebel army. They retreated, and the woman was given a guarantee that her rent would never be raised.

A SHORT WALK
AROUND
LA FENICE

Distance 1.5 km (1 mile) **Time** 25 minutes
Nearest Vaporetto San Marco

West of the bustling Piazza San Marco, there is a labyrinth of alleys to explore. At the centre of this part of the *sestiere* is Campo San Fantin, flanked by the Renaissance church of San Fantin. Nearby is the Ateneo Veneto, formerly a *scuola* (school) whose members had the unenviable role of escorting prisoners to the scaffold. The narrow streets around these sights are home to some wonderful little shops, while the Calle Larga XXII Marzo, further south, features some of the biggest names in Italian fashion. The quarter in general has some excellent restaurants but, being San Marco, the prices in the majority of establish-ments are fairly steep.

Campo San Fantin has a late Renaissance church, **San Fantin**, *with a particularly beautiful apse designed by Jacopo Sansovino.*

La Fenice (p92), *Venice's most famous opera house, is now beautifully restored after it was destroyed by fire for a second time in 1996.*

The **Rio delle Veste** *leads past the rear of the theatre. This is the route taken by those fortunate enough to arrive for their night out by gondola.*

CAMPO SAN MANTIN

CD CORTESIA

CALLE D VERONA

RIO D VERONA

CAMPO SAN FANTIN

START
FINISH

CALLE DELLA FENICE

RIO DELLE VEST

RIO S MARIA D GIGLIO

CAMPIELLO SANTA MARIA ZOBENIGO

RIO DELL' ALBERO

↑ Exterior of La Fenice, Venice's most famous theatre and opera house

The carvings on **Santa Maria Zobenigo** (p91) *feature the Barbaro family, who paid for the church façade. Ground-level reliefs show towns where the family held high-ranking posts.*

The statue of Daniele Manin, leader of the 1848 uprising, stands on **Campo Manin** gazing towards the house where he once lived.

Locator Map
For more detail see p74

Tucked away off the main street, **Palazzo Contarini del Bovolo** (p90) *is tricky to find, but worth seeking out for its fairy-tale external stairway.*

CALLE D LOCANDE

CALLE DEI FUSERI

RIO DI SAN LUCA

RIO FUSERI

C DEL FRUTTAROL

C DEI BARCAROLI

| 0 metres | 50 |
| 0 yards | 50 |

N ↑

Did You Know?

In December 1807, La Fenice hosted a ball for the French emperor, Napoleon Bonaparte.

DI PISCINA

PISC DI FREZZERIA

CALLE BOGNOLO

FREZZERIA

Frezzeria, *in medieval times, was the street where citizens went to purchase their frecce (arrows). Its shops now sell chic clothes.*

RIO DEI BARCAROLI

CALLE D VESTE

PISC S MOISE

CAMPO SAN MOISE

SAL SAN MOISE

The exuberant Baroque façade of **San Moisè** (p90) *was funded by a legacy from the patrician Vincenzo Fini, whose bust features above a side door.*

CALLE LARGA XXII MARZO

Calle Larga XXII Marzo *was named after 22 March 1848, the day of Manin's rebellion. Today the street is best known for its fashionable designer boutiques.*

→
The view from the arcade at the top of Palazzo Contarini del Bovolo

SAN POLO AND SANTA CROCE

The *sestieri* of San Polo and Santa Croce, bordered by the upper sweep of the Grand Canal, were both named after churches that stood within their boundaries – San Polo, originally constructed in the 9th century and heavily remodelled in the centuries to follow, and Santa Croce, established by refugees fleeing the Lombards in the 6th century, only to be demolished by Napoleon in 1808.

The first inhabitants are said to have settled on the cluster of small islands called Rivus Altus (high bank) or Rialto. When markets were established in the 11th century, the quarter became the commercial hub of Venice, giving the area its reputation as the bazaar of Europe. Almost anything could be traded here, from gold and jewellery to spices, dyes and unusual delicacies from far-flung lands. In 1514 a fire raged through the Rialto, destroying everything except the church. Rebuilding started straight away, restoring the market and surrounding area to its former glory.

San Polo continues to be one of the liveliest *sestieri* of the city, with its market stalls, busy shops and local bars. The bustle of the market gives way to a maze of narrow alleys opening on to squares. Santa Croce for the most part is an area of narrow, tightly packed streets and squares where you will see a more local side of Venetian life. Its grandest palazzos line the Grand Canal. On its western edge, on a self-contained island, is the Piazzale Roma – one of the city's main transport hubs.

SAN POLO AND SANTA CROCE

Must Sees

1 Santa Maria Gloriosa dei Frari
2 Scuola Grande di San Rocco
3 Rialto

Experience More

4 San Cassiano
5 San Rocco
6 San Polo
7 Campo San Polo
8 Casa di Goldoni
9 San Giovanni Evangelista
10 Palazzetto Bru Zane
11 San Giacomo dell'Orio
12 San Nicolò da Tolentino
13 Museo di Storia Naturale
14 Museo di Palazzo Mocenigo
15 San Stae
16 Ca' Pesaro

Eat

1 Al Nono Risorto
2 La Zucca
3 Antiche Carampane

Drink

4 Al Prosecco
5 Bacareto Da Lele
6 Cip & Ciop Osteria Venezia
7 Hostaria Vecio Biavarol
8 Osteria Da Filo
9 Osteria della Rivetta

Shop

10 DoppioFondo
11 Il Pavone di Paolo Pelosin
12 Legatoria Polliero

SANTA MARIA GLORIOSA DEI FRARI

📍D6 🏛Campo dei Frari 🚊San Tomà 🕐9am-6pm Mon-Sat, 1-6pm Sun & religious hols 🚫During Mass, 1 Jan, 25 Dec 🌐basilicadeifrari.it

More commonly known as the Frari (a corruption of *frati*, meaning "brothers"), this vast Gothic church dwarfs the eastern side of San Polo. The airy interior is striking for the sheer size and quality of its works of art, including masterpieces by Titian and Giovanni Bellini, a statue by Donatello and several grandoise tombs.

The first church on this site was built by Franciscan friars in 1250–1338, but was replaced by a much larger building in the 15th century. The labyrinthine monastery and courtyards adjoining the church have been home to Venice's State Archives since the fall of the Republic. Its 300 rooms are loaded with precious records documenting the history of Venice right back to the 9th century.

Donatello's sculpture of St John the Baptist (1438) appears in the altar of the chapel immediately to the right of the apse.

The Monks' Choir consists of three-tiered stalls (1468), carved with bas-reliefs of saints and Venetian city scenes.

The campanile is 83 m (262 ft) high, the tallest in the city after that of San Marco.

Titian's spectacular work Assumption of the Virgin *(1518) draws the eye through the Monks' Choir to the altar, and heavenwards.*

Pietro Lombardo and Bartolomeo Bon carved this rood screen (1475) and its decorative marble figures.

The Madonna di Ca' Pesaro *(1526) shows Titian's mastery of light and colour.*

Canova's pyramidal tomb is based on a design he planned, but never constructed, as a monument for Titian.

The Gothic church of Santa Maria Gloriosa dei Frari ↑

1

2

① The entrance to Santa Maria Gloriosa dei Frari faces the Rio dei Frari canal.

② Titian's famous *Assumption of the Virgin* dominates the apse.

③ The sacristy's altarpiece, *Madonna and Child* (1488), by Bellini, is one of Venice's most beautiful Renaissance paintings.

④ The church's former monastery houses Venice's State Archives.

Courtyard and former monastery

3

4

2 ✎ 🛍

SCUOLA GRANDE DI SAN ROCCO

📍 D6 🏛 Campo San Rocco 🚆 San Tomà 🕐 9:30am–5:30pm daily
📅 1 Jan, 25 Dec 🌐 scuolagrandesanrocco.it

Dazzling in the morning sun, the early Renaissance façade of this historic building, home to masterpieces by Jacopo Tintoretto, is a marvel of intertwined sculpted stone wreaths and crouching elephants dwarfed by stately columns.

Founded in honour of St Roch (San Rocco), the Scuola was set up as a charitable institution for the sick. Construction began in 1515 under Bartolomeo Bon and was completed in 1549 by Scarpagnino, financed by donations from Venetians who believed St Roch, the patron saint of contagious disease, would save them from the plague. In 1564 Tintoretto was commissioned to decorate the walls and ceilings of the Scuola. His paintings have no labels, but a useful plan is available (in multiple languages) for free at the entrance. To see the paintings in chronological order, start in the Sala dell'Albergo, followed by the Upper Hall and finally the Ground-Floor Hall.

23

The number of years it took Tintoretto to complete the Scuola's paintings.

NOT JUST TINTORETTO

With the overwhelming number of paintings by Tintoretto, it's easy to forget the Scuola holds other artistic treasures, such as Titian's dreamlike *Annunciation* (around 1535). Two masterpieces by Tiepolo hang on the stairs leading to the Treasury. One of the Scuola's greatest pieces is Giorgione's *Christ Carrying the Cross* (below). Once considered miraculous by Venetians, who prayed for cures in front of it, it is a truly moving and magnificent work.

Sala dell'Albergo

▷ A competition was held in 1564 to select an artist to paint the central ceiling panel of the Sala dell'Albergo in the Scuola. To the fury of his rivals, Tintoretto installed his painting prior to judging. He won the commission and was later made a member of the Scuola. Over the next 23 years, Tintoretto decorated the entire building. The winning painting, *St Roch in Glory*, can be seen on the ceiling of the Sala dell'Albergo. The most moving work in the cycle is *The Crucifixion* (1565), of which Henry James wrote: "Surely no single picture contains more of human life."

Upper Hall

▽ Scarpagnino's great staircase (1544–6) leads to the Upper Hall, where the ceiling paintings portray scenes from the Old Testament. The three large central square paintings represent *Moses Striking Water from the Rock*, *The Miracle of the Bronze Serpent* and *The Gathering of the Manna*, all alluding to the Scuola's charitable aims. The vast wall paintings in the hall feature episodes from the New Testament, including *The Temptation of Christ* and *Adoration of the Shepherds*.

Ground-Floor Hall

▽ This final cycle, executed in 1582–7, consists of eight paintings illustrating the life of Mary. The series starts with an *Annunciation* and ends with an *Assumption*, which was restored some years ago. The tranquil scenes of *St Mary of Egypt*, *St Mary Magdalene* and *The Flight into Egypt* are remarkable for their serenity. In all three paintings, the landscapes, rendered with rapid strokes, play a major role.

←

The ornate façade of the Scuola Grande di San Rocco on Campo San Rocco

RIALTO

⚲G5 🚊Rialto

The commercial hub of Venice, the Rialto takes its name from *rivo alto* (high bank) and was one of the first areas of Venice to be inhabited. A financial and then a market district, it remains one of the city's busiest and most bustling areas. Locals and visitors alike shop at the colourful stalls of the Erberia (fruit and vegetable market) and Pescheria (fish market), and gather on the famous Rialto Bridge, browsing for souvenirs or taking a break to watch the swirl of activity on the Grand Canal below.

→
Gondola boats bobbing on the Grand Canal, with the Rialto Bridge in the background

| 0 metres | 100 |
| 0 yards | 100 |

N ↑

Fondaco dei Tedeschi, originally a warehouse and lodgings for German traders, is now a luxury department store.

↑ The Grand Canal through the Rialto district

Palazzo Camerlenghi, built in 1528, was once the offices of the camerlenghi (city treasurers). The ground floor was the state prison.

③

Riva del Vin is one of the few spots to sit and relax on the banks of the Grand Canal.

Palazzo Barzizza, rebuilt in the 17th century, still preserves its early 13th-century façade.

①

②

Riva del Ferro is where barges unloaded ferro (iron).

Did You Know?

An early wooden Rialto bridge collapsed under the weight of a wedding party in 1444.

① San Giacomo di Rialto

⌂ Campo San Giacomo, San Polo ☎ 041 275 04 62 🕒 9am–5pm Mon–Sat ⊘ During Mass

The first church to be built on this site was allegedly founded in the 5th century, making it the oldest church in Venice. The present building dates from between the 11th and 12th centuries, while major restoration work took place in 1601. The original Gothic portico and huge 15th-century 24-hour clock on its façade are the church's most striking features.

The crouching stone figure on the far side of the square is the so-called Gobbo (hunchback) of the Rialto. In the 16th century this was a welcome sight for minor offenders who were forced to run the gauntlet from Piazza San Marco to this square at the Rialto.

② Rialto Bridge

Very few visitors leave Venice without crossing the iconic Rialto Bridge. The oldest of the four crossings over the Grand Canal, it is a wonderful place to watch the constant activity of boats on the water below. Stone bridges were built in Venice as early as the 12th century, but it was not until 1588, after the collapse, decay or sabotage of earlier wooden structures, that a competition was held for the design of a new Rialto bridge to be built in stone. Andrea Palladio, Jacopo Sansovino and Michelangelo were the eminent contenders, but after months of deliberation it was the aptly named Antonio da Ponte who won the commission. Work was completed on the 48-m (157-ft) bridge in 1591. Until 1854, when the Accademia Bridge was constructed, the Rialto Bridge was the only means of crossing the Grand Canal on foot. Prior to this, pedestrians would have to be ferried across the canal on gondola boats.

③ Rialto Market

⌂ San Polo 🕒 Fruit and vegetable market: 7:30am–1pm Mon–Sat; Fish market: 7:30am–1pm Tue–Sat

Venetians have come to the Erberia fruit and vegetable market to buy fresh produce for hundreds of years. Heavily laden barges arrive at dawn and offload their crates on to the quayside by the Grand Canal. Local produce includes red *radicchio* from Treviso and succulent asparagus and baby artichokes from the islands of Sant'Erasmo and Le Vignole. In the adjoining Pescheria fish market are pilchards, anchovies, octopus, squid, crabs, clams and other lagoon seafood for sale.

INSIDER TIP
Rialto Market

To see the market in full bustling swing, visitors must arrive early in the morning – by noon the vendors are already starting to pack up.

EXPERIENCE MORE

4 San Cassiano

F5 ▲Campo San Cassiano, San Polo
041 721 408 ⛴San Stae
🕓9am-noon & 3-7pm daily

The medieval church of San Cassiano is a bizarre mix of architectural styles. Of the original church, only the campanile survives. Jacopo Tintoretto's powerful *Crucifixion* (1568) is displayed in the sacristy.

The *campo* in which the church stands was well-known for its numerous brothels in the 1500s; it is now a peaceful square.

5 San Rocco

D6 ▲Campo San Rocco, San Polo ⛴San Tomà
🕓9:30am-5:30pm Mon-Sat, 1:30-5:30pm Sun
🌐scuolagrandesanrocco.it

Sharing the little square with the celebrated Scuola Grande di San Rocco (*p104*) is the

church of the same name. Designed by Bartolomeo Bon in 1489 and largely rebuilt in 1725, the exterior is a unique blend of various architectural styles. The ornate façade was added in 1765-71.

Inside, the main interest lies in Tintoretto's paintings in the chancel, which depict scenes from the life of St Roch, a 14th-century pilgrim said to have ministered to the sick on his journey to Rome, and hence patron saint of contagious diseases. Of these the most notable is *St Roch Curing the Plague Victims* (1549).

↑ The bell tower of San Cassiano overlooking the canal of the same name

6 San Polo

E6 ▲Campo San Polo ⛴San Silvestro
🕓10:30am-1:30pm & 2:30-5pm Mon-Sat; last adm: 10 mins before closing
🌐chorusvenezia.org

Founded in the 9th century, rebuilt in the 15th and revamped in the early 19th in Neo-Classical style, the church of San Polo lacks any sense of homogeneity. Yet it is worth visiting for individual features such as the lovely Gothic portal and the Romanesque lions at the foot of the 14th-century campanile – one holds a serpent between its paws, the other a human head.

Inside, follow the signs for the *Via Crucis del Tiepolo* – 14 canvases of the Stations of the Cross by Giandomenico Tiepolo. The church also has paintings by Veronese, Palma il Giovane (the Younger) and a dark and dramatic *Last Supper* by Tintoretto.

7 Campo San Polo

E5, E6 ⛴San Silvestro

The spacious square of San Polo, a popular venue for

↑ Campo San Polo, Venice's second-largest square after San Marco, and *(inset)* a flea market stall

Carnival festivities today, has long been host to spectacular events. As far back as the 15th century it was the venue for festivities, masquerades, balls and ceremonies.

The most dramatic event was the assassination of Lorenzino de' Medici in 1548. He had taken refuge in Venice after brutally killing his cousin Alessandro, Duke of Florence. Lorenzino was stabbed in the square by two assassins who were in the service of Cosimo de' Medici, and both were handsomely rewarded by the Florentine duke.

On the eastern side of the square is the beautiful Gothic Palazzo Soranzo. This was originally two palaces – the one on the left is the older.

Palazzo Corner Mocenigo, which is situated in the northwest corner (No. 2128), was once the residence of the eccentric English writer Frederick Rolfe (1860–1913),

alias Baron Corvo. He was thrown out of his lodgings when his English hostess read his manuscript of *The Desire and Pursuit of the Whole* – a cruel satirization of English society in Venice.

---

8 ⟨⟩ 📷

Casa di Goldoni

📍E6 🏛 Palazzo Centani, Rio Terà' dei Nomboli, San Polo 2794 🚉 San Tomà 🕐 10am–4pm Thu–Tue 🌐 carlogoldoni.visitmuve.it

Carlo Goldoni, one of the city's favourite sons, wrote over 250 comedies, many based on *commedia dell'arte* figures. Goldoni was born in the beautiful Gothic Palazzo Centani (or Zantani) in 1707. The house was left to the city in 1931 and is now a centre for theatrical studies and has a collection of theatrical memorabilia. The enchanting courtyard has a 15th-century open stairway and a superb wellhead, which features carved lions and a coat of arms bearing a hedgehog.

DRINK

Al Prosecco
Sample a superb range of wines and top-notch meals in a pretty square.

♀E4 ♠Campo San Giacomo dell'Orio 1503 ♨Sun �W alprosecco.com

Bacareto Da Lele
Students flock here for reasonably priced beers and wine by the glass.

♀C5/6 ♠Campo dei Tolentini ♨Sun

Cip & Ciop Osteria Venezia
This *osteria* has a southern look, but the *cichetti* are very much Venetian.

♀D4 ♠Calle Larga dei Bari 1162

Hostaria Vecio Biavarol
A champion of the "slow food" movement, this joint serves cold cuts, cheese and quality wines.

♀C5 ♠Fondamenta dei Tolentini 225

Osteria Da Filo
Another popular student hangout, with live music on Wednesdays.

♀E5 ♠Calle dell Tintor 1539 ♨Breakfast, lunch

Osteria della Rivetta
This convivial *osteria* is a favourite with locals thanks to its bar snacks.

♀C5 ♠Calle Sechera 637/A ♨Mon W allarivetta.it

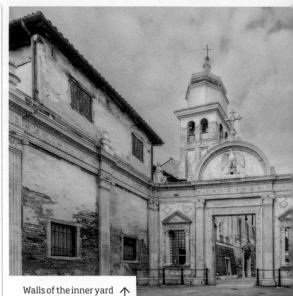

Walls of the inner yard of the church of San Giovanni Evangelista ↑

⑨ San Giovanni Evangelista

♀D5 ♠Campiello de la Scuola, San Polo ⛴San Tomà ⏰9:30am-1pm & 2-5:30pm if no events are being held (check website) W scuolasangiovanni.it

A confraternity of flagellants founded the Scuola of St John the Evangelist in 1261. Today, the complex comprises a church, *scuola*, a bookshop and courtyard. Separating the square from the street is Pietro Lombardo's elegant white and grey screen and portal (1480), and in the arch crowning the portal a carved eagle representing St John the Evangelist takes pride of place.

The main hall of the Scuola is reached via a splendid 15th-century double stairway by Mauro Coducci (1498). Large, dark canvases decorate the ceiling and walls of the 18th-century hall. The Scuola's greatest art treasure, the cycle of paintings depicting *The*

INSIDER TIP
Walk and Talk

Immerse yourself in Venice while learning Italian at the Venice Italian School in San Polo. Classes involve chats over aperitivo and strolls around the neighbourhood (*www.venice italianschool.com*).

Stories of the Cross, is now on display in the Accademia gallery (*p140*). It formerly embellished the oratory (located just off the main hall) where the Reliquary of the True Cross is still carefully preserved.

---

⑩ Palazzetto Bru Zane

♀D5 ♠Calle dell'Olio, San Polo 2368 ⛴San Tomà W bru-zane.com

Years of extensive restoration works have returned this 17th-century palazzetto to its

San Giacomo dell'Orio

⑪ ⌖

📍E4 🏛Campo San Giacomo dell'Orio, Santa Croce 🚉Riva di Biasio or San Stae ⏰10:30am-5pm Mon-Sat; last adm: 10 mins before closing 🌐chorusvenezia.org

This church is a focal point of a quiet quarter of Santa Croce. The name *dell'Orio* may derive from an *alloro* (laurel tree) that once stood near the church.

Founded in the 9th century, rebuilt in 1225 and repeatedly modified, it exhibits a rare mix of architectural styles. The basilica ground plan, campanile and Byzantine columns survive from the 13th century. The ship's keel roof and the columns are from the Gothic period and the apses are Renaissance. The sacristy ceiling was decorated by Veronese and there are some gripping altar paintings. The main altarpiece, *Virgin Mary and Child with Apostles and Saints*, was painted in 1546 by Lorenzo Lotto, an artist who was born in Venice but travelled widely in search of commissions; as a result, few of his works are found in Venice.

former glory, and the unique acoustics of the Bru Zane's 100-seat auditorium attract world-famous musicians from around the globe once again. Previously home to the Habsburgs, one of the most prominent dynasties of Europe from the 15th to the 20th century, and still bearing their crest on the doorbell, Bru Zane was bought by the Swiss Fondation Bru and now houses the prestigious Centre de Musique Romantique Française. Although the name suggests a particular focus on French romantic music, there are regular forays into many other genres and eras.

The palace also has a delightful leafy courtyard with plenty of open-air seating that can be enjoyed whether you are coming for the music or not. Free guided tours of the palace are held in English every Thursday at 3:30pm.

→

Corinthian capitals on the Classical façade of San Nicolò da Tolentino

Did You Know?

The Flagellants were medieval religious zealots who sought penance by whipping themselves.

⑫

San Nicolò da Tolentino

📍C5 🏛Campo dei Tolentini, Santa Croce 🚉Piazzale Roma 📞041 522 21 60 ⏰3:30-6pm Mon-Sat, 10am-12:30pm Sun 🔔During Mass

Close to Piazzale Roma is this imposing 17th-century church with a huge Classical portico. The interior, magnificently decorated with 17th-century paintings, is the resting place of Francesco Morosini (d 1678), Venetian patriarch and doge.

A cannonball embedded in the façade is a memento of an Austrian bombardment during the siege of 1849.

HIDDEN GEM
Heaven Scent

As well as its perfume rooms, Museo di Palazzo Mocenigo offers two-hour perfume workshops in multiple languages. Participants are shown how to make their own perfume with a kit that they can take home.

Museo di Storia Naturale

📍E4 🏛Canal Grande, Santa Croce 1730 🚤San Stae ⏰10am–6pm Tue–Sun 🌐msn.visitmuve.it

The Museo di Storia Naturale (Natural History Museum) has occupied the Fondacio dei Turchi since 1923. In the museum's collection – consisting of over two million pieces – are stuffed animals, crustacea and dinosaur fossils, and a section on lagoon life. Prize exhibits include a skeleton of an *Ouranosaurus nigeriensis*, 7 m (23 ft) long and 3.6 m (12 ft) tall, and a fossil of a *Sarcosuchus imperator* – an ancestor

of the crocodile. The building itself has a chequered history. In the 13th century it was one of the largest palazzos on the Grand Canal. In 1381 it was bought by the state for the Dukes of Ferrara and its lavish rooms were used for banquets and state functions. In 1621 the Turks set it up as a *fondaco* (warehouse), but when commerce with Asia declined, the structure fell into disrepair until, roused by John Ruskin's passionate interest, the Austrians began restoration work in the 1850s.

Museo di Palazzo Mocenigo

📍E4 🏛Salizada San Stae, Santa Croce 1992 🚤San Stae ⏰10am–6pm Tue–Sun; last adm: 4pm 🌐mocenigo.visitmuve.it

One of the oldest Venetian families, the Mocenigos produced seven doges. There were various branches of the family,

one of which resided in this 17th-century mansion. Count Alvise Nicolò Mocenigo, the last of this particular branch, died in 1954, bequeathing the palace to the Comune di Venezia (city authorities).

The entrance façade is unremarkable, but the interior is elegantly furnished and gives you a rare opportunity of seeing inside a palazzo preserved more or less as it was in the 18th century. The frescoed ceilings and other works of art are celebrations of the family's achievements. The illustrious Mocenigos are portrayed in a frieze around the *portego* (porch) on the first floor.

The Museo del Tessuto e del Costume inside the house contains antique fabrics and exquisitely made costumes. It also has five fascinating rooms dedicated to the history of perfumes and

The Museo di Storia Naturale, and *(inset)* the butterflies on display here ↓

EAT

Al Nono Risorto
Traditional dishes at decent prices. Check out the wisteria-clad courtyard.

🔴F5 🅰Sottoportico di Siora Bettina, Santa Croce 2338 🆆alnono risortovenezia.com

€€€

La Zucca
Though the menu is pretty meaty, this fabulous neighbourhood restaurant was one of the first to be vegetarian-friendly.

🔴E4 🅰Ponte del Megio, Santa Croce 1762 🆆lazucca.it

€€€

Antiche Carampane
Difficult to find, but worth it, this Venetian stalwart serves up fish dishes with style.

🔴F5 🅰Rio Terà delle Carampane, San Polo 1911 🆆antiche carampane.it

€€€

perfume-making, with videos, sensorial experiences and a wonderful collection of perfume bottles.

San Stae

🔴F4 🅰Campo San Stae, Santa Croce 🚏San Stae 🕒2:30–5pm Wed-Thu 🔒1 Jan, 25 Dec 🆆chorus venezia.org

Restored in 1977–8 by the Pro Venezia Foundation, San Stae (or Sant'Eustachio) has a spick-and-span sculpted façade. It was built in 1709 by Domenico Rossi, and works by Piazzetta, Tiepolo and other celebrated 18th-century artists adorn the chancel. Near the second altar on the left is a bust of Antonio Foscarini, who was executed for treason in 1622 but then pardoned the following year.

Ca' Pesaro

🔴F4 🅰Canal Grande, Santa Croce 2076 🚏San Stae 🕒10am–6pm Tue-Sun 🆆capesaro.visitmuve.it

It took 58 years to complete this magnificent Baroque palace. Built for the Pesaro family, it was the masterpiece of Baldassare Longhena, who worked on it until his death in 1682. Antonio Gaspari then took over Longhena's design, eventually completing the structure in 1710.

In the 19th century the Duchess of Bevilacqua La Masa bequeathed the palace to the city for exhibiting the works of unestablished Venetian artists. The Galleria Internazionale d'Arte Moderna was founded in 1897. Today this features a permanent exhibition of artists such as Bonnard, Matisse, Miró, Klee, Klimt and Kandinsky, in addition to works by celebrated Italian artists of the 19th and 20th centuries.

The building also contains the Museo d'Arte Orientale, which has an eclectic collection of Chinese and Japanese artifacts – the latter is one of the largest from the Edo period found in Europe – collected by the Count of Bardi during his 19th-century travels.

A SHORT WALK
SAN POLO

Distance 2 km (1.5 miles) **Time** 35 minutes
Nearest Vaporetto San Stae

The Rialto Bridge and markets dominate this area of Venice, and are a huge draw for locals and visitors alike. Traditionally the city's commercial quarter, it was here that bankers, brokers and merchants once conducted their affairs. Today, the streets are no longer lined with stalls selling spices and fine fabrics, but the food markets and pasta shops are an enticing sight. The old-fashioned standing-only bars called *bacari* are filled with locals, especially at aperitivo time. To the south is the lively Riva del Vin where tourists tend to congregate.

Inside **San Cassiano** (p108) *church is a carved altar (1696) and* Crucifixion *by Tintoretto (1568).*

START

The crooked **Ponte Storto** *leads under a portico to Calle Stretta, a narrow alley that is only 1 m (3 ft) wide in places.*

SAN CASSIANO

CAMPO SAN CASSIANO

C D CRISTI

CALLE DEL CAMPANILE

CALLE DEI BOTTERI

RIO DI

R T D CAMPANE

CAMPIELLO ALBRIZZI

C SALVATI

BECCARIE

RIO DELLE

RUGA RAVANO

C DELL'OLIO

CAMPO SANT' APONAL

C DE LUGANEGHER

CAMPO SAN SILVESTRO

Sant'Aponal, *founded in the 11th century, rebuilt in the 15th, is now deconsecrated.*

Riva del Vin *is one of the few accessible quaysides along the Grand Canal.*

SAN SILVESTRO

↑ Campo San Cassiano, a world away from the buzzing Riva del Vin

0 metres   75   N
0 yards   75   ↑

Locator Map
For more detail see p100

The markets at the **Rialto** (p107) have been in operation for centuries. The Pescheria sells fresh fish and seafood, and the Erberia sells fruit and vegetables.

The statue of **Gobbo of the Rialto**, the "hunchback", was sculpted in 1541.

Since its installation in 1410, the clock on **San Giacomo di Rialto** (p107) has been a notoriously poor timekeeper.

The **Calle della Madonna** looks distinctly medieval with its overhanging first floors.

A beloved landmark of the Grand Canal, the **Rialto Bridge** (p107) marks the geographical centre of the city.

FMTA DELL OLIO

CAMPO DELLA PESCHERIA

C BECCARIE

RIALTO MERCATO

RUGA DEI SPEZIERI

RUGA DEGLI ORESI

SAN GIOVANNI

RUGA VECCHIA

CALLE D MADONNA

FINISH

RIVA DEL VIN

CANAL GRANDE

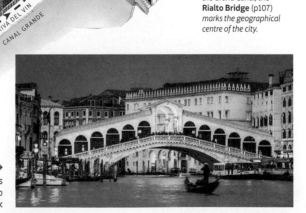

→
A gondola passes under the Rialto Bridge at dusk

CASTELLO

The largest of Venice's *sestieri*, Castello stretches from San Marco and Cannaregio in the west to the modern blocks of Sant'Elena in the east. The area takes its name from the 8th-century fortress that previously stood on what is now San Pietro, the island that was once the religious focus of the city. The church here was the episcopal see from the 9th century and the city's cathedral from 1451 to 1807.

The industrial hub of Castello was the Arsenale, then the greatest shipyard in the world, where Venice produced its indomitable fleet of warships. It was the heart of La Serenissima's maritime power, but following the Fall of the Republic in 1797, Napoleon destroyed the docks. He also stripped the *Bucintoro* (the ceremonial ship of the doge), and had its cannons and bronzes melted down to contribute to victory monuments celebrating the French Revolution. Castello's most popular and commercial area is the Riva degli Schiavoni promenade, which looks out over the lagoon. Behind the waterfront it is comparatively quiet, characterized by narrow alleys, faded palazzos and fine churches, including the great Santi Giovanni e Paolo.

CORTE CARITÀ

CORTE DEL FUMO

CANNAREGIO
p154

🚻 Ospedale

Canale delle Fondamente Nuove

San Lazzaro ai dei Mendicanti

Ospedale Civile

Santi Maria dei Miracoli

Scuola Grande di San Marco **13**

Santi Giovanni e Paolo **1**

Statue of Colleoni **11**

15 Ospedaletto

San Francesco della Vigna **14**

5

BARBARIA DELLE TOLE

C ZEN

Rio di Sah

Giovanni Laterano

CASTELLO

Campo Santa Maria Formosa **12**

12 **11**

San Lorenzo **17**

Santa Maria Formosa

Palazzo Grimani **10**

Scuola di San Giorgio degli Schiavoni **16**

Santa Maria della Fava

Fondazione Querini Stampalia **9**

5

8

6

Museo Guidi

4

San Giorgio dei Greci **3**

Calle d. Madonna **1**

SAN MARCO
p72

Museo Diocesano d'Arte Sacra **6**

3

San Zaccaria **5**

Campo San Zaccaria

San Giovanni in Bragora **18**

2

Basilica di San Marco

8 Bridge of Sighs

2 Hotel Danieli

10 La Pietà **4**

9

7

PIAZZA SAN MARCO

Palazzo Ducale

8 Ponte della Paglia

7 Riva degli Schiavoni

RIVA DEGLI SCHIAVONI

Zecca

ℹ️

🚻

San Marco-Zaccaria 🚏

Arsenale 🚏

7

San Marco-Giardinetti 🚏

San Marco-Vallaresso 🚏

Bacino di San Marco

Canale di

8

CASTELLO

San Giorgio

CAMPO SAN GIORGIO

San Giorgio Maggiore

SAN GIORGIO MAGGIORE

9

0 metres 250
0 yards 250

N ↑

H   J   K   L

CASTELLO

Must See
1. Santi Giovanni e Paolo

Experience More
2. Hotel Danieli
3. San Giorgio del Greci
4. La Pietà
5. San Zaccaria
6. Museo Diocesano d'Arte Sacra
7. Riva degli Schiavoni
8. Ponte della Paglia and Bridge of Sighs
9. Fondazione Querini Stampalia
10. Palazzo Grimani
11. Statue of Colleoni
12. Campo Santa Maria Formosa
13. Scuola Grande di San Marco
14. San Francesco della Vigna
15. Ospedaletto
16. Scuola di San Giorgio degli Schiavoni
17. San Lorenzo
18. San Giovanni in Bragora
19. Via Guiseppe Garibaldi
20. San Pietro di Castello
21. Arsenale
22. Museo Storico Navale

Eat
1. Da Remigio
2. Al Covo
3. Alla Rivetta
4. Aciugheta
5. Osteria Oliva Nera
6. Ristorante Giorgione
7. Oriental Bar & Bistrot

Stay
8. Aqua Palace
9. Hotel Metropole
10. Londra Palace

Shop
11. Libreria Acqua Alta
12. Papier Maché

❶ ⊗ 🏛

SANTI GIOVANNI E PAOLO

📍 J5 🏠 Campo Santi Giovanni e Paolo (also signposted San Zanipolo) �FondamenteNuove, Ospedale Civile 🕒 9am-6pm Mon-Sat, noon-6pm Sun ⏰ 12:30-4pm Easter &25 Dec 🌐 santigiovanniepaolo.it

Known colloquially as San Zanipolo, the vast and austere Santi Giovanni e Paolo vies with the Frari for the top spot as Venice's greatest Gothic church. Located in the Castello area, it is slightly off the tourist track, meaning it is often very quiet.

Known as the Pantheon of Venice, this striking church, built by the Dominicans in the 14th century, houses monuments to more than 25 doges. Among these are several fine works of art, executed by the Lombardi family and other leading sculptors. On arrival, visitors enter through a doorway decorated with Byzantine reliefs and carvings by celebrated Italian sculptor Bartolomeo Bon. The doorway itself is thought to be one of Venice's earliest Renaissance architectural works. The commanding bronze statue at the opposite end of the church is a monument to Doge Sebastiano Venier, who was Commander of the Fleet at Lepanto. A mere few steps away lies the tomb of Andrea Vendramin, created by Pietro Lombardo in 1476–8, in the form of a Roman triumphal arch.

Further up on the right is the grand Cappella di San Domenico, containing St Catherine of Siena's foot in a precious reliquary. The chapel's ceiling was frescoed by Giovanni Battista Piazzetta; his *Glory of St Dominic*, painted in 1727, displays a mastery of colour, perspective and foreshortening that is said to have had a profound influence on the young Tiepolo.

LOST FOREVER

Like many buildings in Venice, this basilica has suffered its share of fires, none more devastating than the one of 15 August 1867 in the rosary chapel, built in 1582 to commemorate the Venetian Republic's victory in Lepanto. Not only was the chapel entirely gutted, masterpieces by Titian, Tintoretto and Giovanni Bellini placed there for safekeeping were all lost. The fire is believed to have been started by anti-Catholic arsonists, and restoration work on the chapel was not completed until 1959.

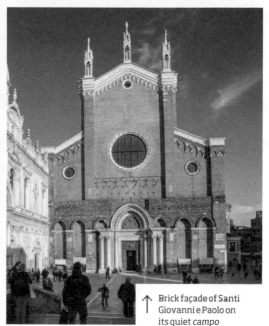

← The serene interior is packed with works by Venetian artists

↑ Brick façade of Santi Giovanni e Paolo on its quiet *campo*

Highlights

Lorenzo Lotto
The right transept contains Lorenzo Lotto's *St Antonine Distributing Alms* (1542), bursting with angels and cherubs.

Cima da Conegliano
▽ The bright colours of Cima da Conegliano's *Coronation of the Virgin* (1490) remain vibrant and remarkable.

Giovanni Bellini
△ Giovanni Bellini's magnificent polyptych of *San Vincenzo Ferrerei* (1465) still hangs in its original frame.

Alvise Vivarini
The sacristy houses Alvise Vivarini's exquisite *Christ Carrying the Cross* (1474), restored by Save Venice.

Paolo Veronese
△ Paolo Veronese has not one, but three ceiling panels in the rosary chapel.

EXPERIENCE MORE

STAY

Castello's grand hotels are sheer indulgence, with canal views and rooftop terraces, fine dining, sumptuous decor and meticulous service.

Aqua Palace
📍H6 🏛Calle della Malvasia 5492
🌐aquapalace.it

€€€

Hotel Metropole
📍K7 🏛Riva degli Schiavoni 4149
🌐hotelmetropole.com

€€€

Londra Palace
📍K7 🏛Riva degli Schiavoni 4171
🌐londrapalace.com

€€€

2
Hotel Danieli

📍J7 🏛Riva degli Schiavoni 4196 🚏San Zaccaria
🌐hoteldanieli.com

One of the most celebrated hotels in all of Europe, Hotel Danieli's deep-pink façade is a landmark on the Riva degli Schiavoni. Built in the 14th century, it became famous as the venue for the first opera performed in Venice, Monteverdi's *Proserpina Rapita* (1630). The palace – described as "the most noble in Venice" – became a hotel in 1822 and soon gained popularity with the literary and artistic set. Over the years, famous guests have included the likes of Balzac, Proust, Dickens, Cocteau, Ruskin, Debussy and Wagner. In the 1830s Room 10 witnessed an episode in the love affair between the French poet and dramatist Alfred de Musset, and novelist George Sand: when de Musset fell ill after a surfeit of orgies, Sand ran off with her Venetian doctor.

↑ The ornate interior of Hotel Danieli, and *(inset)* its iconic deep-pink façade

3 ✍
San Giorgio dei Greci

📍J/K7 🏛Campo dei Grei 3422 ☎041 523 95 69 🚏San Zaccaria 🕐9am-12:30pm & 2:30-4:30pm Mon & Wed-Sun (Sun am for Mass only)

The most remarkable feature of this 16th-century Greek church is the listing campanile, which looks as if it is about to topple into the Rio dei Greci. Inside is the *matroneo* – the gallery where, in keeping with Greek Orthodox custom, the women sat apart from the men. Note also the iconostasis separating the sanctuary from the nave. The nearby Scuola di San Nicolò dei Greci, redesigned in 1678, is now the **Museo delle Icone** of the Hellenic Institute.

Museo delle Icone
☎ 041 522 65 81 ○10am–6pm Sat–Mon

La Pietà

📍K7 🏛Riva degli Schiavoni 🚏San Zaccaria ○10:30am–1pm & 2:30–5:30pm daily; Guided tours: from noon Tue–Fri 🌐pietavenezia.org

The church of La Pietà (or Santa Maria della Visitazione) dates from the 15th century. It was rebuilt in 1745–60 by Giorgio Massari, and the Classical façade was added in 1906. It has an elegant oval interior. The resplendent ceiling fresco, *Triumph of Faith* (1755), was painted by Giambattista Tiepolo.

The church formed part of the Ospedale della Pietà, a convent, music school and foundling home for orphans; a large bas-relief by Marsili above the main entrance represents Charity. The institution was so popular that a warning plaque threatening damnation to parents who passed off their children as orphans was placed on the side wall.

From 1703 until 1740, celebrated composer Antonio Vivaldi directed the musical groups and wrote numerous pieces for the Pietà choir, and the church became famous for its performances.

It is now a popular venue for concerts, with a special emphasis on Vivaldi. These are held throughout the year, usually on Mondays and Thursdays.

→

The Flamboyant Gothic San Zaccaria dominates the quiet campo

San Zaccaria's adjoining Benedictine convent, which had close links with the church, became quite notorious for the riotous behaviour of its nuns.

San Zaccaria

📍J6 🏛Campo San Zaccaria ☎041 522 12 57 🚏San Zaccaria ○10am–noon & 4–6pm Mon–Sat, 4–6pm Sun

Set in a quiet square a stone's throw from the Riva degli Schiavoni, this church blends Flamboyant Gothic and Classical Renaissance styles. Founded in the 9th century, San Zaccaria was completely rebuilt between 1444 and 1515. Antonio Gambello began the façade in Gothic style and, when Gambello died in 1481, Mauro Coducci completed the upper section, adding all the Classical detail.

San Zaccaria's adjoining Benedictine convent, which had close links with the church, became quite notorious for the riotous behaviour of its nuns. The majority of them were Venetian nobility, sent to the convent to avoid the expense of a dowry. Every Easter the doge came with his entourage to San Zaccaria – a custom which originated as an expression of gratitude to the nuns, who had relinquished part of their garden so that Piazza San Marco could be enlarged.

The artistic highlight of the interior (illuminate with coins in the meter) is Giovanni Bellini's sumptuously coloured *Madonna and Child with Saints* (1505).

On the right of the church is a door to the Chapel of St Athanasius, which leads to the Chapel of San Tarasio. The chapel is decorated with vault frescoes (1442) by Andrea del Castagno, and Gothic polyptychs painted in 1443–4 by Antonio Vivarini and Giovanni d'Alemagna. The relics of eight doges lie buried in the water logged crypt. There is a small charge to visit the chapels and crypt.

6

Museo Diocesano d'Arte Sacra

📍 J7 🏛 Sant'Apollonia, Ponte della Canonica 🚤 San Zaccaria ⏰ 10am–1pm & 3–6pm Thu–Fri, 10am–6pm Sat 🔒 Public hols 🌐 veneziaupt.org

An architectural gem in a city that brims with architectural wonders, the cloister of Sant'Apollonia is the only Romanesque building in Venice. Only a few steps from Piazza San Marco, it provides a quiet retreat from the Piazza.

The monastery was once the home of Benedictine monks. In 1976 its cloisters became the home of the Diocesan Museum of Sacred Art, founded to provide a haven for works of art from closed or deconsecrated churches. The collection includes paintings, statues, crucifixes and many pieces of valuable silver. There are two workshops, staffed by volunteers who restore the paintings and statues. The collection is ever-changing, but among the major permanent exhibits are works by Luca Giordano (1634–1705), which came from the Church

---

🏔 GREAT VIEW
Gaze Across the Lagoon

It might be a cliché, but nothing can beat the lovely view across the blue waters of the Venetian Lagoon to the island of San Giorgio Maggiore from the Riva degli Schiavoni.

---

of Sant'Aponal, an impressive late 15th-century crucifix from San Pietro di Castello, and a 16th-century wood and crystal tabernacle.

7

Riva degli Schiavoni

📍 J/K7 🚤 San Zaccaria

The sweeping promenade that forms the southern quayside of Castello was named after the traders from Schiavonia (Dalmatia) who used to moor their boats and barges here. For those who arrive in Venice by water, this

↓ People enjoying a sunny afternoon along the Riva degli Schiavoni

---

long, curving quayside is a spectacular introduction to the charms of the city.

Originally formed from silt dredged up from the lagoon, the quay was widened and paved in the 18th century to create an elegant promenade. At its western end, close to Piazza San Marco, it teems with tourists thronging the souvenir stalls and people hurrying to vaporetto stops.

The Riva degli Schiavoni has always been busy with boats. Canaletto's drawings in the 1740s and 1750s show the Riva bustling with gondolas, sailing boats and barges. The gondolas are still here, but it is also chock-a-block with water taxis, vaporettos, excursion boats and tugs. Naval ships and the massive – and controversial – forms of ocean liners can also often be seen. After huge local protest, from 2021, giant cruise ships were banned from St Mark's Basin.

The modern annexe of the Hotel Danieli (p122) caused a great furore when it was built in 1948. Intruding on a waterfront graced by fine Venetian palaces and mansions, its stark outline is still something of an eyesore. The annexe occupies the spot where Doge Vitale Michiel II was stabbed to death in 1172. Three centuries earlier, in 864, Doge Pietro Tradonico had suffered the same fate in nearby Campo San Zaccaria.

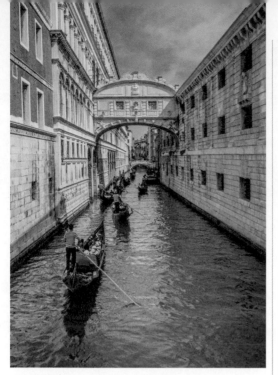

Gondolas glide along the Rio di Palazzo below the Ponte dei Sospiri (Bridge of Sighs)

8
Ponte della Paglia and Bridge of Sighs

Q J7 **🚊** San Zaccaria

The name of the Ponte della Paglia may derive from the boats that once moored here to off-load their cargoes of *paglia* (straw). Originally built in 1360, the existing structure dates from 1847. According to legend, the Bridge of Sighs, built in 1600 to link the Palazzo Ducale (*p82*) with the New Prisons, takes its name from the lamentations of the prisoners as they made their way over to the offices of the feared State Inquisitors, catching what might be their last glimpse of Venice through the stone grilled windows. Access to the bridge is available to the public via the Palazzo Ducale.

Did You Know?

In 1819, an escaped circus elephant sought refuge in Riva degli Schiavoni's Church of Sant'Antonin.

9
Fondazione Querini Stampalia

Q J6 **🚪** Campo Santa Maria Formosa 5252 **🚊** San Zaccaria **🕐** 10am–6pm Tue–Sun; Library: 10am–8pm Tue–Fri, 10am–7pm Sat & Sun **🌐** querinistampalia.org

The large Palazzo Querini Stampalia was commissioned in the 16th century by the descendants of the Venetian Querini family. Being great art lovers, they filled their palace with all manner of fine paintings. In 1868 the last member of the dynasty bequeathed the palace and the family art to the foundation that bears his name. The paintings include works by Giovanni Bellini, Giambattista Tiepolo and some vignettes by Pietro and Alessandro Longhi. The library on the first floor is a public facility with over 200,000 books, plus newspapers and magazines: bring photo ID so that the staff can issue you with a reader's card.

EAT

Da Remigio
Venetian seafood is on the menu at this charming trattoria; the *risotto di pesce* is a particular highlight.

Q K6 **🚪** Salizzada dei Greci 3416 **📞** 041 523 00 89 **🕐** Breakfast, Mon dinner, Tue

€€€

Al Covo
Tucked away in a hidden square, a husband-and-wife team focus on fish. Save room for one of Diane's desserts.

Q L7 **🚪** Campiello della Pescaria 3968 **🕐** Breakfast, Tue & Wed **🌐** ristorantealcovo.com

€€€

Alla Rivetta
A popular haunt of gondoliers, the tiny Alla Rivetta serves seasonal fish, including *canoce* (mantis shrimp) and *folpetti* (baby octopus).

Q J6 **🚪** Ponte San Provolo 4625 **🕐** Breakfast, Mon **🌐** allarivetta.it

€€€

↑ The fabulous ceiling of Palazzo Grimani's Tribuna room, modelled on Rome's Pantheon

MAURO CODUCCI

Little is known about Italian architect Mauro Coducci, who designed both the church of Santa Maria Formosa and the delightful façade of the Scuolo Grande di San Marco. Yet this enigmatic man from Bergamo has left an indelible mark on Venice. In 1469 he started building the church on the island of San Michele (p182), thus creating the first truly Renaissance building in Venice. His other projects include the church of San Zaccaria (p123) and the Ca' Vendramin Calergi palace.

⑩ Palazzo Grimani

📍 J6 🏛 Ramo Grimani, 4858 Castello 🚤 San Zaccaria, Ospedale Civile 🕐 10am-7pm Tue-Sun 🌐 palazzogrimani.org

Palazzo Grimani was once a famous residence-museum. The building housed a fine collection of antiquities collected by the two Grimani brothers, Giovanni, Patriarch of Acquileia, and Vettore, Procurator de Supra for the Venetian Republic, who renovated their grandfather's palace in the mid-16th century. The result is a magnificent work of architecture, which combines Tuscan and Roman elements with the original Venetian ones. The Roman courtyard and staircase are its finest examples.

Many of the Grimani brothers' treasures are now housed in the Museo Archeologico (p88), but even though the rooms are unfurnished, they are a delight: the decoration is rich, with elaborate marble and stuccowork, statues, fireplaces and stunning frescoes. Of particular note are the Tribuna and the Sala a Fogliami (Foliage Room). Temporary exhibitions are also held at the palazzo.

⑪ Statue of Colleoni

📍 J5 🏛 Campo Santi Giovanni e Paolo 🚤 Ospedale Civile

Bartolomeo Colleoni, the famous condottiere (commander of mercenaries) who became general-in-chief of the Republic of Venice in 1454, left his fortune to the Republic on condition that his statue was placed in front of San Marco. A prominent statue in the Piazza would have broken with precedent, so the Senate cunningly had Colleoni raised before the Scuola di San Marco instead of the basilica. A touchstone of early Renaissance sculpture, the equestrian statue of the commander is by the Florentine Andrea del Verrocchio and, after his death, was cast in bronze by Alessandro Leopardi. The statue has a strong sense of power and movement which ranks it alongside works of Donatello.

⑫ Campo Santa Maria Formosa

📍 J5, J6 🚤 Fondamente Nuove, Rialto

Spacious, sunny and flanked by handsome palaces, this market square is one of the most characteristic campi of Venice. On the southern side is the church of **Santa Maria Formosa**, distinctive for its swelling apses. Built on ancient foundations, the

← Late 15th-century statue of Bartolomeo Colleoni, general-in-chief of the Republic church was designed by Mauro Coducci in 1492, but took over a century to assume its current form. Unusually, it has two main façades – one overlooking the *campo*, the other the canal. Its most notable feature is the stone face at its foot.

Inside, Palma il Vecchio's polyptych *St Barbara and Saints* (around 1523) ranks among great Venetian masterpieces. Palma's portrayal of the dignified figure of St Barbara glorifies Venice's ideal female beauty. St Barbara was the patron saint of soldiers: in wartime they prayed to her for protection; in victory they came for thanksgiving.

Santa Maria Formosa

⏱10:30am–5pm Mon–Sat
🌐chorusvenezia.org

⓭

Scuola Grande di San Marco

📍J5 🏛Campo Santi Giovanni e Paolo
🚏Ospedale Civile
⏱9:30am–5:30pm Tue–Sat
🌐scuolagrandesanmarco.it

Few hospitals have as rich and unusual a façade as that

↑ The soaring marble façade of the Scuola Grande di San Marco

of Venice's Ospedale Civile. It was built originally as the seat of one of the six great confraternities of the city, but this 13th-century building was destroyed by fire in 1485. The Scuola was rebuilt in its current form at the end of the 15th century. The delightful asymmetrical façade, with its arcades, marble panels and trompe-l'œil effects, was the work of Pietro Lombardo working in conjunction with Giovanni Buora. The upper order was finished by Italian architect Mauro Coducci in 1495.

The interior was revamped in the 19th century and, since then, most of the artistic masterpieces the Scuola once contained have been dispersed. The library, featuring a fine carved 16th-century ceiling, is now a Museum of the History of Medicine, displaying antique texts and instruments. The hospital chapel, the Church of San Lazzaro dei Mendicanti, contains an early Tintoretto, *Saint Ursula and the 11,000 Virgins*, together with works by Veronese.

SHOP

Libreria Acqua Alta

Chaos reigns in this whimsical bookshop. Bathtubs and boats are filled with books, a staircase of tomes leads you to a towering view in the courtyard and cats lounge across bookshelves.

📍J5 🏛Calle Lunga Santa Maria Formosa 5176/b
📞041 296 08 41

Papier Mâché

Merging traditional techniques with contemporary design, this Venetian studio and shop has been producing masks for over 30 years. Handpainted ceramics and wooden frames are also available here.

📍J5 🏛Calle Lunga Santa Maria Formosa 5174/b
🌐papiermache.it

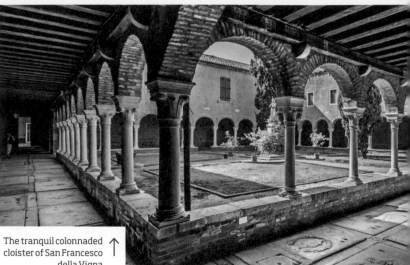

The tranquil colonnaded cloister of San Francesco della Vigna ↑

14

San Francesco della Vigna

📍L5 🏛️Campo di San Francesco della Vigna 📞041 520 61 02 🚤Celestia 🕐8am-12:30pm & 3-7pm daily

The name "della Vigna" derives from a vineyard that was bequeathed to the Franciscans in 1253. The church which the order built here in the 13th century was rebuilt under Jacopo Sansovino in 1534, with a façade added in 1562–72 by Palladio. The interior has a rich collection of works of art, including sculpture by Alessandro Vittoria, Paolo Veronese's *The Holy Family with Saints* (1562) and Antonio da Negroponte's *Virgin and Child* (around 1450). The

Did You Know?

Usefully meaning both "hello" and "goodbye", the word "*ciao*" originated in Venice.

Madonna and Child with Saints (1507) by Giovanni Bellini hangs near the cloister.

15

Ospedaletto

📍J5 🏛️Calle Barbaria delle Tole, 6691 Castello 📞041 532 29 20 🚤Ospedale Civile 🕐On request via bookings (call ahead)

Beyond the south flank of Santi Giovanni e Paolo *(p120)* is the façade of the Ospedaletto or Santa Maria dei Derelitti. The Ospedaletto was set up by the Republic in 1527 as a charitable institution to care for the sick and aged, and to educate orphans and abandoned girls. Such an education consisted largely of the study of music. The girls performed in choirs and orchestras, bringing in funds for the 1776 *Sala della Musica*, which became the main performance venue and has frescoes by Jacopo Guarana.

The church, which formed part of the Ospedaletto, was built by Andrea Palladio in 1575. Its façade was added in 1674 by Baldassare Longhena. The huge, monstrous heads on the façade have been

described as dark, distorted and anti-Classical grotesques, likened to deformed figures and swollen fruit. The interior of the church is decorated with notable 18th-century paintings, including *The Sacrifice of Isaac* (1720) by Giambattista Tiepolo.

16

Scuola di San Giorgio degli Schiavoni

📍K6 🏛️Calle Furlani, Castello 3959A 🚤San Zaccaria 🕐10am-5:30pm Wed-Mon (book ahead) 🌐scuoladalmatavene zia.com

Within this surprisingly simple *scuola* are some of the finest paintings of Vittore Carpaccio, which were commissioned by the Schiavoni community in Venice in the 15th century.

From the earliest days of the Republic, Venice forged trade links with the nearby coastal region of Schiavonia (Dalmatia) across the Adriatic. By 1420 permanent Venetian rule was established there, and many of the Schiavoni came to live in Venice. By the mid-15th century the Slav

> From the earliest days of the Republic, Venice forged trade links with the nearby coastal region of Schiavonia (Dalmatia) across the Adriatic Sea.

colony In the city had grown considerably and the state gave permission for them to found their own confraternity.

The Scuola was first established in 1451. It is a delightful spot to admire exceptional artworks by Carpaccio, and it has changed very little since it was rebuilt in 1551. The canvases show scenes from the lives of saints. Outstanding among them are *St George Slaying the Dragon*, *St Jerome Leading the Tamed Lion to the Monastery* and *The Vision of St Jerome*.

⑰
San Lorenzo

📍K5/6 🏛Campo San Lorenzo 🚤San Zaccaria 🕐11am–6pm Wed–Sun 🌐ocean-space.org

The church of San Lorenzo's only claim to fame is as the alleged burial place of Marco Polo. Unfortunately, there is nothing to show for it because

→

Walking on water: an infilled canal now forms Via Giuseppe Garibaldi

his sarcophagus disappeared during rebuilding in 1592. Bar occasional use during Biennales, the church has lain empty for decades, the foundations of the medieval structure and marble floor having been badly damaged by water seeping in from the adjacent canal. However, the deconsecrated church has now undergone extensive restoration thanks to the Thyssen-Bornemisza Art Contemporary Foundation's Ocean Space project, which focuses on issues surrounding climate change and the ocean. As well as art exhibitions, the San Lorenzo space houses educational and outreach programmes, as well as public workshops and climate-change initiatives.

⑱
San Giovanni in Bragora

📍K7 🏛Campo Bandiera e Moro ☎041 520 59 06 🚤Arsenale 🕐9:15–11:45am & 3:30–6pm Mon–Sat, 9:15–11:45am Sun

The foundations of this simple church date back to ancient times but the existing building is essentially Gothic (1475–9).

The intimate interior has major works of art which demonstrate the transition from Gothic to early Renaissance. Bartolomeo Vivarini's altarpiece, *Madonna and Child with Saints* (1478), is clearly Gothic. In stark contrast with this is Cima da Conegliano's *Baptism of Christ* (1492–5) on the main altar. This large-scale narrative scene, in a realistic landscape, set a precedent for later Renaissance painters.

⑲
Via Giuseppe Garibaldi

📍M8, M7, N7 🚤Giardini

This broad street, now a hot spot for restaurants and nightlife, was created by Napoleon in 1808 by filling in a canal. John Cabot and his son Sebastian, the Italian navigators who in 1497 found what they thought to be the coast of China (but in reality was the Labrador coast of Newfoundland), once lived here. Near the end of the street a bronze monument of Garibaldi by Augusto Benvenuti (1885) marks the northern end of the Viale Garibaldi, which leads to the public gardens.

⑳ San Pietro di Castello

⌖ P7 **⌂ Calle Seconda de la Fava 70, Castello** **🚉 San Pietro di Castello** **🕐 10:30am–5pm Mon–Sat** **🌐 chorusvenezia.org**

The old church of San Pietro di Castello and its free-standing, tilting campanile overlook a grassy square. The church, probably founded in the 7th century, became the cathedral of Venice and remained so until 1807, when San Marco took its place. The existing church, built to a Palladian design in the mid-16th century, has several notable features. These include the Lando Chapel, the Vendramin Chapel and the marble throne from an Arabic tombstone, originally said to have been the Seat of St Peter. In the south of the square is Mauro Coducci's elegant stone campanile, which was built in 1482–8; the cupola was added in 1670. Beside the church, the Palazzo Patriarcale was turned into barracks by Napoleon. The old cloisters are overgrown and strung with washing lines and fishing nets.

㉑ Arsenale

⌖ L6/M7, M6 **🚉 Arsenale**

Heart of the city's maritime power, the Arsenale was founded in the 12th century and enlarged in the 14th to 16th centuries to become the greatest naval shipyard in the world. The word "arsenal" derives from the Arabic *darsina'a*, house of industry – which indeed it was. At its height in the 16th century, a workforce of 16,000, the *arsenalotti*, was employed to construct, equip and repair the great Venetian galleys. One of the first production lines in Europe, it was like a city within a city, with workshops, warehouses, foundries and docks. Surrounded by crenellated walls, the site today is largely unused, except during the Architecture Biennale. The gateway, built in the form of a triumphal arch in 1460 by Antonio Gambello, and the vast site are the only evidence of its former splendour.

The two lions guarding the entrance were pillaged from Piraeus (near Athens) in 1687. A third lion, bald and sitting upright, bears runic inscriptions on his haunches, and is thought to have been carved by Scandinavian mercenaries who fought for the Byzantine emperor.

By the 17th century, when the seeds of Venetian decline were well and truly sown, the *arsenalotti* numbered only 1,000. Following the fall of the Republic in 1797, Napoleon destroyed the docks. In 1980, Arsenale served as an exhibition site of the first Biennale d'Architettura, today a famed international architecture and art show. From 1999,

---

THE ASSEMBLY-LINE SYSTEM

During the Arsenale's heyday, a Venetian galley could be constructed and fully equipped with remarkable speed and efficiency. From the early 16th century, the hulls, which were built in the New Arsenal, were towed past a series of buildings in the Old Arsenal to be equipped in turn with rigging, ammunition and food supplies. By 1570, when Venice was faced with the Turkish threat to take Cyprus, the Arsenale was so fast that it could turn out an entire galley in 24 hours. Henry III of France witnessed the system's efficiency in 1574 when the *arsenalotti* completed a galley in the time it took for him to partake in a state feast.

↓ Exterior wall of the Arsenale complex of former shipyards

↑ Celebrating the maritime splendour of the past, Venice's Museo Storico Navale

the Arsenale has been renovated, allowing sections of the area previously closed to be opened to the public, including the Giardino delle Vergini and the Sale d'Armi.

The bridge by the arched gateway affords views of the shipyard, while vaporetto 4.1 and 4.2 follow the perimeter wall.

⸻

Museo Storico Navale

♀ L7 ⌂ Riva San Biagio, Arsenale, Castello 2148 🚊 Arsenale ⏰ 11am–6pm Wed-Mon 🖥 visitmuve.it

It was the Austrians who, in 1815, first had the idea of assembling the remnants of the Venetian navy to create a historical naval museum.

To a series of models of vessels produced in the 17th century by the Arsenale they added all the naval paraphernalia they could obtain, including friezes preserved from famous galleys of the past, a variety of maritime firearms and a replica of the doge's ceremonial barge, the *Bucintoro*.

The collection has been housed in an ex-warehouse on the waterfront since 1958, and is now divided into the history of the Venetian navy, the Italian navy from 1860 to today, Adriatic vessels and a Swedish room. The layout and displays are excellent and there are informative explanations in English.

EAT

Aciugheta
Tasty *cichetti* and pizza in a friendly setting.

♀ J6 ⌂ Campo Santi Filippo e Giacomo 4359 🖥 aciugheta.com

€€€

⸻

Osteria Oliva Nera
A charming spot, with tables outdoors in summer.

♀ K6 ⌂ Salizzada dei Greci 3447 🗓 Wed 🖥 olivanera.com

€€€

⸻

Ristorante Giorgione
This lively restaurant serves hearty seafood.

♀ M7/8 ⌂ Via Garibaldi 1533 🗓 Wed 🖥 ristorantegiorgione.it

€€€

⸻

Oriental Bar & Bistrot
Exquisite drinks and cuisine in the Hotel Metropole.

♀ K7 ⌂ Riva degli Schiavoni 4149 🖥 hotelmetropole.com

€€€

A SHORT WALK
CASTELLO

Distance 1 km (half a mile) **Time** 10 minutes
Nearest Vaporetto San Zaccaria

A stroll along the Riva degli Schiavoni is an integral part of a visit to Venice. Glorious views of San Giorgio Maggiore compensate for the commercialized aspects of the quayside: souvenir stalls, excursion touts and an abundance of tourists. Associations with literary figures are plentiful. Petrarch lived at No. 4145, Henry James was offered lodgings at No. 4161, and John Ruskin stayed at the Hotel Danieli. Inland, the quiet, unassuming streets and squares of Castello provide a contrast to the bustling waterfront.

Palazzo Trevisan-Cappello, *used as a showroom for Murano glass, was the home of Bianca Cappello, wife of Francesco de' Medici.*

The **Museo Diocesano d'Arte Sacra** *(p124) is housed in the cloisters of the ancient Benedictine monastery of Sant'Apollonia.*

START

CAMPO SS
FILIPPO E GIACOMO

CALLE DRIO LA CHIESA

SALIZZADA SAN PROVOL

Did You Know?

Legend says if you kiss on a gondola under the Bridge of Sighs at sunset, eternal love is yours.

CALLE DEGLI ALBANESI

CALLE DELLE RASSE

RIO DEL PALAZZO

RIO DEL VIN

People throng the Istrian stone **Ponte della Paglia** *(p125) – the "straw bridge" – for the best views of the neighbouring Bridge of Sighs, the covered bridge that links the Palazzo Ducale to the old prisons.*

RIVA DEGLI
SCHIAVONI

The paved quayside of **Riva degli Schiavoni** *(p124) was established over 600 years ago, and widened in 1782.*

SAN
ZACCARIA
PAGLIA

SAN
ZACCARIA
DANIELI

Joseph da Niel, after whom **Hotel Danieli** *(p122) is named, turned Palazzo Dandolo into a hub for 19th-century writers and artists.*

| 0 metres | 75 |
| 0 yards | 75 |

N ↑

CASTELLO

↑ Serene and unassuming
Campo Santa Maria
Formosa, Castello

Overlooking the quiet Fondamenta Osmarin is a fine Venetian Gothic palace – **Palazzo Priuli**. *The corner window is particularly beautiful, but the early 16th-century façade frescoes have now disappeared.*

Subsidence is the main cause of Venice's tilting bell towers; that of **San Giorgio dei Greci** (p122) *looks particularly perilous.*

The Gothic façade of **San Zaccaria** (p123) *features Renaissance details by Coducci.*

In Vivaldi's day, **La Pietà** (p123) *became world famous for the superb quality of its musical performances.*

RIO SAN PROVOLO

F.MTA DELL'OSMARIN

CALLE DEI GRECI

CAMPO SAN PROVOLO

CAMPO SAN ZACCARIA

CALLE BOSELLO

RIO DEI GRECI

CALLE DELLA PIETA

RIVA DEGLI SCHIAVONI

■ **FINISH**

SAN ZACCARIA JOLANDA

MVE

Pensione Wildner
is where Henry James completed Portrait of a Lady *(1881).*

The **Statue of Vittorio Emanuele II**,
the first king of a united Italy, was sculpted by Ettore Ferrari in 1887.

↑ The Campanile of San Giorgio dei Greci towers over the Rio dei Greci

A LONG WALK
EASTERN CASTELLO

Distance 5 km (3 miles) **Walking time**
1 hour **Terrain** Paved and relatively flat
Nearest Vaporetto Arsenale

This peaceful stroll takes you from the animated Castello quayside to the quieter eastern limits of the city. The focal point of the tour is the solitary island of San Pietro di Castello, site of the former cathedral of Venice. From here you head south to the island of Sant'Elena with its historic church and Venice's football stadium, and return via the public gardens along the scenic waterfront. There are a handful of simple cafés along the route; most are found on Via Giuseppe Garibaldi. Caffè Paradiso at the entrance to the Giardini Pubblici has excellent views, and the shady parks are a welcome retreat from the bustle of the city.

Locator Map
For more detail see p118

Campo Ruga is a *pretty, residential square, tucked between two quiet canals.*

Pause on the bridge for distant views of the **Arsenale** (p130).

Via Giuseppe Garibaldi (p129)

START FINISH

John Cabot Home

The first house on the right was **the home of John Cabot** *and his son Sebastian, the Italian navigators who in 1497 found what they thought to be the coast of China (it was actually the Labrador coast of Newfoundland).*

Garibaldi Monument

A bronze **monument of Garibaldi** *by Augusto Benvenuti (1885) marks the northern end of the Viale Garibaldi, which leads to the public gardens.*

Giardini

La Donna Partigiana

La Donna Partigiana *is a semi-submerged bronze memorial to all the women who lost their lives in World War II. It can only be seen at low tide.*

San Giuseppe

The church of **San Giuseppe**. *On the rare occasions it is open you can see Vincenzo Scamozzi's monument to Doge Marino Grimani.*

Giardini Pubblici

← Plant lovers adore the lush interior of the historic greenhouse in the popular Giardini Pubblici

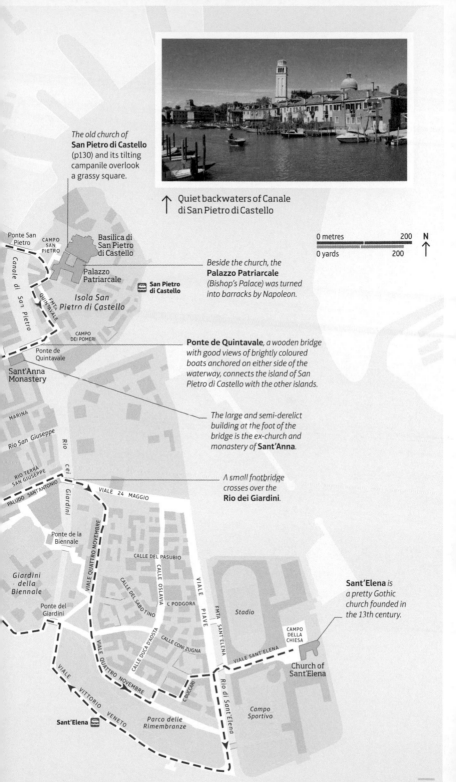

The old church of **San Pietro di Castello** (p130) and its tilting campanile overlook a grassy square.

↑ Quiet backwaters of Canale di San Pietro di Castello

Ponte San Pietro

CAMPO SAN PIETRO

Basilica di San Pietro di Castello

Palazzo Patriarcale

San Pietro di Castello

Canale di San Pietro

FMTA QUINTAVALE

Isola San Pietro di Castello

CAMPO DEI POMERI

Ponte de Quintavale

Sant'Anna Monastery

MARINA

Rio San Giuseppe

RIO

RIO TERRA SAN GIUSEPPE

PALUDO SANT'ANTONIO

Giardini

cei

VIALE 24 MAGGIO

Ponte de la Biennale

VIALE QUATTRO NOVEMBRE

CALLE DEL PASUBIO

CALLE DEL SABOTINO

CALLE OSLAVIA

C PODGORA

VIALE

FMTA SANT'ELENA

PIAVE

Stadio

CAMPO DELLA CHIESA

Giardini della Biennale

Ponte del Giardini

CALLE DUCA D'AOSTA

CALLE CONI ZUGNA

VIALE QUATTRO NOVEMBRE

VIALE SANT'ELENA

Church of Sant'Elena

VIALE

C BUCCARI

Rio di Sant'Elena

Campo Sportivo

VITTORIO VENETO

Parco delle Rimembranze

Sant'Elena

Beside the church, the **Palazzo Patriarcale** (Bishop's Palace) was turned into barracks by Napoleon.

Ponte de Quintavale, a wooden bridge with good views of brightly coloured boats anchored on either side of the waterway, connects the island of San Pietro di Castello with the other islands.

The large and semi-derelict building at the foot of the bridge is the ex-church and monastery of **Sant'Anna**.

A small footbridge crosses over the **Rio dei Giardini**.

Sant'Elena is a pretty Gothic church founded in the 13th century.

0 metres 200
0 yards 200
N ↑

DORSODURO

Dorsoduro is named after the solid subsoil on which this area has been built up – the name translates from Italian to "hard backbone". Venice's first settlers selected this spot to build their homes precisely due to its comparatively high land. Dorsoduro was originally centred around the wide Giudecca Canal facing Giudecca island to the south. From the 6th century, dwellings sprang up along both canal banks and the Zattere, Dorsoduro's long southern quayside once lined with warehouses, became a focal point of Venetian life. It was only at the turn of the 11th century that settlements then spread across the Grand Canal to the north into San Marco.

The establishment of the Accademia in 1750 linked Dorsoduro to the wealthy *sestiere* of San Marco via the Ponte dell'Accademia, bringing prosperity and foreign interest to the immediate area. In contrast, the western side of Dorsoduro and Giudecca remained more industrialized until the end of World War II, when factories and shipyards went into decline. Giudecca is now a quiet residential neighbourhood.

A

PONTE DELLA LIBERTA

CAMPO SANT'ANDREA

Canale di Santa Maria Maggiore

R. T. SANT'ANDREA

FONDAMENTA

RIO TERRA DEI PENSIERI

FONDAMENTA DELLE PROCURATIE

FOND DELL'ARZERE

RIO TERRA DEI SCACCH

RIO DELL'ARZERE

CT MAGGIORE

C CAMERINI

San Nicolò
dei Mendicoli **15**

Campiello Tron **7**

2

FONDAMENTA BARBARIGO

FMTA LIZZA
RIO DI SAN NICOLÒ

FOND. DE PESCHERIA

FMTA DEI DABI

BANCHINA DEL PORTO COMMERCIALE

B

Stazione Ferrovie
dello Stato
Santa Lucia

Ferrovia

Piazzale
Roma

FOND. DI SANTA CHIARA

Ponte della
Costituzione

Piazzale
Roma

**PIAZZALE
ROMA**

FONDA SANT'ANDREA

DELLE BURCHIELLE

FONDAMENTA

RIO TERRA DEI PENSIERI

FMTA CAZZOLA

CALLE LARGA RAGUSEI

FONDAMENTA DEI CERERI

Rio del Tintor

CHIOTTI

CALLE DEI GUARDIANI

RIO DEL SOCCORSO

FONDAMENTA

CALLE RAGUSEI

Rio Briati

Rio dei Carmini **1**

FMTA. DEL SOCCORSO

DORSODURO

RIO DI SAN SEBASTIANO

RIO DI SAN

FMTA S. SEBASTIANO

FOND. DE PESCHERIA

Angelo
Raffaele **3**

13

CAMPO
ANGELO
RAFFAELE

CALLE D. FRATI

14

**San
Sebastiano**

SAL. A SAN BASEGIO

C. BALASTRO

CALLE DELLA MASENA

CALLE D. MORTI

CALLE CHIESA

San Basilio

FMTA. ZATTERE PONTE LUNGO

CALLE DEI CARTELLOTTI

C

FONDAMENTA SANTA LUCIA

C. LUNGA
C. CHIOFFETTA

Rio Marin

FONDAMENTA SAN SIMEON PICCOLO

C. BERGAMASCHI

CAMPO DELLA LANA

Rio di San Zuane

C. SAN ZUANE

San Nicolò
da Tolentino

Giardino
Papadopoli

FONDAMENTA PAPADOPOLI

RIO DEL MAGAZEN

**SAN POLO AND
SANTA CROCE**
p98

Rio Nuovo
DEL RIO NUOVO

Rio di Ca' Foscari

San
Pantalon **8**

CAMPO SAN
PANTALON

Ex-Chiesa di
Santa Margherita

CORTE
CONTARINI

CALLE NUOVA

FMTA
FOSCARINI

CALLE
D. FORNO

FMTA
MALCANTON

10

CALLE DEL
MAGAZEN

CALLE SAONERI

CALLE CAPPELLER

Campo Santa
Margherita

Casa dei Varoteri

Scuola Grande
dei Carmini **11**

R. T. SANT'APONAL

CORTE
D. FORNO

RIO TERRA
BOTTEGHE

CALLE D.

Santa Maria
dei Carmini **12**

CALLE
DELLO SQUERO

Ponte dei
Pugni **5**

6

Campo San
Barnaba

CALLE LUNGA SAN BARNABA

CALLE

CAMPO
SQUERO

Rio Malpaga

RIO TERRA OGNISSANTI

C. DELL'AVOGARIA

Rio

RIO
del Gaffaro

FONDAMENTA

Rio Ognissanti

FOND. DELLE EREMITE

FONDAMENTA DI BORGO

RIO delle EREMITE

FONDAMENTA
BONTINI

San
Trovaso **17**

16

Squero di
San Trovaso

CALLE TREVISAN

V-A-C Foundation
Zattere

18

Zattere

Zattere

Molino Stucky

Hilton Molino
Stucky

RIO DI SAN BIAGIO

FONDAMENTA SAN BIAGIO

D

C. LARGA DEI BARI

C. LUNGA
C. CHIOFFETTA

SANTA CROCE

CAMPO
SAN ROCCO

CALLE DEI PRETI CROSERA **5**

8

CALLE DEL MAGAZEN

CALLE

Canale della

GIUDECCA

Sant'
Eufemia

Inset (bottom left)

DORSODURO

DORSODURO

Must Sees
1. Accademia
2. Peggy Guggenheim Collection

Experience More
3. Santa Maria della Salute
4. Campiello Barbaro
5. Ponte dei Pugni
6. Campo San Barnaba
7. Punta della Dogana
8. San Pantalon
9. Ca' Rezzonico
10. Campo Santa Margherita
11. Scuola Grande dei Carmini
12. Santa Maria dei Carmini
13. Angelo Raffaele
14. San Sebastiano
15. San Nicolò dei Mendicoli
16. Squero di San Trovaso
17. San Trovaso
18. Zattere
19. Santa Maria della Visitazione
20. Gesuati

Eat
1. Da Codroma
2. Osteria Bakan
3. Trattoria Anzolo Raffaele

Drink
4. Cantine del Vino già Schiavi
5. Malvasia all'Adriatico Mar
6. Osteria ai Pugni

Stay
7. B&B Le Terese
8. Pensione Accademia Villa Maravegie

❶ ⬦ 🅜 🛍

ACCADEMIA

📍E8 🏛 Campo della Carità 🚉 Accademia 🕒 8:15am–2pm Mon, 8:15am–7:15pm Tue–Sun 🚫 1 Jan, 25 Dec 🌐 gallerieaccademia.it

A dazzling collection of masterpieces spanning the full development of Venetian art from Byzantine to Renaissance, Baroque and Rococo, the Accademia is Venice's answer to the Uffizi in Florence – and with works by Titian, Bellini and Giorgione, it is equally unmissable.

The largest collection of Venetian art in existence, the Gallerie dell'Accademia is housed in three former religious buildings. The basis of the collection was the Accademia di Belle Arti, founded in 1750 by the painter Giambattista Piazzetta, who started the collection to serve as models for the art school; in 1807 it was boosted by Napoleon with the addition of many masterpieces salvaged from the churches and monasteries that he suppressed. That same year the collection was moved to its present premises.

The opening of the downstairs galleries in 2015 was the first stage of an ambitious expansion plan. These interactive galleries present the art of the 17th, 18th and 19th centuries, grouped around themes such as portraiture, with rooms devoted to the work of Hayez, Canova and Palladio, as well as a room on ceiling paintings, including a masterpiece by Veronese.

> 💬 INSIDER TIP
> **Let There Be Light**
>
> The paintings in the museum depend on natural light. For the best viewing experience, visit on a bright, sunny morning.

$\rightarrow$
Admiring Veronese's
*Feast in the House
of Levi* (1573)

1507

▽ The unknown meaning of Giorgione's *Tempest* has been vexing art historians for centuries.

1496

△ Though his *St Ursula* cycle is the Accademia's real treasure, Carpaccio's *Miracle of the Cross at the Rialto* is remarkable for its depiction of a Black gondolier.

1530

△ Another famously haunting piece is Lorenzo Lotto's *Portrait of a Young Man*, known for his penetrative stare.

1534

△ Commissioned by the fraternity of the Scuola Grande di Santa Maria della Carità, Titian's magnificent *Presentation of the Virgin* still hangs proudly in its original home.

GALLERY GUIDE

The current programme of restoration work is ongoing, so be prepared for absent paintings or sections of the gallery that are temporarily closed off. The additional ground-floor galleries are arranged thematically, while upstairs a second gallery (Quadreria) is arranged chronologically and contains works by artists such as Bellini. Guided visits are free of charge but it is recommended to book in advance. Entry to the gallery is free on local public holidays and during National Museum Week in March.

↑ Entrance to the Accademia Gallery on Campo della Carità

EXPLORING THE ACCADEMIA'S COLLECTION

Spanning more than five centuries, the fascinating collection of paintings in the Accademia provides a complete spectrum of the Venetian school, from the medieval Byzantine period through the Renaissance to the Baroque and Rococo. Upstairs, the order is more or less chronological, while the downstairs rooms are arranged thematically.

Byzantine and International Gothic

In Room 1, Paolo Veneziano, the true founder of the Venetian school and the most important Venetian painter of the 14th century, displays a blend of Western and Eastern influences in his *Coronation of the Virgin* (1325). The linear rhythms are unmistakably Gothic, yet the glowing gold background is distinctly Byzantine. In the same room, Michele Giambono's *Coronation of the Virgin* (1448) is characterized by delicate naturalistic detail.

↑ *Coronation of the Virgin in Paradise* (1450) by da Venezia in Room 1

Early Renaissance

Central to Venetian art in the 15th century was the *Sacra Conversazione*, where the Madonna is portrayed in a unified composition with saints: Giovanni Bellini's altarpiece for San Giobbe (around 1487) in Room 2 is a fine example. Giovanni, the younger Bellini, was influenced by the controlled rational style and mastery of perspective in the works of his brother-in-law, Andrea Mantegna, whose work *St George* (around 1460) is in Room 23. To Mantegna's rationality and harsh realism Giovanni added humanity. This is seen in his Madonna paintings (Rooms 4 and 23).

Out on a limb from the main 16th-century Venetian tradition was the enigmatic Lorenzo Lotto, best known for portraits conveying moods of psychological unrest, such as his melancholic *Portrait of a Gentleman* (around 1525) in Room 7. More in the Venetian tradition, Palma il Vecchio's sumptuous *Sacra Conversazione* in Room 8, painted around the same time, shows the influence of the early work of Titian.

High Renaissance

Occupying an entire wall of Room 10, the *Feast in the House of Levi* by Paolo Veronese (1573) was commissioned as *The Last Supper*. However, the hedonistic details in the painting were not well received and Veronese was ordered to remove the profane content of the picture. Instead, he simply changed the title.

Jacopo Tintoretto made his reputation with *The Miracle of the Slave* (1548), also in Room 10. This was the first of a series of works painted for the Scuola Grande di San Marco (p127). In the same room, see Veronese's use of colour in the *Mystical Marriage of St Catherine* (around 1575).

ROSALBA CARRIERA

Venetian artist Rosalba Carriera's career took off in the 17th-century, when her pastel portraits earned her international acclaim throughout Europe, particularly in Vienna and Paris. It was here that she painted fellow painter Antoine Watteau among many others. She was the most successful female artist of her time.

Baroque, Genre and Landscapes

Venice suffered from a distinct lack of local Baroque painters, but a few non-Venetians kept the Venetian school alive during the 17th century. The most notable among these artists was celebrated Genoese painter Bernardo Strozzi (1581–1644). The artist was a great admirer of the work of Veronese, as can be seen in his *Feast at the House of Simon* (1629) in Room 11. Also represented in this room is Giambattista Tiepolo, the greatest Venetian painter of the 18th century.

Ceremonial Paintings

Rooms 20 and 21 feature two great cycles of paintings from the late 16th century.

↑ Tintoretto's *Miracle of the Slave* (1548) depicting St Mark's benevolence

Room 20 houses *The Stories of the Cross* by many of Venice's leading artists, commissioned by the Scuola di San Giovanni Evangelista, including *The Procession in St Mark's Square* (1496) by Gentile Bellini. Another, Vittore Carpaccio's *Healing of the Madman* (around 1496), depicts the Rialto Bridge, which collapsed in 1524. The second series, which features detailed *Scenes from the Legend of St Ursula* (1490s) by Carpaccio in Room 21, provides a fascinatingly poignant kaleidoscope of life.

Masterpieces

Room 23 brings together some of the most famous master-pieces of the collection. These include Andrea Mantegna's *St George* (around 1460), Bellini's *Madonna of the Little Trees* (around 1487) and Giorgione's famous *Tempest* (around 1507). The inventive young Giorgione was influenced by Bellini, but went way beyond his master. In the atmospheric *Tempest*, his treatment of the landscape and the use of the figures to intensify that mood was an innovation replicated by many artists working in the 16th century and well beyond.

Sala dell'Albergo

When the Scuola della Carità became the site of the Academy of Art in the early 19th century, the Scuola's *albergo* (where students lodged) retained its original panelling and 15th-century ceiling. The huge *Presentation of the Virgin* (1538) is one of surprisingly few Titians in the gallery. The walls are also adorned with a grandiose triptych (1446) by Antonio Vivarini and Giovanni d'Alemagna.

↑ The colourful triptych (1446) adorning the walls of the Sala dell'Albergo

Did You Know?

Leonardo da Vinci's ink-on-paper *The Vitruvian Man* is stored safely in the Accademia's Cabinet of drawings and prints.

→ Façade of Peggy Guggenheim and *(inset)* abstract painting by Tancredi

② 🎨 🅜 🖥 🛍

PEGGY GUGGENHEIM COLLECTION

📍 F8 🏛 Palazzo Venier dei Leoni 🚤 Accademia 🕙 10am–6pm Wed–Mon
🚫 25 Dec 🌐 guggenheim-venice.it

The light-filled rooms and the modern canvases of the Peggy Guggenheim Collection stand in stark contrast to the Renaissance paintings of Venice's churches and museums. One of the city's most visited sights, it houses works by more than 200 modern and contemporary artists, representing avant-garde movements such as Cubism, Futurism and Surrealism.

Intended as a four-storey palace, the Palazzo Venier dei Leoni never rose beyond the ground floor – hence its nickname, Il Palazzo Nonfinito. In 1949 it was bought by American millionairess Peggy Guggenheim, a collector, dealer and patron of the arts. A perspicacious and high-spirited woman, she befriended and furthered the careers of many Abstract and Surrealist artists. She bequeathed her vast collection of modern European and American art to her uncle Solomon R Guggenheim's foundation in 1979, stipulating that it remain in Venice. The museum was inaugurated in 1980.

The collection is one of Europe's leading modern art galleries. It consists of 200 pieces, representing almost every modern art movement, by artists such as Picasso, Braque, Miró, de Chirico, Magritte, Dalí, Kandinsky, Balla, Severini, Picabia, Delaunay, Pollock, Duchamp, Klee, Mondrian, Malevich, Calder and Rothko.

Sculpture features prominently throughout the house and garden. The most provocative piece is Marino Marini's *Angelo della Città* (Angel of the City, 1948), a prominently displayed man sitting on a horse, erect in all respects.

EXPERIENCE MORE

3

Santa Maria della Salute

⊞ G8 ⌂ Campo della Salute ⊞ Salute ⊙ 9am-noon, 3-5:30pm daily ⊞ basilica salutevenezia.it

This great Baroque church standing at the entrance of the Grand Canal is one of the most imposing architectural landmarks of Venice. Henry James likened it to "some great lady on the threshold of her salon".

The church was built in thanksgiving for the city's deliverance from the plague of 1630, hence the name *Salute*, meaning "health and salvation". Every 21 November, in celebration of the occasion, worshippers approach across a bridge of boats spanning the mouth of the canal. Baldassare Longhena began the church in 1630. It was completed in 1687, five years after his death.

The interior consists of a large octagonal space and six chapels radiating from the ambulatory. The altar's sculptural group by Giusto Le Corte represents the Virgin and Child protecting Venice from the plague. Some of the best works, such as

Titian's ceiling paintings of *Cain and Abel, Abraham and Isaac* and *David and Goliath* (1540–49), are beyond the altar, where visitors are not allowed. The Pinacoteca Manfrediniana, next door to the sacristy, is home to a number of works by Veronese and Titian.

4

Campiello Barbaro

⊞ F8 ⊞ Salute

This enchanting little square is flanked on one side by the wisteria-clad walls of Ca' Dario, a Grand Canal palace. The square's tree-studded centre draws an interesting and eclectic crowd of university students, historians, street artists and locals on evening strolls.

170

The total number of canals that crisscross the city of Venice.

PEGGY GUGGENHEIM

Peggy Guggenheim (1898-1979) came to Europe in 1921, quickly fitting into Bohemian Paris. Resolving to "buy a picture a day", she amassed an extensive collection before she made Venice her home in 1947, hosting exhibits and supporting local artists. She is fondly remembered by locals for her faithful dogs and for owning the city's last private gondola.

↑ The sun sinking behind the spectacular walls of Santa Maria della Salute

DRINK

Cantine del Vino già Schiavi

This outstanding vintner's doubles as a wine bar, and it's one of the best in town. There are no seats, so you're served where you stand.

📍E8 🏠Fondamenta Nani 992 🕐Sun
🌐cantinaschiavi.com

Malvasia all'Adriatico Mar

This tiny bar squeezes in delicious snacks, light meals and unusual wines - ask Francesco to guide you through the exceptional list.

📍D6 🏠Calle Crosera 3771 📞041 476 43 22

Osteria ai Pugni

A lively bar beloved of locals and offering over 50 different wines to choose from. Tasty snacks are also served.

📍D7 🏠Fondamenta Gherardini 2836
📞346 960 77 85

---

⑤

Ponte dei Pugni

📍D7 🏠Fondamenta Gherardini 🚉Ca' Rezzonico

Venice has several Ponti dei Pugni (bridges of fists), but this is the most famous. Spanning the peaceful Rio San Barnaba, the small bridge is distinguished by two pairs of footprints that are set in white stone on the top of the bridge. These mark the starting positions for the fights that took place between rival factions. Formerly there were no balustrades and contenders hurled each other straight into the water. The battles became so bloodthirsty that they were banned in 1705.

---

⑥

Campo San Barnaba

📍D7 🚉Ca' Rezzonico

The Parish of San Barnaba, with its central canalside square, was known in the 18th century as the home of impoverished Venetian patricians who were lured by the low rents. Some relied on state support or begging, while others worked in the state gambling house.

Today the square and canal, with its vegetable barge, are quietly appealing. The church (open Mon–Sat mornings) is fairly simple in design, apart from a Tiepolesque ceiling.

---

⑦

Punta della Dogana

📍G8 🏠Campo della Salute 🚉Salute 🕐10am-7pm Wed-Mon 🚫25 Dec
🌐pinaultcollection.com

The building that housed the sea customs post was originally constructed in the 15th century to inspect the cargo of ships that intended to enter Venice. However, the customs house that visitors see today was built in the late 17th century and replaced a tower that guarded the entrance to the Grand Canal. On the corner tower of the house, two bronze Atlases support a striking golden ball.

The Punta della Dogana continued to serve as a customs house until the 1980s. After standing empty for many years, it was bought in 2007 by French billionaire François Pinault, owner of the famous Palazzo Grassi *(p93)*, and now hosts temporary displays of modern art.

---

⑧

San Pantalon

📍D6 🏠Campo San Pantalon 🚉San Tomà, Piazzale Roma 🕐10am-12:30pm & 3:30-6pm Sat-Thu 🌐sanpantalon.it

The overwhelming feature of this late 17th-century church is the painted ceiling, remarkable for its illusionistic effects. It comprises a total of 40 scenes (admirers claim it as the world's largest work of art on canvas), depicting the martyrdom of the physician St Pantalon. The artist, Gian Antonio Fumiani, took 24 years (1680–1704) to achieve this masterpiece, but then allegedly fell to his death from the scaffolding.

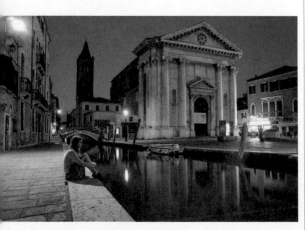

↑ The canal that cuts through picturesque Campo San Barnaba

↑ Visitors exploring the exquisite marble halls of Ca' Rezzonico

Paolo Veronese's emotive painting *St Pantalon Healing a Boy* was his final work of art (1587). To see Antonio Vivarini and Giovanni d'Alemagna's *Coronation of the Virgin* (1444) and *The Annunciation* (1350), attributed to Paolo Veneziano, ask the custodian for access to the Cappella del Sacro Chiodo (Chapel of the Holy Nail).

Ca' Rezzonico

📍 E7 🚪 Fondamenta Rezzonico 3136 🚤 Ca' Rezzonico 🕐 Apr–Oct: 10am–6pm Wed–Mon; Nov–Mar: 10am–4:30pm 🌐 carezzonico.visitmuve.it

This richly furnished Baroque palace is one of the most splendid in Venice. It is also one of the few palaces in the city that opens its doors to the public, and since 1934 it has housed the museum of 18th-century Venice.

The building was begun by Baldassare Longhena (architect of the Santa Maria della Salute, *p145*) in 1667, but the funds of the Bon family, who commissioned it, ran dry before the second floor was started. In 1712, the unfinished palace was bought by the Rezzonicos,

a Genoese family of merchants-turned-bankers. A large portion of their fortune was spent on the purchase, construction and decoration of the palace. By 1758 it was in a fit state for the Rezzonicos to throw the first of the huge parties for which they later became renowned.

The palace was bought by the poet Robert Browning and his son, who was married to an American heiress. Unfortunately, Browning died of bronchitis in 1889, just a year after he had purchased the palace.

The outstanding attraction in the palace today is Giorgio Massari's ballroom, which occupies the entire breadth of the building. It has been beautifully restored and is embellished with gilded chandeliers and a ceiling with trompe-l'œil frescoes.

Eighteenth-century paintings occupy the *piano nobile* (second floor). A whole room is devoted to Pietro Longhi's portrayals of everyday Venetian life. Other paintings worthy of note are Francesco Guardi's *Nuns' Parlour* (1768) and one of the few Canalettos

in Venice, his *View of the Rio dei Mendicanti* (1725). On the floor above is a reconstructed 18th-century apothecary's shop and a puppet theatre.

---

⑩

Campo Santa Margherita

📍 D7 🚤 Ca' Rezzonico

The sprawling square of Santa Margherita, lined with houses from the 14th and 15th centuries, is the lively hub of western Dorsoduro. Market stalls, offbeat shops and cafés attract a young crowd.

The former church of Santa Margherita, now an auditorium owned by the university, lies to the north of the square. Visitors can see sculptural fragments from the original 18th-century church, including gargoyles, on the truncated campanile and adjacent house. The *Scuola dei Varotari* (Scuola of the Tanners), in the centre of the square, has a faded relief of the Madonna della Misericordia protecting the tanners.

> The sprawling square of Santa Margherita, lined with houses from the 14th and 15th centuries, is the lively hub of western Dorsoduro.

↑ A frescoed ceiling within Scuola Grande dei Carmini, painted by Giambattista Tiepolo

11

Scuola Grande dei Carmini

📍C7 🏛Campo Carmini 🚏Ca' Rezzonico 🕐10am-5pm daily 🔒Religious hols 🌐scuolagrandecarmini.it

The headquarters of the Carmelite confraternity was built beside their church in 1663. In the 1740s Giambattista Tiepolo was commissioned to decorate the ceiling of the *salone* (hall) on the upper floor. The nine ceiling paintings that he produced so impressed the Carmelites that Tiepolo was promptly made an honorary member of the brotherhood. The ceiling shows *St Simeon Stock Receiving the Scapular of the Carmelite Order from the Virgin*. The Carmelites honoured St Simeon Stock because he re-established the order in Europe after its 13th-century expulsion from the Holy Land.

The archive rooms also contain remarkable art and elaborate woodwork, with ceiling and wall paintings by Giustino Menescardi and caryatids by Giacomo Piazzetta.

12

Santa Maria dei Carmini

📍C7 🏛Campo Carmini 📞0415226553 🚏Ca' Rezzonico, San Basilio 🕐7:15am-noon & 4-7pm daily

Known also as Santa Maria dei Carmelo, this church was built in the 14th century but has since undergone extensive alterations. The most prominent external feature is the lofty campanile, whose perilous tilt was skilfully rectified in 1688. The interior is large, sombre and richly decorated, with the nave adorned with

Contrasting with the remote and run-down area that surrounds it, San Nicolò dei Mendicoli is one of the most charming and delightful churches in Venice.

EAT

Da Codroma
Expect quality cooking at this neighbourhood fish restaurant.

📍C7 🏛Fondamenta Briati 2540 📞041 524 6789 🔒Mon

€€€

Osteria Bakan
Behind a humble exterior lies this fabulous restaurant.

📍B7 🏛Corte Maggiore 2314a 📞0415647658 🔒Breakfast, Mon

€€€

Trattoria Anzolo Raffaele
Head here for meat-heavy mains and a superb regional wine list.

📍B8 🏛Campo dell'Angelo Raffaele 1722 🔒Wed 🌐trattoria anzoloraffaele.it

€€€

gilded statues, and a series of paintings illustrating the history of the Carmelite Order.

There are two interesting paintings in the church's side altars. Cima da Conegliano's *Adoration of the Shepherds* (around 1509) is in the second altar on the right (coins in the light meter are essential). In the second altar on the left is Lorenzo Lotto's *St Nicholas of Bari with Saints Lucy and John the Baptist* (around 1529). This painting demonstrates the artist's religious devotion and his love of nature. On the right-hand side of this highly detailed landscape, there is a tiny depiction of St George killing the dragon. To the right is a *Holy Family* by Paolo Veronese.

13
Angelo San Raffaele

📍B8 🏛Campo Angelo Raffaele ☎041 522 85 48 🚤San Basilio 🕐10am–noon & 3–5:30pm Mon–Sat, 9am–noon Sun & public hols

The main attraction of this 17th-century church is the series of panel paintings on the organ balustrade. These were executed in 1749 by Antonio Guardi, brother of the more famous Francesco, and tell the tale of Tobias, the blind prophet cured by the archangel Raphael, after whom the church is named.

14
San Sebastiano

📍B/C8 🏛Campo San Sebastiano 🚤San Basilio 🕐10:30am–5pm Mon–Sat 🌐chorusvenezia.org

This 16th-century church has one of the most colourful interiors of Venice. Veronese, who was commissioned to decorate the sacristy ceiling, the nave ceiling, the frieze, the

east end of the choir, the high altar, the doors of the organ panels and the chancel – in that order. The paintings are typical of Veronese: rich and radiant, with sumptuous costumes and colours. Among the finest of his works are the three ceiling paintings of Esther, Queen of Xerxes I of Persia. Appropriately, Veronese is buried here, alongside the organ.

15
San Nicolò dei Mendicoli

📍A7/8 🏛Campo San Nicolò ☎041 270 24 64 🚤San Basilio 🕐10am–noon & 3–5:30pm Mon–Sat, 9am–noon Sun & public hols

Contrasting with the remote and run-down area that surrounds it, San Nicolò dei

> The walls of San Nicolò dei Mendicoli, and (inset) its ornate, ↓ carved interiors

Mendicoli is one of the most charming and delightful churches in Venice. Originally constructed in the 12th century, it has been rebuilt extensively over the centuries; the porch on the north flank dates from the 15th century.

Thanks to the Venice in Peril Fund, in the 1970s the church underwent one of the most comprehensive restoration programmes since the floods of 1966. The floor, which was 30 cm (1 ft) below the level of the canals, was rebuilt and raised slightly to prevent further damage; the roofs and lower walls were reconstructed; and paintings and statues restored.

The interior is richly embellished, especially the nave with its 16th-century gilded wood statues, which included the figure of San Nicolò himself. On the upper walls is a series of paintings of the life of Christ by Alvise dal Friso and other pupils of Veronese.

16

Squero di San Trovaso

📍 **D8** 🚪 **Rio San Trovaso**
🚤 **Zattere**

This is one of the few surviving gondola workshops in Venice, and the most picturesque. Its Tyrolean look dates from the days when crafters came down from the Cadore area of the Dolomites (p246).

Tours run during the week and must be booked in advance, but from the far side of the Rio San Trovaso it is possible to watch the upturned gondolas being given their scraping and tarring treatment. Nowadays, only around 10 boats are made each year, but there is still plenty to see.

📷 **PICTURE PERFECT**
Shipyard Snaps

The Squero di San Trovaso boatyard is one of the most photographed spots in Venice. For the best results, go in the morning when the sun is shining on the boatyard and stand on Fondamenta Priuli.

17

San Trovaso

📍 **D8** 🚪 **Campo San Trovaso**
📞 **041 522 21 33** 🚤 **Zattere or Accademia** ⏰ **Times vary, call ahead**

The church of Santi Gervasio e Protasio, which in the Venetian dialect is slurred to "San Trovaso", was built in 1590. It has two identical façades, one overlooking a canal, the other a quiet square. The church stood on neutral ground between the parishes of the rival factions of the Castellani and Nicolotti families, and tradition has it that this necessitated a separate entrance for each party.

The interior houses some late paintings by Jacopo Tintoretto, and Michele Giambono's 15th-century work, *St Chrysogonus on Horseback*, is situated in the chapel.

18

Zattere

📍 **D9** 🚤 **Zattere or San Basilio**

Stretching along the southern part of the *sestiere*, the Zattere is the long quayside looking across to the island of Giudecca. The name derives from the *zattere* (rafts) made of and carrying timber from the Republic's forests. After skilful navigation along the River Piave, the rafts were dismantled on arrival in Venice. On a sunny day it is a pleasure to sit at a waterside café here, looking across to the Church of the Redentore or watching the water buses as they cross back and forth between the shores.

Overlooking the Giudecca Canal, the Russian-run **V-A-C Foundation Zattere** is a space for contemporary art events with a focus on engaging with the Venetian population. Throughout the year, exhibitions, workshops and film screenings take place – all free of charge – in this well-restored palace. On the ground floor is the sudest 1401 restaurant, run by refugees, and a garden that reproduces the Venetian lagoon habitat.

V-A-C Foundation Zattere
🎫 📍 **D8** 🚪 **Fondamenta Zattere al Ponte Longo** 🔧 **For renovation** 🌐 **v-a-c.ru**

→

The picturesque canalside Squero di San Trovaso

19

Santa Maria della Visitazione

◉ E9 **⌂ Fondamenta delle Zattere** **☎ 041 522 40 77** **⛴ Zattere** **⏱ 10:30am–4:30pm Mon–Sat**

Situated beside the Gesuati, this Renaissance church was built between 1494 and 1524 by the Order of the Gesuati. Inside the church is a fine wooden ceiling painted by 16th-century Umbrian and Tuscan artists. The exterior *bocca di leone* to the right of the façade is one of several "lion's mouth" denunciation boxes surviving from the rule of the Council of Ten *(p84)*; this one was used to complain about the state of the streets.

↑ The decorative façade of Gesuati church, looking out over the turquoise water

20 🖉

Gesuati

◉ E9 **⌂ Fondamenta delle Zattere** **⛴ Zattere** **⏱ 10:30am–5pm Mon–Sat** **🌐 chorus venezia.org**

Not to be confused with the Gesuiti *(p166)*, this church was built by the Dominicans, who took possession of the site in the 17th century when the Gesuati Order was suppressed. Work began in 1726 and the stately façade reflects that of Palladio's Redentore church across the Giudecca Canal. It is the most conspicuous landmark of the long Zattere quayside. The interior of the church is richly decorated. Tiepolo's frescoed ceiling, *The Life of St Dominic* (1737–39), demonstrates the artist's mastery of light and colour. Just as impressive (and far easier to see) is his *Virgin with Saints* (1740), which is situated in the first chapel on the right. The church also features two altar paintings by Sebastiano Ricci and Giambattista Piazzetta.

A SHORT WALK
DORSODURO

Distance 1.5 km (1 mile) **Time** 25 minutes
Nearest Vaporetto Ca' Rezzonico

Lively Campo Santo Margherita is at the heart of the *sestiere* of Dorsoduro. The square bustles with activity, particularly in the morning, when the market stalls are open, and in the evening when it is the haunt of students from nearby Ca' Foscari, now part of the University of Venice. The surrounding streets contain several spectacular buildings, most notably Ca' Rezzonico and the Scuola Grande dei Carmini, which has decorations by Tiepolo. Of the area's waterways, the delightful Rio San Barnaba is best appreciated from the Ponte dei Pugni, near the barge selling fruit and vegetables – itself a time-honoured Venetian sight. To discover the quieter part of the *sestiere*, travel east of the Peggy Guggenheim Collection for shaded squares and picturesque residences.

Campo Santa Margherita *is an ideal place for relaxing in a café.*

Scuola Grande dei Carmini (p148) *contains nine ceiling panels in the hall on the upper floor, painted by Tiepolo for the Carmelite confraternity.*

Palazzo Zenobio, *built at the end of the 17th century, is used for temporary exhibitions. With permission, visitors can see the fine 18th-century ballroom.*

The church of **Santa Maria dei Carmini** *has a Gothic side porch carved with Byzantine reliefs.*

Fondamenta Gherardini *runs beside the Rio San Barnaba, one of the prettiest canals in the sestiere.*

CALLE RENIER · C DELLA CHIESA · RIO DI SANTA MARGHERITA · C D CAFFETTIER · C DEL FORNO · CAMPO SANTA MARGHERITA · R T SANT APONAL · CAMPO DEI CARMINI · START · CALLE D PAZIENZA · R T SCOAZZERA · FMTA D SQUERO · RIO SAN BARNABA · FONDAMENTA GHERARDINI · C LUNGA SAN BARNABA

0 metres 75
0 yards 75
N ↑

Locator Map
For more detail see p138

DORSODURO

↑ Sunlight dapples the canal
by Campo San Barnaba

RIO DI CA' FOSCARI

C D ASEO

SAONERI

DEL MAGAZEN

C DELLA VIDA

C D BOTTEGHE

DORSODURO

Ca' Foscari *was
completed in 1437 for
Doge Francesco.*

CANAL GRANDE

Palazzo Giustinian
*was home to Wagner
in 1858.*

CALLE BERNARDO

*The ballroom of Ca'
Rezzonico covers the
width of the palazzo.*

CAMPO
SAN
BARNABA

FINISH

CALLE DEL TRAGHETTO

San Barnaba (p146), *a tiny islet
within Venice, is a thriving community,
with its own floating barge stall
crammed with fresh produce.*

Ponte dei Pugni (p146) *was a traditional
setting for fist fights between rival factions.
They were finally banned in 1705
for being too violent.*

Did You Know?

Dorsoduro has a high
student population, which
means the *sestiere* has a
vibrant nightlife.

CANNAREGIO

The city's most northerly *sestiere*, Cannaregio
derives its name either from the red-coloured
Italian *canne*, meaning canes or reeds, which grew
here centuries ago, or perhaps from Canale Regio
or "Royal Canal" – the former name of what is now
the Canale di Cannaregio. This waterway was the
main entry to Venice prior to the building of the
Santa Lucia train station, which now sits at the
western edge of Cannaregio and links Venice with
the mainland. During the 11th century, major
devel-opment took place, and the main canal was
drained to allow the adjoining waterways to be
dredged. Elegant palazzos faced the Grand Canal,
but this area was primarily working class and
residential, with some manufacturing buildings.
In 1516, Venice's Jewish population was confined
to one of Cannaregio's islets in an enclosed area
known as the Ghetto. Such restrictions continued
for more than 270 years, until Napoleon Bonaparte
annexed the Republic in 1797, ridding the area of
all its gates and allowing residents the freedom to
live where they chose.

Today, over a third of the city's population lives
in Cannaregio. For the most part it is an unspoiled
area, divided by wide canals, crisscrossed by alleys,
and characterized by small stores, simple bars and
artisans' workshops.

CANNAREGIO

Must Sees
① Ca' d'Oro
② The Ghetto
③ Santa Maria dei Miracoli

Experience More
④ Campo dei Mori
⑤ Madonna dell'Orto
⑥ Fondamenta della Sensa
⑦ San Marziale
⑧ Gesuiti
⑨ Fondamente Nuove
⑩ Oratorio dei Crociferi
⑪ San Giovanni Grisostomo
⑫ Scalzi
⑬ Santi Apostoli
⑭ Palazzo Labia
⑮ Teatro Malibran
⑯ San Giobbe

Eat
① Al Timon All'Antica Mola
② Osteria Al Cicheto
③ Ostaria Da Rioba
④ Paradiso Perduto

Drink
⑤ Un Mondo di Vino
⑥ Osteria ai Tronchi
⑦ Hostaria Bacanera

Shop
⑧ Codex
⑨ Mori & Bozzi
⑩ Nicolao Atelier
⑪ Sullaluna

Map Grid References

F
G
H
J

1
2
3
4
5
6
7

0 metres 250
0 yards 250

N

Canale delle Fondamente Nuove

Orto

CAMPIELLO PIAVE

CALLE GRADISCA

FMTA MADONNA DELL'ORTO
Madonna

CALLE LARGA PIAVE

5 Madonna dell'Orto

dell'Orto

4 Palazzo Mastelli

Campo dei Mori

DELLA SENSA
Rio della

FMTA DEI MORI

Casa del Tintoretto

10 **3**
CALLE LARGA

FONDAMENTA DELLA MISERICORDIA
Rio della

4 **11**

C.D. FOSCOLO

CORTE VECCHIA
CEE D. CONT.

FMTA DELL'ABBAZIA

Santa Maria della Misericordia

Sacca della Misericordia

FOND. GASPARO CONTARINI

FOND. D. MUTI

CAMPO DELL'ABBAZIA

Rio della Sensa

FONDAMENTA NUOVE

CALLE MARCO FOSCARINI

CALLE LUNGA SANTA CATERINA

CALLE D. CADENE

SAL. DEI SPECCHIERI

Fondamente Nuove

9

FOND. CANAL
Rio dei Servi

C. MADDALENA

7 San Marziale

FMTA VENDRAMIN

VIA VITTORIO EMANUELE

Rio di Noale

Rio della Racchetta

CALLE DELLA RACCHETTA

CORTE 5O VECCHIO

FONDAMENTA SANTA CATERINA
Rio d)

Santa Caterina

Oratorio dei Crociferi **10**

CAMPO DEI GESUITI

Gesuiti **8**

CALLE DEI VOLTI

Rio dei Gesuiti

Fondamente Nove

FONDAMENTA NUOVE

CALLE LARGA DEI BOTTERI

CALLE DELLA PIETÀ

CORTE CARITA
C.D. VOLTO

C. LARGA BERLENDIS

CALLE DEL FUMO

CALLE DELLO SQUERO

CALLE DEI MENDICANTI

Rio dei Mendicanti

San Stae

CAMPO SAN STAE

FMTA CHIESA FMTA SAN FELICE
Rio di Con felice

CAMPO S FELICE

CALLE DELLE VELE

CALLE PRIULI

C.S FELICE

C. DEL FORNO

STRADA NOVA

Santa Sofia

CALLE DEI TAGLIAPIETRA

6

CALLE DEL REMER

C.D. MADONNA

C.D. VARISCO

C.D. FORNO

C.D. POSTA

CALLE APOSTOLI

CALLE STELLA

CALLE DEI BIRI

CALLE TERRA DELLE

CORTE DEI PALUDO

CORTE 2a

CALLE DELLA TESTA

NUOVE

Santi Giovanni e Paolo

Ca' d'Oro
1

Ca' d'Oro

CAMPO SANTA SOFIA

Palazzo Sagredo

CAMPO DEI SANTI APOSTOLI

13

Santi Apostoli

R.T.D. FRANCESCHI

R.T.D.S. APOSTOLI

CPLO. D. CASON
7

Rio dei

SAL. SAN CANCIANO
5

CAMPO SANTA MARIA NOVA

CALLE WIDMAN

CAMPIELLO WIDMAN

CALLE BONDI

C. LARGA G. GALLINA

Santi Giovanni e Paolo

Ca' Pesaro

CALLE DEL CAPITELLO
FMTA DELL'ORO

CALLE DEL FORNO

C.D. OCA

CAMPO SANTA SOFIA

SALIZADA DEL PISTOR

CALLE DEL FORNO

SAL. SAN GIOVANNI CRISOSTOMO

Santa Maria dei Miracoli **3**

CALLE CASTELLI

C. DELLE ERBE

CAMPO SAN CASSIANO

Rio delle Beccarie

RUGA DEI SPEZIALI

Rialto Mercato

Fabbriche Nuove

RUGA VECCHIA S. GIOVANNI

RUGA DEL RAVANO

CAMPO RIALTO NUOVO

San Giovanni Grisostomo **11**

CORTE 2a D. MILION

Teatro Malibran **15**

CAMPO SAN MARINA

CALLE MARTINENGO

C. DI BARGOZZA

CASTELLO
p116

RIO TERRA RAMPANI

CALLE DEI BOTTERI

Ponte di Rialto

Rialto

RIVA DEL VIN

RIVA DEL FERRO

SAN MARCO
p72

SALIZZADA S. LIO

CASTELLO

SAN POLO

CAMPO SAN APONAL

CPLO. MELON

CALLE DOLFIN

Rio delle Madonnetta

San Silvestro

RIVA D. CARBON

C. DEL CARBON

C. BEMBO

C. DEL LOVO

SAN MARCO

CALLE MAZZINI

CAMPO SAN LUCA

San Salvatore

CALLE DEI FABBRI

Palazzo Grimani

Rio di

CAMPO SAN LUCA

San Salvatore

Sant'Angelo

SAL. CHIESA E TEATRO

CPLO DEL TEATRO

CAMPO SANT'ANGELO

CAMPO MANIN

Rio

CALLE DELLA MANDOLA

CALLE DEI FUSERI

CALLE DEL FRUTTAROL

CAMPO SAN GALLO

CALLE FREZZERIA

PIAZZA SAN MARCO

CANNAREGIO

CA' D'ORO

📍G4 🚏Canal Grande (Calle Ca' d'Oro) 🚤Ca' d'Oro ⏰10am-7pm Tue-Sat
🚫1 Jan, 1 May, 25 Dec 🌐cadoro.org

The original lapis lazuli, vermilion and gold façade has long faded, but the delicate Gothic architecture of this "golden palace" is intact, with exquisite marble tracery and arcaded loggias crafted by 15th-century stonemasons.

One of the great showpieces of the Grand Canal, the Ca' d'Oro (or House of Gold) is the finest example of Venetian Gothic architecture in the city. The façade, with its finely carved ogee windows, lofty pinnacles and striking marble tracery, has unmistakable Islamic influences.

In the course of the 16th century the house was remodelled by a succession of owners, but by the early 18th century was semi-derelict. In 1846 the Russian Prince Troubetzkoy bought it for the famous ballerina Marie Taglioni. Under her direction, the Ca' d'Oro suffered barbaric remodelling in 1894. It was finally rescued by Baron Giorgio Franchetti who lovingly restored it to its former glory. Restoration of the façade is now complete, revealing the building's intricate design.

Behind the palace's beautiful façade is a courtyard paved with coloured tesserae. Inside is the Galleria Giorgio Franchetti, which houses a collection of paintings, sculptures and ceramics donated to the state by the Baron in 1916, along with the building. One highlight is Andrea Mantegna's painting *St Sebastian* (1506) in the portico leading to a loggia overlooking the Grand Canal. An ornate 15th-century staircase leads to 16th-century Flemish tapestries on the second floor.

Did You Know?

Ca is an abbreviation of *casa*, meaning "home". This is used to denote grand palazzos, not humble dwellings.

→
Glorious sunset over the Grand Canal and Ca' d'Oro

① Ca' d'Oro's intricately carved balcony overlooking the Grand Canal.

② Visitors exploring the Ca' d'Oro Art Gallery.

③ Detail of the impressive mosaic tiling inside the ground-floor loggia.

2

3

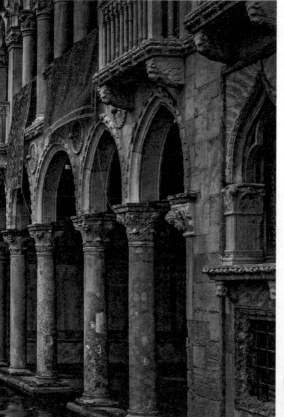

GALLERY GUIDE

On the first floor, pride of place is given to Andrea Mantegna's *St Sebastian* (1506). The *portego* (gallery) opening on to the Grand Canal is a showroom of sculpture. Among the finest pieces are bronze reliefs by the Paduan sculptor Il Riccio (1470–1532), and Tullio Lombardo's marble *Double Portrait* (around 1493). The upper floor houses paintings by numerous Venetian artists, including a Venus by Titian, two Venetian views by Guardi and fresco fragments by Titian.

SHOP

Codex
Delicate ink drawings
are sold in this store.

📍E2 🏠Fondamenta
degli Ormesini 2799
🌐codexvenezia.it

Mori & Bozzi
A haven for
fashionistas.

📍E/F3 🏠Rio Terà de la
Maddalena 2367
📞041 715 261

Nicolao Atelier
The place to go for
Carnevale costumes.

📍F2 🏠Fondamenta de
la Misericordia 2590
🌐nicolao.com

Sullaluna
Quirky bookshop
and vegetarian cafè.

📍F3 🏠Fondamenta de
la Misericordia 2535
🌐sullalunavenezia.it

---

2 🛍

THE GHETTO

📍D2, D3 🚏Ponte Guglie 🏛Museo Ebraico: Campo del Ghetto Nuovo; open 10am-
5:30pm Mon-Wed, Fri & Sun, 11am-6:30pm Thu; www.ghettovenezia.com

Once home to a thriving Jewish population, the Ghetto lost its significance in
1866 when Venice's Jewish community was granted citizenship and allowed to
disperse. Today, it is home to the religious and administrative institutions of the
community, and its five synagogues can be visited along with the Jewish museum.

In 1516 the Council of Ten decreed that
all Jewish people in Venice be confined to
an islet of Cannaregio. The quarter was
cut off from outside contact, its entrances
manned by Christian guards. By day the Jewish
people held here were allowed out of the
Ghetto, but at all times they were made to
wear identifying badges and caps. As the
population expanded, the Ghetto's buildings
rose vertically and spread into the Ghetto
Vecchio and the neighbouring Ghetto Nuovo.

By the mid-17th century the population
numbered over 5,000. It wasn't until 1866
that Venice's Jewish population was granted
its freedom.

The Museo Ebraico houses an expansive
collection of historic artifacts from the 17th
to 19th centuries. A guided tour of the quarter's synagogues departs from the museum
daily (except on Saturdays), allowing a
fascinating glimpse into the past life of
the Ghetto.

Did You Know?

The area was named after a *geto* (foundry), a term later applied to other Jewish enclaves around the world.

↑ A quiet evening on Fondamenta Ormesini, Ghetto Nuovo

↑ The gilded oval interior of the Great German Synagogue, the oldest synagogue in Venice

LEONE DA MODENA

Modena (1571–1648) was a respected rabbi, musician and printer. An opponent of the mystical approach to Judaism, he gave sermons in Italian to attract non-Jewish people and Christian scholars. His account of how life was in the Jewish Ghetto provides a deep insight into the social and economic conditions of early modern Venice.

3 🏛️

SANTA MARIA DEI MIRACOLI

📍 H5 🏛️ Campiello dei Miracoli 🚏 Fondamente Nuove
or Rialto 🕐 10:30am–5pm Mon–Sat 🌐 chorusvenezia.org

A "jewellery box" of marble slabs and exquisite bas-reliefs, this Renaissance church was named after an alleged miracle-working icon from 1409, which reputedly brought a drowned man back to life and erased a woman's fatal wounds. The sculpture is now enshrined on the main altar of the church.

An exquisite masterpiece of the early Renaissance, Santa Maria dei Miracoli is the favourite church of many Venetians, and was the subject of a major restoration programme funded by the American Save Venice organization in the early 1990s. Tucked away in a winding maze of alleys and waterways in eastern Cannaregio, it is small and somewhat elusive, but well worth the trip.

The façade is decorated in various coloured marbles, with fine bas-reliefs and sculpture. It was built in 1481–9 by the architect Pietro Lombardo and his sons to enshrine *The Virgin and Child* (1408), a painting believed to have miraculous powers. The picture, by Nicolò di Pietro, can still be seen high above the altar.

The stunning interior of the Miracoli is best visited in the morning when pale shafts of light stream in through the windows. It is embellished by pink, white and grey marble and crowned by a barrel-vaulted ceiling, featuring portraits of saints and prophets. Tullio Lombardo's balustrade is decorated by carved figures of St Francis, Archangel Gabriel, the Virgin and St Clare. The screen around the high altar and the medallions of the Evangelists in the cupola spandrels are also by Lombardo.

↑ Banding in this stone carving gives the impression that the Madonna is weeping

EARLY RENAISSANCE ARCHITECTURE

One of the best examples of the early Venetian Renaissance, the Miracoli's façade is a harmonious tapestry of decorated panels and multicoloured polished stone. Inside, the ceiling gleams with gilt miniatures of holy figures.

The semicircular crowning lunette emphasizes the church's jewel-box appearance.

A false loggia is formed of Ionic arches, inset with windows.

The marble panels are fixed to the bricks by metal hooks. This method, which prevents the build-up of damp and salt water behind the panels, dates from the Renaissance.

→ Ornate façade of the Santa Maria dei Miracoli

The Miracoli's impressive barrel-vaulted ceiling, featuring over 50 frescoed portraits, and ↓ *(inset)* its colossal exterior

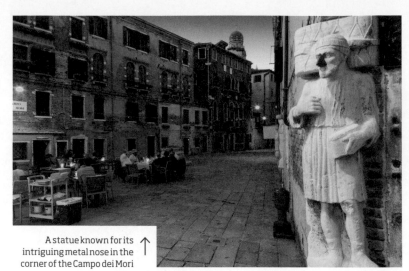

A statue known for its intriguing metal nose in the corner of the Campo dei Mori ↑

EXPERIENCE MORE

④ Campo dei Mori

◉ F2 🚻 Madonna dell'Orto

According to popular tradition, the "Mori" were the three Mastelli brothers who came from the Morea (the Peloponnese). The brothers, who were silk merchants by trade, took refuge in Venice in 1112 and built the Palazzo Mastelli, visible from Fondamenta Gasparo Contarini and recognizable by its camel bas-relief. The brothers' stone figures are embedded in the wall of the *campo* on its eastern side. The corner figure with the makeshift rusty metal nose (added in the 19th century) is "Signor Antonio Rioba", who, like the Roman Pasquino, was

> According to popular tradition, the "Mori" were the three Mastelli brothers who came from the Morea (the Peloponnese).

the focus of malicious fun and satire. A fourth merchant with a large turban faces the Rio della Sensa on the façade of Tintoretto's house (*p170*).

⑤ Madonna dell'Orto

◉ F2 🏛 Campo Madonna dell'Orto 🚻 Madonna dell'Orto ⏰ 10am–5pm Mon–Sat 🚫 1 Jan, Easter, 15 Aug, 25 Dec

This lovely Gothic church is frequently referred to as the English Church in Venice, for it was British funds that helped restore the building after the 1966 floods. The original church, founded in the mid-14th century, was dedicated to St Christopher, patron saint of travellers, to protect the boatmen who ferried passengers to the islands in the northern lagoon. The dedication was changed and the church reconstructed in the early 15th century following the discovery, in a nearby garden (*orto*), of a statue of the Virgin Mary said to

have miraculous powers. A 15th-century statue of St Christopher still stands above the portal, however.

The interior is large, light and uncluttered. The greatest treasures are the works of art by Tintoretto, who was a parishioner of the church. His tomb lies in the chapel to the right of the chancel.

The most dramatic of his works are the towering paintings in the chancel (1562–4). In the painting *The Adoration of the Golden Calf* on the left wall, the figure carrying the calf, fourth from the left, is said to depict Tintoretto himself.

Inside the chapel of San Mauro visitors can see the radically restored statue of the Madonna that inspired the reconstruction of the church. The vacant space opposite the entrance belongs to Giovanni Bellini's *Madonna with Child* (around 1478), which was stolen for the third time in 1993.

6

Fondamenta della Sensa

⧉ E2 🚊 Madonna dell'Orto

When the marshy lands of Cannaregio were drained in the Middle Ages, three long, straight canals were created, running parallel to each other. The middle of these is the Rio della Sensa, which stretches from the Sacca di Sant'Alvise at its western end to the Canale della Misericordia in the east. The Fondamenta cuts through a quiet quarter of Cannaregio. With its small grocery shops, and simple local bars and *trattorie*, the neighbourhood feels far removed from San Marco.

Now occupied by the city's working class, this area is still interspersed with fine (but neglected) palaces that once belonged to the wealthy Venetians who lived here.

7

San Marziale

⧉ F3 🚶 Campiello San Marziale 🚊 San Marcuola ⧗ By appt

A Baroque church on medieval foundations, San Marziale was rebuilt between 1693 and 1721. It is visited mainly for the ceiling frescoes by Sebastiano Ricci, a painter of the decorative Rococo style. Executed between 1700 and 1705, relatively early in Ricci's career, these foreshortened frescoes combine the Venetian tradition with flamboyant Rococo flourishes. Sadly, though, the vivid colours for which Ricci was known have been sullied by decades of grime. The central painting shows *The Glory of Saint Martial*, while the side paintings relate to the image of the Virgin.

EAT

Al Timon All'Antica Mola

Hit the bar for pescatarian snacks, or sample Venetian staples in the main restaurant.

⧉ E2 🏠 Fondamenta dei Ormesini 2800 ⧗ 5pm–1am daily 🌐 altimon.it

€€€

Osteria Al Cicheto

There's a small but excellent menu at this traditional *bacaro*, with a focus on local wines and artisanal produce.

⧉ C4 🏠 Calle de la Misericordia 367a ⧗ Sun 🌐 osteria-al-cicheto.it

€€€

Ostaria Da Rioba

Head here for inventive dishes in a classic setting, with a strong line in creative raw seafood. Reservations required.

⧉ F2 🏠 Fondamenta della Misericordia 2553 ⧗ Mon 🌐 darioba.com

€€€

Paradiso Perduto

A no-frills fish restaurant with great prices and a friendly atmosphere.

⧉ F3 🏠 Fondamenta della Misericordia 2450 ⧗ Tue & Wed 🌐 ilparadisoperduto. wordpress.com

€€€

←
Visitors paddling the canal in front of the brick façade of the Madonna dell'Orto

↑ The spectacular interiors of the Gesuiti, and *(inset)* its imposing façade

8

Gesuiti

📍 H3 🏛 Salizada dei Spechieri 4877 ☎ 041 528 6579 🚏 Fondamente Nuove 🕐 10am-12:30pm & 4:30-6:30pm Mon-Thu, 10am-1pm & 3-7pm Fri-Sun

The Jesuits' close links with the papacy provoked Venetian hostility during the 17th century, and for 50 years they were refused entry to the city. However, in 1714 they were permitted to build this church in the north of Venice, on the site of a 12th-century church that had originally belonged to the Order of the Crociferi. Consecrated as Santa Maria Assunta, the church is always referred to simply as the Gesuiti; thus it is often confused with the Gesuati in Dorsoduro *(p151)*.

Domenico Rossi's imposing Baroque exterior gives only a hint of the opulence inside. The green and white marble, carved in parts like great folds of fabric, gives the dramatic impression that the interior is clothed in damask.

Titian's *Martyrdom of St Lawrence* (around 1555), which hangs above the first altar on the left, is worth a closer look, and has been described by the art historian Hugh Honour as "the first successful nocturne in the history of art".

9

Fondamente Nuove

📍 H3 🚏 Fondamente Nuove

The Fondamente Nuove or "New Quays" are over 400 years old. This chain of waterside streets borders the northern lagoon for one kilometre (over half a mile), from the solitary Sacca della Misericordia to the Rio di Santa Giustina in Castello

on the eastern side. Before the construction of the quays in the 1580s, this was a desirable residential area where the air was said to be healthy and the houses had gardens sloping down to the lagoon.

One of the residents of this neighbourhood was Titian, who lived from 1531 until his death in 1576 in a now demolished house at Calle Larga dei Botteri No. 5182–3 (an ornately carved plaque marks the site).

Today the quaysides are aesthetically uninspiring but they do provide splendid views of the northern lagoon and – on a clear day – the spectacular peaks of the Dolomites. The island most easily visible from the quays is San Michele in Isola *(p182)*, with its dark, stately cypress trees rising high above the cemetery walls.

Did You Know?

Titian lived at the Vatican for six months while working on two portraits of Pope Paul III.

Oratorio dei Crociferi

⚑H3 **⌂**Campo dei Gesuiti 4905 **☎**041 934 67 48 **🚤**Fondamente Nuove **🕐**For guided tours only; times vary, check website (book ahead) **🌐**gioielli nascostidivenezia.it

Founded in the 13th century as a hospital for returning Crusaders, the Oratorio dei Crociferi (built for the order of the Bearers of the Cross) was turned into a charitable institution for old people in the 15th century.

Between 1583 and 1591 the artist Palma il Giovane, commissioned by the Crociferi, decorated the chapel with a cycle of paintings depicting crucial events in the history of this religious order. They were terribly damaged in the floods of 1966, but were restored and the chapel reopened in 1984.

The inscriptions on the walls of some of the surrounding houses in the square are those of art and craft guilds, such as silk weavers and tailors, whose works formerly occupied the buildings.

---

⑪
San Giovanni Grisostomo

⚑H5 **⌂**Campo San Giovanni Grisostomo **☎**041 309 66 05 **🚤**Rialto **🕐**10am–6:30pm Mon– Sat, 11:30am–6:30pm Sun **🕐**During Mass

This terracotta-coloured church is near the Rialto. Built between 1479 and 1504, it was Mauro Coducci's last work.

The interior, built on a Greek-cross plan, is dark and intimate. Notable works of art that hang here include Giovanni Bellini's *St Jerome*

with *Saints Christopher and Augustine* (1513), which is found above the first altar on the right. Influenced by Giorgione, this was probably Bellini's last painting. Another artist inspired by Giorgione was Sebastiano del Piombo, whose *St John Chrysostom and Six Saints* (1509–11) is above the high altar. Some believe that the figures of St John the Baptist and St Liberal were painted by Giorgione himself.

DRINK

Un Mondo di Vino
This spot is usually packed, and deservedly so. Make your way to the bar for a scrumptious *cichetto*. There are also dozens of wines available by the glass.

⚑H4/5 **⌂**Salizada San Canzian 5984/a **🌐**bacarounmondo divino.it

---

Osteria ai Tronchi
Visitors here can choose between a bargain glass of delicious house wine for around €1, or the myriad more sophisticated options. If you're peckish, dig in to snacks and sandwiches.

⚑H4 **⌂**Calle del Spezier 4792 **☎**041 528 27 27 **🕐**Sun

Hostaria Bacanera
This local favourite is part wine bar, part restaurant, and a formidable selection of wines are served by knowledgeable staff. On Tuesdays, head down to enjoy some live music.

⚑H4 **⌂**Campiello de la Cason 4506 **🕐**Breakfast, Mon & Tue **🌐**bacanera.it

↑ The peach tower of San Giovanni Grisostomo, rising above the surrounding narrow streets

MARCO POLO

Born in around 1254 near the Rialto, Marco Polo left Venice at the age of 18 for his voyage to the court of the Emperor Kublai Khan. He returned in 1295, bringing with him a fortune in jewels and a host of fabulous stories. While a prisoner of war in 1298 he compiled an account of his travels, which became *Le Livre des Merveilles*. Though many disbelieved his tales of the East, the book was an instant hit. His nickname became Marco Il Milione (of the million lies).

and sculptures. The impressive ceiling painting, *The Council of Ephesus* by Ettore Tito (1934), replaced Giambattista Tiepolo's fresco of *The Translation of the Holy House to Loreto* (1743–5), which was destroyed by the Austrian bombardment of 24 October 1915.

⑬
Santi Apostoli

🔲 G4 🏠 Campo Santi Apostoli 📞 041 523 82 97 🚊 Ca' d'Oro 🕐 7:30–11:30am & 5–7pm Mon–Sat

The Campo Santi Apostoli is an important crossroad for pedestrians en route to the Rialto or the railway station. Its church is architecturally unremarkable and little remains of the 16th-century building. A notable exception, however, is the enchanting

⑫
Scalzi

🔲 C4 🏠 Fondamenta Scalzi 📞 041 822 40 06 🚊 Ferrovia 🕐 7:45am–12:30pm & 4–7pm daily

Beside the modern railway station stands the church of Santa Maria di Nazareth, known as the Scalzi. The *scalzi* were "barefooted"

Carmelite friars who came to Venice during the 1670s and commissioned their church to be built on the Grand Canal.

Designed by Baldassare Longhena, the huge Baroque interior is an over-elaboration of marble, gilded woodwork

→ The impressive Baroque façade of the church of Santa Maria di Nazareth, or Scalzi late 15th-century Renaissance Corner Chapel on the right of the nave, believed to have been designed by Mauro Coducci. The chapel contains *The Communion of St Lucy* by Giambattista Tiepolo (1748), the tomb of Marco Corner, probably by Tullio Lombardo (1511), and an inscription to Corner's daughter, Caterina Cornaro, Queen of Cyprus, who was buried here before she was moved to the Church of San Salvatore *(p93)*.

⑭ Palazzo Labia

📍 **D3** 🏠 **Fondamenta Labia (entrance on Campo San Geremia)** ☎ **041 529 87 11** 🚏 **Ponte Guglie** ⏰ **By appt (call ahead)**

The Labias were a wealthy family of Catalonian merchants, who bought their way into the

Venetian patriciate in 1646. Towards the end of the century they built their Baroque palace, with a splendid façade, on the wide Cannaregio Canal, close to its junction with the Grand Canal.

In 1745–50 the ballroom was frescoed by Giambattista Tiepolo. The wonderfully painted scenes are taken from the life of Cleopatra but the setting is Venice, and the queen's attire is that of a 16th-century noblewoman.

Passed from one owner to another, the palace gradually lost all trace of its former grandeur and has variously served as a religious foundation, a school and a homeless shelter. Since 1964, the Palazzo Labia has served as the office of the Italian broadcasting network, RAI, which also undertook its restoration.

⑮ Teatro Malibran

📍 **H5** 🏠 **Campiello del Teatro 5873** 🌐 **teatrola fenice.it**

Tucked behind a bustling thoroughfare is the charming Teatro Malibran. Built on the site of Marco Polo's former home, this theatre originally went by the name of Teatro Grisostomo, after the nearby church. The theatre first opened its doors in 1678 and was one of three such venues owned by the powerful Grimani family. In 1819 the theatre was sold, lavishly restored and reopened with Rossini's *La Gazza Ladra*.

The famous soprano Maria Garcia Malibran came to perform at the theatre in 1835, and the building was renamed in her honour. When La Fenice tragically burned down in 1996, the Malibran was used as a replacement and continues to work in tandem with the renowned opera house, hosting a number of performances throughout the year.

⑯ San Giobbe

📍 **C3** 🏠 **Campo San Giobbe** 🚏 **Ponte dei 3 Archi** ⏰ **10:30am–1pm Mon, Tue, Fri & Sat** 🚫 **1 Jan, Easter, 15 Aug, 25 Dec** 🌐 **chorus venezia.org**

The church of San Giobbe stands in a remote *campo* full of cats. The early Gothic structure of the church was modified in the 1470s by Pietro Lombardo, who added Renaissance elements to the design, such as the saints over the portal. The Martini chapel, which is located second on the left, displays clear Tuscan influences and is decorated with Della Robbia-style glazed terracotta. The altarpieces by Giovanni Bellini and Vittore Carpaccio were removed when Napoleon suppressed the monastery of San Giobbe, and these highly valuable pieces are now on display in the Accademia gallery *(p140)*.

→

A statue from San Giobbe, by Pietro Lombardo

A SHORT WALK
AROUND CANNAREGIO

Distance 1.5 km (1 mile) **Time** 25 minutes
Nearest Vaporetto Madonna dell'Orto

Surprisingly few tourists find their way to this unspoiled quarter of northern Cannaregio. This is the more humble, peaceful side of Venice, where clean washing is strung over the waterways and the streets are flanked by the faded façades of shuttered houses, from which the comforting smell of home-cooking wafts out onto the streets, the envy of many a passer-by. All along the spacious *fondamente*, little shops stock basic groceries and unassuming bars are always filled with Venetians. The quarter's cultural highlight is the lovely Gothic church of Madonna dell'Orto, Tintoretto's parish church.

One of the finest Gothic churches in Venice, **Madonna dell'Orto** (p164) *has a richly decorated façade and a wealth of works by such artists as Tintoretto.*

START

Fondamenta della Sensa (p165) *is a peaceful backwater with typically Venetian peeling façades.*

Campo dei Mori (p164) *is named after the stone statues of three Moors (Mori) which are carved on its walls.*

Tintoretto lived with his family in this house, **No. 3399 Fondamenta dei Mori***, from 1574 until his death.*

Ceiling paintings by Sebastiano Ricci (1700–25) and a bizarre Baroque altar adorn the Baroque church of **San Marziale** (p165).

FINISH

0 metres	50	N
0 yards	50	↑

↑ Walking along Fondamenta della Sensa and Rio della Sensa in Cannaregio

Locator Map
For more detail see p156

Fondamenta Gasparo Contarini *is named after the cardinal, diplomat and scholar who lived at Palazzo Contarini dal Zaffo in the 16th century.*

↑ Quiet Campo dell'Abbazia della Misericordia and its church

Did You Know?

Madonna dell'Orto once held a Bellini masterpiece. Stolen in 1993, it is yet to be recovered.

La Sacca della Misericordia *is an artificial dock with 290 moorings for local boats. It looks out at the cemetery island of San Michele.*

Venetian oarsmen usually practise their technique on the lagoon, but they can also be seen on Cannaregio's quieter canals, such as the **Rio Madonna dell'Orto**.

Campo dell'Abbazia, *a peaceful open square with decorative herringbone floor tiles, is overlooked by the Scuola Vecchia della Misericordia and a deconsecrated church.*

Fondamenta della Misericordia *was built in the Middle Ages.*

THE LAGOON ISLANDS

Shrouded in myth and superstition, the lagoon was once the preserve of fishers and hunters. But marauders in the 5th and 6th centuries CE drove mainland dwellers to the safety of the marshy lagoon. They made their home in this watery environment, which was protected from the open sea by thin *lidi* (sandbanks), created from silt washed down by the rivers of the Po Delta. In the 13th century the first *murazzi* were built – seawalls of angular stone that safeguard the *lidi* from erosion. Experiments with tidal barriers continue in an effort to combat the ever-present threat of flooding caused predominantly by high tides in the Adriatic and strong sirocco winds from the south.

The thriving communities that once lived and traded here are long gone. Many of the islands, formerly used as sites for monasteries, hospitals or powder factories, are now abandoned, but a handful of them have been rehabilitated – one as a university and others as luxury resorts.

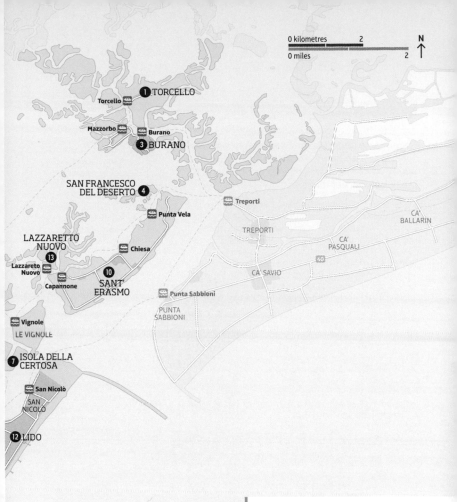

❶ ⊘

TORCELLO

🚢 12 from Fondamenta Nuove, then 9 from Burano
📞 041 73 07 61 ⏰ Basilica and museum: 10:30am–5:30pm daily

A 40-minute ferry ride from Cannaregio in Venice, Torcello's green fields, tranquil canals and pastel-hued houses offer a welcome escape from the bustling streets of the city.

Established between the 5th and 6th centuries, Torcello grew into a thriving colony, with palaces, churches and a population said to have reached 20,000. But with the rise of Venice the island went into decline. Today, Torcello is home to a handful of gardeners and fishers, and all that remains of this once vigorous community is the Byzantine cathedral, the church of Santa Fosca, and the memory of its former glory.

The striking Basilica di Santa Maria dell'Assunta – the lagoon's oldest building – was founded in 639, but underwent radical restructuring in 1008. It retains its Romanesque form, light-brick walls and an arcaded 9th-century portico. Here, some of the most breathtaking Byzantine mosaics in the world reward those who visit.

The cathedral's 55-m (180-ft) campanile offers spectacular views over the vast expanse of the lagoon to the Adriatic Sea, Venice itself and even north to the Alps on a clear winter's day. Inside are astonishing 12th- and 13th-century Domesday Mosaic, which depict scenes of devils and angels.

ATTILA THE HUN

The King of the Huns ruled over an empire that stretched from the Alps to the Caspian Sea. As part of his campaign against the Roman empire, Attila attacked Milan, Verona and Padua, and refugees fled to Torcello. Legend has it that a marble armchair in front of the Cathedral was his throne.

The Apse Mosaic, of a 13th-century Madonna set against a gold background, is one of the most moving mosaics in Venice.

The huge and highly decorative Domesday Mosaic, depicting the Last Judgement, covers the entire west wall.

The present basilica dates from 1008, but includes many earlier features. The marble pulpit is made of fragments from the first, 7th-century church.

The exquisite Byzantine marble panels of the Iconostasis (rood screen) are carved with peacocks, lions and flowers. A highlight is a detailed relief showing two peacocks drinking from the fountain of life.

Santa Maria dell'Assunta and the church of Santa Fosca ↑

① The elegant Santa Fosca was based on a Greek-cross design.

② Santa Fosca heightens Torcello's peaceful atmosphere.

③ The only path in Torcello runs alongside the canal.

Built in the 11th and 12th centuries on a Greek-cross plan, Santa Fosca has a lovely portico and a serene Byzantine interior.

The central dome and cross-sections are supported by columns of Greek marble with fine Corinthian capitals.

24

The tiny population of Torcello today.

It was said that Attila, the 5th-century king of the Huns, used this marble seat as his throne.

Old church treasures and some archaeological fragments are housed in the Museo dell'Estuario.

GLASS-BLOWING

A main attraction of a trip to Murano is a demonstration of glass-blowing, where you can watch in amazement while a glass-blower takes a blob of molten paste and, by twisting and blowing, transforms it into a vase, wine goblet or similar work of art. The display is followed by a tour of the showroom. Since it's free, visitors are expected to make a purchase; do bear in mind that there is no obligation to buy. The best time to visit is during Venice Glass Week in September.

↑ Murano's handcrafted glassware makes an excellent souvenir

2 🛍️

MURANO

🚊 4.1, 4.2 or 12 from Fondamente Nuove; 3 from Piazzale Roma ℹ️ Basilica dei Santi Maria e Donato: Campo San Donato, 041 73 90 56, open 9am–6pm Mon–Sat, 12:30–6pm Sun & public hols; Museo del Vetro: Palazzo Giustinian, Fondamenta Giustinian, times vary, check website, www.museovetro.visitmuve.it

Murano, like Venice, comprises a cluster of islands, connected by bridges. It has been the centre of Venetian glass-making since the 13th century.

Murano owes its prosperity entirely to glass. Venetians honed the craft due to their close connection with the Byzantine Empire between the 7th and 9th centuries, when the first glass factory was built on Torcello. In 1291, all glass-making activity was moved to Murano to prevent the significant fire hazard to the city and protect the trade's sought-after technological secrets – particularly in regard to making mirrors. By the 15th century the Venetians had created "cristallo", the clearest glass in the world and Murano was Europe's dominant glass-making centre. Though some of its factories are now derelict, the area still produces vast quantities of glass.

To see the early origins of glass-making visit the Basilica dei Santi Maria e Donato, which features a golden glass mosaic dome. The church's floor, or pavimento, incorporates fragments of ancient glass from the island's foundries into its imagery. Follow the rest of Murano's story at the Museo del Vetro, which displays a wonderful collection of antique, modern and contemporary pieces of glass.

1️⃣ Basilica dei Santa Maria e San Donato overlooking the square.

2️⃣ Colourful exhibits on display in the Museo del Vetro.

3️⃣ Traditional Murano glass retailer.

EXPERIENCE MORE

3

Burano

🚌 12 from Fondamente Nuove; 14 from San Zaccaria via Lido and Punta Sabbioni

Burano is the most colourful of the lagoon islands. Lying in a lonely expanse of the northern lagoon, it is distinguished from a distance by the tall, tilted tower of its church. In contrast to the tranquil Torcello (p176), the island is densely populated, its waterways lined by brightly painted houses.

A tour of the island's sights will take an hour or so. The street from the ferry stop takes visitors to the main thoroughfare, Via Baldassare Galuppi, named after the Burano-born composer (1706–85). The street is lined with traditional lace and linen stalls and open-air trattorias serving fresh fish.

4

San Francesco del Deserto

🚌 12 from Fondamente Nuove

This oasis of lush greenery, inhabited by nine friars, lies just south of the island of Burano. The multilingual friars give tours of the island's old church and the lovely gardens, which contain a tree said to have sprouted from the staff of St Francis of Assisi. To watch lacemakers at work, visit the **Museo del Merletto** housed in a historic palace that was once the home of the famed Burano Lace School.

> Burano is the most colourful of the lagoon islands. Lying in a lonely expanse of the northern lagoon, it is distinguished from a distance by the tall, tilted tower of its church.

Museo del Merletto
📍 Piazza Galuppi 187
🕐 Noon–6pm Thu–Sun
🌐 museomerletto. visitmuve.it

5

Giudecca

🚌 2, 4.1 or 4.2

In the days of the Republic, the island of Giudecca was a pleasure ground of palaces and gardens. Today it is very much a suburb of the city, with its narrow alleys, an interesting mix of apartments,

Visitors admiring the vibrant houses that fringe Burano's waterways

← Visitors admiring the vibrant houses that fringe Burano's waterways

TOP 3 CULTURAL SPACES IN GIUDECCA

Casa dei Tre Oci
🏠 Fondamente Zitelle 43
Ⓦ berggruen.org
Home to the Berggruen Institute which hosts global thinkers and photography exhibits.

Galleria Michela Rizzo
🏠 Fondamenta S. Biagio
Ⓦ galleriamichelarizzo.net
A gallery championing international and Venetian artists.

Spazio Punch
🏠 Giudecca 800/o
Ⓦ spaziopunch.com
Spazio Punch stages live events in this former brewery.

faded palazzos and luxury hotels. Many of its old factories have been converted into modern housing. However, the long, wide quayside skirting the city side of the island makes a very pleasant promenade and offers stunning views of Venice across the water.

The island was originally named Spinalunga (long spine) on account of its shape. The name Giudecca, once thought to have referred to the Jewish people, or *giudei*, who lived here in the 13th century, is more likely to have originated from the word *giudicati*, meaning "the judged". This referred to troublesome aristocrats who, as early as the 9th century, were banished to the island.

Hotel Cipriani, among the most luxurious places to stay in Venice, is discreetly located at the tip of the island. At Giudecca's western end looms the massive Neo-Gothic ruin of the Molino Stucky. It was built in 1895 as a flour mill by the Swiss entrepreneur Giovanni Stucky, an unpopular employer who was murdered by one of his workers in 1910. The mill ceased functioning in 1954. Following extensive renovations, it reopened in 2007 as a luxury hotel with a rooftop pool.

The main monument in Giudecca is Palladio's church of **Il Redentore** (The Redeemer). It was built in 1577–92 in thanksgiving for the end of the 1576 plague, which wiped out a third of the city's population. The Classical interior presents a marked contrast to the ornate style of most Venetian churches. The main paintings, by Paolo Veronese and Alvise Vivarini, are in the sacristy to the right of the choir.

Il Redentore
♿ 🏠 Campo Redentore
🚏 Redentore ⏰ 10am–1:30pm & 2:30–5pm Mon–Sat 🚫 1 Jan, 25 Dec Ⓦ chorusvenezia.org

↑ Enjoying a sunset dinner at a scenic, waterside restaurant in Giudecca

6

San Michele

🚌 **4.1 or 4.2 from Fondamente Nuove**

Studded with dark cypresses and enclosed within high terracotta walls, the cemetery island of San Michele lies just across the water from Venice's Fondamente Nuove *(p166)*. The bodies of Venetians were traditionally buried in church graveyards in Venice, but, for reasons of hygiene and space, San Michele and its neighbour were designated cemeteries in the 19th century.

The church of San Michele in Isola stands by the landing stage. Designed by Mauro Coducci, it was the first church in Venice to be faced in white Istrian stone. With its carved tombstones and chapels, the cemetery holds a curious

fascination. Some graves have suffered neglect, but most are well-tended and enlivened by a riot of flowers.

The most famous graves are those of foreigners: Ezra Pound (1885–1972), in the *Evangelisti* (Protestant) section, and Sergei Diaghilev (1872–1929) and Igor Stravinsky (1882–1971) in the *Greci* or Orthodox section. These bodies have been allowed to rest in peace. Most others are

dug up after about ten years to make way for new arrivals, and the bones taken to the ossuary island of Sant'Ariano. Today, however, due to a lack of space, most Venetians are buried on the mainland.

FRA MAURO

The monastery of San Michele was home to Camaldolese monks from 1212, before being handed over to the Franciscan Order. One of the monastery's most famous residents was Fra Mauro, who in about 1450 created one of the most beautiful and detailed maps of the world without ever having left his island home. Thanks to the constant flow of merchants and seamen arriving in Venice from all over the world, Fra Mauro was able to piece together their accounts of the countries and regions they had seen on their travels, and thus produce his world map. This magnificent example of medieval cartography has undergone painstaking restoration and today is housed at the Biblioteca Nazionale Marciana *(p87)* in Piazza San Marco.

7

Isola della Certosa

🚌 **4.1 or 4.2; request stop**

La Certosa is named after the wealthy order of Carthusian monks who once had a grand monastery here, complete with a church full of ducal tombs and artworks. This was all lost

The grand arched gates of San Michele's cemetery, and *(inset)* bright floral offerings ↓

→

Inside the library at San Lazzaro degli Armeni, which houses over 40,000 texts

in the intervening years when the island was occupied by the military and sold off to wealthy Europeans, like Prince Charles of Prussia who relocated the cloister to his summer castle in Berlin in 1850.

Now, however, the island has been rehabilitated thanks to funding from the European Union and a public-private partnership with Vento di Venezia. Instead of disused military barracks there is now a smart marina, a sailing club and kayak centre, a beautiful park, a hotel and a very popular alfresco bar run by the acclaimed chef Raffaelle Alajmo.

> San Lazzaro degli Armeni served as an asylum in the 12th century and later became a hospital island for lepers, named after their patron saint, Lazarus.

8

San Servolo

🚢 20 from San Zaccaria

Halfway between San Marco (p76) and the Lido (p184) is the island of San Servolo. Now a centre for teaching traditional crafts, and home to the **Venice International University**, it started life as one of the original monastery islands of Venice. Benedictine monks established a monastery here in the 8th century, and later added a hospital.

In 1725 the island became an asylum and a new hospital was built to house the patients. The Council of Ten (p84) declared that this was to be strictly a shelter for "maniacs of noble family or comfortable circumstances". Meanwhile, the poor were imprisoned or left to their own devices. In 1797 Napoleon scrubbed this discriminatory decree and the asylum became free to all.

In 1980 this spartan island was taken over by the Venice European Centre for the Trades and Professions of Conservation, and in 1996 Venice International University opened its doors here. The historic buildings and the park in which they are set have been extensively restored.

Venice International University

📍 Isola di San Servolo
🚢 20 from San Zaccaria
🌐 univiu.org

9

San Lazzaro degli Armeni

📞 041 526 01 04 🚢 20 (leaves San Zaccaria daily at 3:10pm)

Lying just off the Lido, San Lazzaro degli Armeni is a small monastery island, recognizable by the onion-shaped cupola of its white campanile. The buildings are surrounded by gardens and groves of cypress trees.

This island served as an asylum in the 12th century and later became a hospital island for lepers, named after their patron saint, Lazarus. In 1717 an Armenian monk was forced to flee his homeland, the Morea, when the Turks invaded. Venetian rulers gave him this island as a place of shelter, and he established a religious order here. The Armenians rebuilt the island, setting up a monastery, church and library amid gardens and orchards, and it has remained a centre of learning ever since.

Today, multilingual monks give visitors guided tours of the church, the art collection, the library and the museum, which houses Armenian, Greek, Indian and Egyptian artifacts. The most impressive exhibit is the printing hall where, over 200 years ago, a press produced works in 36 languages. A polyglot press is still in use, producing postcards, maps and prints for visitors.

Did You Know?

Among the artifacts in the museum of the San Lazzaro degli Armeni is a mummy of an Egyptian priest.

↑ The luxurious Kempinski Hotel on the historic island of San Clemente

10

Sant'Erasmo

This green island is known as "Venice's garden" thanks to the dozens of working farms here. This is where many of the vegetables in the Rialto Market (*p107*) originate and the island's enjoyable Festa del Carciofo Violetta (Purple Artichoke Festival), in early May, is held. It also has some narrow beaches and a simple hotel, Il Lato Azzurro (*www.latoazzurro.it*).

11

San Clemente

Founded in 1131 as a refuge for pilgrims and soldiers en route to the Holy Land, the island of San Clemente became the site of a monastery, home to a succession of religious orders. During the Republic, doges frequently met distinguished visitors here, but from 1630, when it was hit by the plague,

it served as a military depot. In the 19th century the island was turned into an asylum; most of the buildings date from that time. Today San Clemente is home to a five-star Kempinski hotel and is only accesssible to guests. It is only minutes away from Piazza San Marco.

12

Lido

🚢 1, 2, 5.1, 5.2 and 6 (summer) to Santa Maria Elisabetta; 17 from Tronchetto to San Nicolò

The Lido is a slender sandbank 12 km (8 miles) long, which forms a natural barrier between Venice and the open sea. It is both a residential suburb of the city and the city's seaside resort. The only island in the lagoon where cars are permitted is linked to the Tronchetto island car park by car ferry. From Venice, the Lido is served by regular vaporettos.

The Lido's main season runs from June to September, the busiest months being July, August and September. In winter most hotels are closed. In the 19th century, before the Lido was developed, the island was a favourite haunt of English poet Lord Byron, author Mary Shelley and other literary figures.

Bathing establishments were gradually opened and by the turn of the 20th century the Lido had become one of Europe's most fashionable seaside resorts, frequented by royalty, film stars and leading lights of the literati. They stayed in the grand hotels, swam in the sea or sat in deckchairs on the sands by the striped *cabanas* (huts). Life in the Lido's heyday was brilliantly evoked in Thomas Mann's book *Death in Venice* (1912). The Hôtel des Bains, where the melancholic character of Von Aschenbach resides, appears in the novel and in Visconti's 1970 film, and is still a prominent landmark, although it has since been converted into private apartments.

The Lido is no longer the prestigious resort it was in the 1930s. Beaches are crowded and ferries packed with day trippers, but the sands, sea and sporting facilities never-theless provide a welcome break from city culture.

The Lido can be covered by bus but a popular form of trans-port is the bicycle. Visitors can hire one from the shop almost opposite the vaporetto stop at Santa Maria Elisabetta.

The east side of the island is fringed by sandy beaches. For passengers arriving by ferry at the main landing stage, these beaches are reached by bus, taxi or on foot along the Gran Viale Santa Maria Elisabetta. This is the main shopping

> By the turn of the 20th century the Lido had become one of Europe's most fashionable seaside resorts, frequented by royalty, film stars and leading lights of the literati.

→

One of the many luxury hotels that are dotted across the Lido street of the Lido. At the end of the Gran Viale, turn left for the beaches of San Nicolò or right along the Lungomare G Marconi, which features the most opulent hotels and the best beaches.

The long straight road parallel to the beach leads southwest to the village of Malamocco. There are some good fish restaurants here, but visitors will find little evidence to suggest that this was once an 8th-century political powerhouse and former seat of the lagoon's government.

The Lido's main quarter of cultural interest is San Nicolò in the north. Across the Porto di Lido, it is possible to see the fortress of Sant'Andrea on the island of Le Vignole, built by Michele Sanmicheli between 1435 and 1449 to guard the main entrance of the lagoon.

It was to the Porto di Lido that the doge was rowed annually to cast a ring into the sea in symbolic marriage each spring. After this he would visit the nearby church and monastery of San Nicolò, which was founded in 1044 and rebuilt in the 16th century.

The nearby **Jewish cemetery** dates from 1386. After centuries of neglect, restoration began in 1999, successfully saving more than 1,000 memorials. Book a guided tour of the cemetery through the Museo Ebraico (p160). The rest of this area is given over to an airfield. The

INTERNATIONAL FILM FESTIVAL

Movie fans flock to the Lido every year for the International Film Festival. First held in 1932, the festival has long attracted big names in the film world, but it has also been plagued by bureaucracy and political in-fighting. There are signs that the event is making a comeback, however, and famous names are now returning. The event takes place in late August/early September, with films shown day and night across the island.

aeroclub located there can organize private flying lessons.

Jewish Cemetery
♿ Ⓜ ☎ 041 71 53 59 ⏰ For guided tours only (call ahead)

13 ♿ Ⓜ

Lazzaretto Nuovo
🚌 13 ⏰ For guided tours only; Apr–Oct: 11am Sat 🌐 lazzarettiveneziani.it

A mere stone's throw from Sant'Erasmo, in the northern lagoon, Lazzaretto Nuovo is one of the few uninhabited islands that can still be visited. Archaeologists here continue to unearth medieval structures dating back to the late 15th century, when the island was used as a quarantine station for crews of ships hailing from distant lands where the plague was rife. Cargoes would be fumigated with rosemary and juniper. During the pestilence that afflicted Venice in 1576, the island was home to around 10,000 victims.

Houses line the canal in Padua

THE VENETO PLAIN

The Veneto Plain sweeps round from the Po river delta in the southwest to the mountains that form the border between Italy and Slovenia. The whole region is crossed by a series of rivers, canals and waterways, all of which converge in the Adriatic Sea. The river-borne silt deposits that created the Venetian Lagoon cover the Veneto, making the land extremely fertile. The Romans established their frontier posts here, and these survive today as the great cities of Vicenza, Padua and Treviso. Their strategic position at the hub of the empire's road network enabled them to prosper under Roman rule, as they continued to do under the benign rule of the Venetian empire more than 1,000 years later.

Wealth from agriculture, commerce and the spoils of war paid for the beautification of these cities through the construction of Renaissance palaces and public buildings, many of them designed by the region's great architect, Andrea Palladio. His villas can be seen all over the Veneto, symbols of the idyllic and leisured existence once enjoyed by the region's aristocrats.

Visitors exploring the Basilica Palladiana, Piazza dei Signori. ↑

❶ VICENZA

🚉🚌 Piazza Stazione ℹ️ Piazza Matteotti 12; www.vicenzae.org

Vicenza is known as the adoptive city of Andrea Palladio (1508–80), who started out as a stonemason and became one of the most influential architects of all time. One of the wealthiest cities in the Veneto, Vicenza is celebrated the world over for its splendid and varied architecture, which shows the extraordinary evolution of Palladio's distinctive style. It also offers an array of elegant shops and cafés to visit.

① Piazza dei Signori

At the heart of Vicenza, the bustling square of Piazza dei Signori is home to a number of architectural landmarks, but it is dominated by the huge Palazzo della Ragione, often referred to as the "Basilica Palladiana". Open to the public, its green, copper-clad roof is shaped like an upturned boat with a balustrade that bristles with the statues of famous Greek and Roman gods. The elegant colonnades were designed by Palladio in 1549 to support the 15th-century town hall, which had begun to subside. This was his first public commission, and his aesthetically pleasing yet practical solution ensured the survival of the building for many generations to come.

The astonishingly slender Torre di Piazza alongside has stood since the 12th century. Opposite is the elegant café Gran Caffè Garibaldi, which is next to Palladio's Loggia del Capitaniato (1571). The Loggia's upper rooms contain the city's council chamber.

② Contrà Porti

Contrà (an abbreviation of *contrada*, or "district") is the local dialect word for "street". On the western side is a series of pretty Gothic buildings with painted windows and ornate balconies, including Palazzo Porto-Colleoni (No. 19). In many ways, these opulent houses reflect Venice's distinctively ornate architecture, a reminder that Vicenza was once part of the Venetian empire.

Several fine Palladian palazzos stand on this street. The Palazzo Thiene (No. 12) of 1545–50, the Palazzo Porto Barbarano (No. 11) of 1570 and the Palazzo Iseppo da Porto (No. 21) of 1552 all illustrate the variety of Palladio's style – Classical elements are common to all three, but each is unique in its architectural execution. The Palazzo Thiene reveals some intriguing details of Palladio's methods: though the building appears to be of stone, close inspection reveals that it is built of cheap lightweight brick, cleverly rendered to look like masonry.

the sun, who appears to fly over the ceiling of the entrance hall. In the upstairs rooms are many Gothic altarpieces, such as Hans Memling's *Crucifixion* (1468–70), the central panel of a triptych whose side panels are now in New York.

In the later rooms are works by the local artist Bartolomeo Montagna (around 1450–1523), including his *Virgin Enthroned with Child, St John the Baptist and Saints Bartholomew, Augustine and Sebastian*.

③
Museo Civico

🏛 Piazza Matteotti 37-9
🕐 Jul-Aug: 10am-6pm Tue-Sun; Sep-Jun: 9am-5pm Tue-Sun 🌐 museicivici vicenza.it

This fine museum is housed in Palladio's Palazzo Chiericati, built in 1550. Inside is a fresco by Domenico Brusazorzi of a naked charioteer, representing

④
Santa Corona

🏛 Contrà Santa Corona
📞 0444 32 08 54 🕐 9am-5:30pm Tue-Sun

This Gothic church was built in 1261 to house what was thought to be a thorn from Christ's Crown of Thorns, donated by Louis IX of France. In the Porto Chapel are numerous notable paintings and the tomb of Luigi da Porto, author of the novel *Giulietta e Romeo*, upon which Shakespeare based his famous play. In the cloister the Museo Naturalistico-Archeologico exhibits natural history and archaeology.

EAT

Al Pestello
This family-run spot is dedicated to modernizing traditional recipes using the best local ingredients.

🏛 Contrà San Stefano 3
🌐 alpestello.it

€€€

Antico Guelfo
This upmarket restaurant is known for its traditional Veneto and modern dishes.

🏛 Contrà Pedemuro San Biagio 90 🕐 Sun dinner, Tue
🌐 anticoguelfo.it

€€€

Osteria Il Cursore
Get local and seasonal produce here, paired with regional dishes.

🏛 Stradella Pozzetto 10
🕐 Tue 🌐 osteria cursore.it

€€€

⑤ 🏛️
Villa Rotonda

🏠 Via della Rotonda 45
🕐 10am-noon & 3-6pm Fri-Sun 🌐 villalarotonda.it

With its symmetrical proportions, this villa, also known as the Villa Capra Valmarana, is the epitome of Palladio's architecture and the most famous of all his villas, being the most widely copied. The design is simple yet satisfying, as is the contrast between the green lawns, white walls and terracotta roof tiles. Built between 1550 and 1552, it has inspired

lookalikes in cities as far away as Delhi and St Petersburg. Fans of *Don Giovanni* will recognize locations used in Joseph Losey's 1979 film. The villa can be reached by bus from town, or on foot, following the path that passes the Villa Valmarana.

⑥
San Lorenzo

🏠 Piazza San Lorenzo
📞 0444 32 19 60 🕐 9:30am-noon & 3:30-6pm Mon-Sat, 10-10:45am & 3:30-6pm Sun

This church's portal is a splendid example of Gothic stone carving, decorated with figures of the Virgin and Child, and St Francis and St Clare. The frescoes inside are damaged, but there are fine tombs. The cloister, to

The iconic colonnades of Andrea Palladio's Villa Rotonda, and *(inset)* its exterior ↓

the north, is a flower-filled haven of calm.

⑦ 🏛️ 🛍️
Palazzo Leoni Montanari

🏠 Contrà Santa Corona 25
🕐 10am-6pm Tue-Sun
🌐 gallerieditalia.com

This Baroque building, completed around 1720, was commissioned by Giovanni Leoni Montanari, who had made his fortune producing and selling cloth. Today the palazzo houses an art gallery renowned for its unique collections of Venetian paintings and Russian icons.

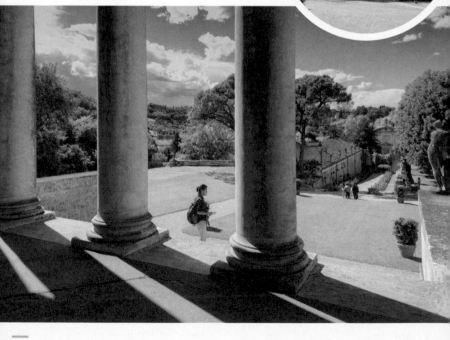

> The wide avenue linking the city to the Basilica di Monte Berico on top of the hill features shady colonnades with many shrines along the route.

↑ The grand entrance hall of the ornately decorated Villa Valmarana ai Nani

⑧
Casa Pigafetta

🏛 Contrà Pigafetta

This breathtaking Spanish Gothic building of 1481 has clover-leaf balconies, gryphon brackets and Moorish windows. The owner, Antonio Pigafetta, sailed round the world with Magellan in 1519–22, being one of only 20 men who survived the voyage. The palace's extraordinary exterior can be admired from the street, but there is no public access to the interior.

⑨
Monte Berico

🏛 Basilica di Monte Berico, Viale X Giugno 87 🕐 7am–noon & 2.30–6pm daily 🌐 monteberico.it

Monte Berico is the green, cypress-clad hill to the south of the city to which wealthy Vicenzans once escaped in the summer to enjoy cooler air and bucolic charms. The wide avenue linking the city to the spectacular Basilica di Monte Berico on top of the hill features shady colonnades with many shrines along the route. The Baroque basilica was built in the 15th century and is dedicated to the Virgin who is said to have appeared during the 1426–8 plague to declare that the city of Vicenza and all who live there would be spared.

Many pilgrims travel to this charming church, where Bartolomeo Montagna's moving *Pietà* fresco (1572) makes an impact within the ornate interior. Other attractions include a fossil collection in the cloister and Veronese's fine painting *The Supper of St Gregory the Great* (1572) in the refectory. The large canvas was violently cut to ribbons by bayonet-wielding soldiers during the revolutionary outbursts of 1848 and has since been painstakingly restored to its former glory.

⑩
Villa Valmarana ai Nani

🏛 Via dei Nani 8 🕐 Times vary, check website 🌐 villavalmarana.com

The wall alongside the Villa Valmarana ai Nani, built in 1688 by Antonio Muttoni, is topped by the figures of little people, which give this building its somewhat unusual name – *ai Nani* translates as "at the Dwarfs". Legend has it that Princess Layana, who was a little person, once lived here, and her parents ensured that the servants and custodians of the villa were also little people.

Inside the villa, the walls are covered with frescoes by Tiepolo, in which pagan gods float on clouds watching scenes from the epics of Homer and Virgil. In the separate *Foresteria* (guest house), the frescoes with themes of peasant life and the seasons, painted by Tiepolo's son, Giandomenico, are equally decorative but more earthily realistic.

The villa can be reached by a 10-minute walk from the basilica on Monte Berico. Head downhill along Via M d'Azeglio to the high-walled convent on the right where the road ends, then take the Via San Bastiano.

THE CITY OF GOLD

Producing around 70 per cent or Europe's gold and precious metal jewellery, Vicenza has long been Italy's capital of jewellery-making. The VicenzaOro *(www. vicenzaoro.org)* gold trade fair takes place twice a year in January and September, when local and international jewellers showcase their glamorous wares. Check out the glittering exhibits at Museo del Gioello inside the Basilica Palladiana on Piazza dei Signori *(p190)*.

⑪ ⊘ 🛍

TEATRO OLIMPICO

📍 Piazza Matteotti 🚌 Piazza Matteotti 🕐 Jul & Aug: 9am–6pm
Tue–Sun; Sep–Jun: 9am–5pm Tue–Sun 🌐 teatrolimpicovicenza.it

The Teatro Olimpico was Palladio's final masterpiece and is a
remarkable piece of work, a showcase of his mastery of style and
perspective. The façade has all the typical Palladian hallmarks and
the interior is an extravaganza of columns, sculptures and ornamen-
tation. Tread the boards while marvelling at the beauty of it all.

Europe's oldest surviving indoor theatre, the Teatro Olimpico
is a remarkable structure. Andrea Palladio began work on
the Teatro in 1579, but he died without finishing it. His pupil,
Vincenzo Scamozzi, completed it in time for its ambitious
opening of Sophocles' tragic drama, *Oedipus Rex*, on 3 March
1585, with the addition of his famous trompe-l'œil scenery.

The Teatro hosts a number of events throughout the year.
In early May it's the turn of Vicenza Jazz, followed by Musical
Weeks, with an emphasis on classical music, from mid-May
to early June. September sees Vicenza in Lirica take to the
stage, while the Vicenza Opera Festival is held in October.

*The gods of Mount
Olympus, after which the
theatre is named, decorate
the walls and ceiling of the
Odeon, a room used for
music recitals.*

Did You Know?

The Teatro Olimpico
appeared in Lasse
Hallström's *Casanova*
(2005), starring
Heath Ledger.

*Positioned behind the stage,
Scamozzi's painted scenery
represents the Greek city of
Thebes. The streets are cleverly
painted in perspective and rise
at a steep angle, giving the
illusion of great length.*

*The toga-clad façade
statues are portraits of
sponsors who paid for the
theatre's construction.*

① The walled entrance to the Teatro Olimpico.

② Visitors strolling through the pristine grounds of the Olympic Theatre courtyard.

③ The theatre's ornate interior, with its frescoed ceiling, was designed to look and feel like an outdoor Roman amphitheatre.

← Illustration of the Teatro Olimpico interior and grounds

The armoury gateway, with its military-style carvings, leads from Piazza Matteotti into the picturesque theatre courtyard.

The courtyard of the former castle is adorned with sculptures donated by members of the Olympic Academy, the learned body that built the theatre.

ANDREA PALLADIO

Andrea Palladio was perhaps the most sought-after architect of the 16th century. Inspired by the treatises of ancient authors such as Vitruvius and Virgil, Palladio designed elegant palaces and villas for his clients that harked back to the Classical Age. His own architectural treatise *The Four Books of Architecture* gained him widespread international recognition.

A SHORT WALK
VICENZA

Distance 3.5 km (2 miles) **Time** 35 minutes
Nearest Bus Vicenza Piazza Matteotti

Vicenza, the fourth-largest city in the Veneto,
is packed to the brim with beautifully propor-
tioned buildings that combine classical sophistication
and rustic simplicity. Walking around this great
Palladian city, one can see the evolution of Andrea
Palladio's distinctive style. In the centre is the
monumental basilica he adapted to serve as the
town hall, while all around are the palaces he built
for Vicenza's wealthy citizens.

*Contrà Porti is
home to some of
the most elegant
palazzos in the city.*

START

FINISH

*Palladio's impressive **Palazzo
Valmarana**, built in 1566, was
originally intended to be three
times larger. It was not completed
until 1680, 100 years after the
architect's death.*

Loggia del Capitaniato
*is a covered arcade
designed by Palladio
in 1571.*

CORSO ANDREA PALLADIO

CONTRÀ CAVOUR

C MUSCHERIA

CONTRÀ PESCH
VECCHI

VIA BATTISTI

CONTRÀ
GARIBALDI

CONTRÀ SAN ANTONIO

CONTRÀ LAMPERTICO

PIAZZA DEL DUOMO

↑ The Duomo, heavily
restored and rebuilt
after World War II

*The **Duomo**, Vicenza's
cathedral, was rebuilt after
bomb damage during World
War II left only the façade
and choir intact.*

| 0 metres | 150 |
| 0 yards | 150 |

N ↑

Encircled by grand 15th-century buildings, **Piazza dei Signori** (p190) *is a lively spot, with a bustling market and cafés.*

The **Torre di Piazza** *is 82 m (269 ft) high. Begun in the 12th century, its height was increased in 1311 and 1444.*

The 15th-century basilica has a magnificent loggia built by Palladio in 1549.

CONTRA S BARBARA

PIAZZA DELLE BIADE

PIAZZA DEI SIGNORI

CONTRA CATENA

C GAZZOLE

PIAZZA DELLE ERBE

CONTRA PIANCOLI

CONTRA SAN PAOLO

CONTRA PONTE SAN MICHELE

CONTRA PESCARIA

ANTONIO PIGAFETTA

RETRONE

↑ Statue of the famous Italian architect Andrea Palladio in the Piazzetta

The **Quartiere delle Barche** *contains numerous attractive palaces built in the 14th-century Venetian Gothic style.*

The elegant **Ponte San Michele** *affords scenic views of the surrounding town.*

Piazza delle Erbe, *the city's market square, is overlooked by a 13th-century torture chamber, the Torre del Tormento.*

Casa Pigafetta (p193) *was the birthplace of Antonio Pigafetta, who in 1519 set sail round the world with Magellan.*

This memorial to Vicenza's most famous citizen, Andrea Palladio, is often surrounded by busy market stalls.

Did You Know?

The city of Vicenza was officially designated a UNESCO World Heritage Site in 1994.

↑ Ponte dei Quattro Papi crosses Padua's canal at dusk

PADUA

Piazzale Boschetti FS ⓘ Piazzale della Stazione; www.unlipadova.it

Padua (Padova) is a university town with an illustrious academic history. Rich in art and architecture, it has two particularly outstanding sights. The magnificent Cappella degli Scrovegni (p205), north of the city centre, is famous for Giotto's lyrical frescoes, and forms part of the complex incorporating the Eremitani church and museums. The Basilica di Sant'Antonio is one of the most popular pilgrimage destinations in Italy.

① La Specola

⌂ Vicolo dell'Osservatorio 5
🕒 For guided tours only; Oct-Apr: 4pm Sat, Sun & public hols; May-Sep: 6pm Sat, Sun & public hols

This attractive medieval tower on the river was turned into an observatory in 1761. The guided tour leads you around antique telescopes, charts and sextants before reaching the octagonal chamber with life-size depictions of eminent astronomers.

② The Ghetto

The area known as "the Ghetto" was cordoned off in 1603 and gates were erected to detain Padua's Jewish inhabitants. They were forced to live there until the segregation order was dropped in 1797, when Napoleon's army arrived and took control of the area.

Today, it is a lovely neighbourhood with pedestrianized cobbled streets full of bars and shops. A plaque on the synagogue in Via Solferino commemorates the 46 Paduan Jews who died in the Holocaust, reminding passers-by of the Ghetto's tragic history.

③
Caffè Pedrocchi

⌂ Via VIII Febbraio 15
🕒 Daily ⓦ caffepedrocchi.it

Grand cafés have long played an important role in the intellectual life of northern Italy, and many philosophical

---

GALILEO GALILEI

Often called "the father of modern science", Galileo (1564-1642) made his home in Padua, where he taught at the university. His astronomic discoveries supported Copernicus's theory that the Earth revolves around the sun. Accused of heresy and forced to recant, he spent the rest of his life under house arrest, though this did not stop his research.

issues have been thrashed out at the Caffè Pedrocchi since it first opened in 1831. Politics superseded philosophy when it became a centre of the Risorgimento movement, dedicated to liberating Italy from Austrian rule; it was the scene of uprisings in 1848, for which several student leaders were sadly executed. Later it became famous as the café that never closed its doors. These days people come to talk, read, play cards or watch the world go by as they eat and drink tempting cuisine from the varied menu.

The beautiful upstairs rooms, decorated in Moorish, Egyptian and Greek styles, are now the premises of the **Museum del Risorgimento e dell'Età Contemporanea**. On display here are historical artifacts from World War II.

Museum del Risorgimento e dell'Età Contemporanea

⊛ 📞 049 820 4580

🕐 9:30am–12:30pm & 3:30–6pm Tue–Sun

🚫 1 Jan, 1 May, 25 & 26 Dec

---

④ 🚲 Ⓜ

Palazzo del Bo

🏠 Via VIII Febbraio 2

🕐 For guided tours only (book ahead) 🌐 unipd.it/bo

Named after a tavern called *Il Bo* (the ox), Padua's main university building is mostly used today for graduation ceremonies. Originally it housed the medical faculty, renowned throughout Europe. Among its famous teachers and students was Gabriele Falloplo (1523–62), after whom the Fallopian tubes are named.

Elena Lucrezia Cornaro Piscopia was the first woman in the world to receive a university degree. She graduated in 1678 – long before women could study at many of Europe's other universities. Her statue can be found on the grand staircase leading to the upper gallery of the 16th-century courtyard.

On the tour, you can expect to see the pulpit that Galileo used when he taught here from 1592 until 1610. It also takes in the world's oldest surviving anatomy theatre, which dates back to 1594.

DRINK

Antonio Ferrari

A modern wine bar with friendly staff. Specializes in divine sparkling wines.

🏠 Via Umberto I, 15
🚫 Tue 🌐 antonio ferrari.it

Enoteca Da Severino

Wide range of wines with an aware staff. Sample a glass with a selection of cheese, or buy a bottle to take home.

🏠 Via del Santo 44
🚫 Lunch, Sun
🌐 enotecaseverino.it

Gran Caffe Diemme

Drinks range from cappuccinos to beer and wine. Cool vibe, friendly atmosphere, and a brilliant location make this a great drinking den.

🏠 Piazza dei Signori 17 📞 049 591 39 09 🚫 Mon

199

⑤
Basilica di Sant'Antonio

🏛 Piazza del Santo
🕐 9am-1pm & 2-6pm
Tue-Sun 🚫 1 Jan, 25 Dec
🌐 santantonio.org/
it/basilica

This striking church, with its minaret-like spires and Byzantine domes, is also known as Il Santo. It was begun in 1232 to house the remains of St Anthony of Padua, a preacher who modelled himself on St Francis of Assisi. Although he was a simple man who rejected worldly wealth, the citizens of Padua constructed one of the most lavish churches in Christendom to serve as his shrine.

The outline of the Basilica di Sant'Antonio reflects the influence of Byzantine architecture; a cone-shaped central dome is surrounded by a further seven domes, rising above a façade that combines Gothic with Romanesque elements. The interior is more conventional, however. Visitors are kept away from the high altar, which features Donatello's magnificent reliefs (1444–5) on the miracles of St Anthony, and his statues of the Virgin, the Crucifixion and several Paduan saints. There is access to St Anthony's tomb in the north transept, and it's hung with offerings and photographs of people who have survived serious

> The outline of the Basilica di Sant'Antonio reflects the influence of Byzantine architecture; a cone-shaped central dome is surrounded by a further seven domes.

illness or car crashes with the saint's help. The walls around the shrine are decorated with large marble reliefs depicting St Anthony's life, carved in 1505–77 by various artists, including Jacopo Sansovino and Tullio Lombardo. These are rather cold by comparison with Altichiero da Zevio's *Crucifixion* fresco (1380s) in the opposite transept. This pageant-like painting of everyday scenes from medieval life depicts people, animals and plants.

---

⑥
Duomo and Baptistry

🏛 Piazza Duomo 📞 049 65 69 14 🕐 10am-6pm daily

Padua's grand Duomo was commissioned from Michelangelo in 1552, but his designs were altered during the construction. Of the 4th-century cathedral which stood on the site, the domed Romanesque Baptistry still survives, with its frescoes by Giusto de'

Menabuoi (around 1376). The frescoes cover biblical stories, such as the Creation, Crucifixion and Resurrection and the Last Judgement.

---

⑦
Statue of Gattamelata

Near the entrance to the basilica stands one of the great Renaissance works. This gritty portrait of the mercenary soldier Gattamelata (whose name means "Honey Cat") was created in 1443–52, to honour a man who in his life did great service to the Venetian Republic. Donatello won fame for the monument, the first large-scale equestrian statue made since Roman times.

---

⑧
Scuola del Santo and Oratorio di San Giorgio

🏛 Piazza del Santo 11
📞 049 822 56 52 🕐 9am-1pm & 2-6pm Tue-Sun

These two linked buildings contain excellent frescoes,

←
The statue of Gattamelata stands beside the fine Basilica di Sant'Antonio

including the earliest documented paintings by Titian. These comprise two scenes from the life of St Anthony in the Scuola del Santo, executed in 1511. The delightful saints' lives and scenes from the life of Christ in the San Giorgio Oratory are the work of two artists, Altichiero da Zevio and Jacopo Avenzo, who painted them in 1378–84.

Eremitani Museums

📍 Piazza Eremitani 8
🚌 🕐 Museums: 9am-7pm daily 🚪 1 Jan, 1 May, 25 & 26 Dec 🌐 cappella degliscrovegni.it

This museum complex occupies a group of 14th-century monastic buildings attached to the church of the Eremitani, a reclusive Augustinian order. The admission ticket includes

↑ Admiring the Eremitani Museums' rich collection of paintings and sculpture

entry to the nearby Cappella degli Scrovegni *(p205)* which overlooks the city's Roman amphitheatre, and to the Archaeology Museum, the Medieval and Modern Art Museum, and the Bottacin Museum, housed in the Palazzo Zuckerman across the road.

The main highlight of the archaeological collection is the temple-like tomb of the Volumni family, dating from the 1st century CE. Among several other Roman tombstones from the Veneto region is one of the young dancer Claudia Toreuma – a fairly dull inscribed column rather than a portrait. The collection also includes some fine mosaics, along with several impressive life-size statues depicting muscular Roman deities and toga-clad dignitaries.

The massive Medieval and Modern Art Museum is well worth a visit. It covers the history of Venetian art, with paintings from Giotto to the 1700s. Another section looks at Giotto and his influence on local art, using the Crucifix from the Cappella degli Scrovegni as its centrepiece. The Crucifix is flanked by an army of angels (late 15th century) painted in gorgeous colours by the artist Guariento. Alongside the museum

complex is the Eremitani church (1276–1306), with its magnificent roof and wall tombs. Interred here is Marco Benavides (1489–1582), a professor of law at the city university whose mausoleum was designed by Ammannati, a Renaissance architect from Florence. Sadly missing from the church are Andrea Mantegna's celebrated frescoes of the lives of St James and St Christopher (1454–7), which were destroyed during a bombing raid in World War II. Two scenes from this magnificent work survive in the Ovetari Chapel, south of the sanctuary. *The Martyrdom of St James* was reconstructed from salvaged fragments, and *The Martyrdom of St Christopher* was removed carefully and stored elsewhere before the bombing. Otherwise only photographs on the walls remain to hint at the quality of the lost works.

3,000
—
The number of paintings housed in the monumental Medieval and Modern Art Museum.

TOP 3 EREMITANI MUSEUMS HIGHLIGHTS

Coin Collections
The Bottacin Museum houses an almost complete set of fine Venetian coinage and rare Roman medallions.

Renaissance Bronzes
The most appealing feature in the brilliant Archaeology Museum is the comical *Drinking Satyr* bronze by Il Riccio (1470–1532).

Molinari's Depiction
The Medieval and Modern Art Museum's painting of Elena Lucrezia Cornaro Piscopia, though not artistically special, is significant for depicting the first woman to graduate in the world.

⑩ 🖉

Orto Botanico

🏛 Via Orto Botanico 15
🕐 Times vary, check
website 🚫 1 Jan, 25 Dec
🌐 ortobotanicopd.it

Founded in 1545, Padua's botanical garden is the oldest in Europe, and it retains much of its original appearance; one of the palm trees dates to 1585. Originally intended for the cultivation of medicinal plants, the pathways now spill over with exotic foliage, shaded by ancient trees. The gardens were used to cultivate the first lilacs (1565), sunflowers (1568) and potatoes (1590) grown in Italy.

The original garden was expanded in 2014 with five biodiversity gardens on the site where the Benedictine vegetable gardens once grew. Containing a variety of microcosms, including a tropical rainforest and arid climates, the biodiversity garden building has been designed to be as environmentally friendly as possible, using natural solar energy and rainwater collection. The biodiversity garden is a great source of

 PICTURE PERFECT
Orchids Abound

The tropical greenhouse in the Orto Botanico has a large selection of orchids. Photograph those with large, bright flowers up close, and save a wider shot for the species with tiny flowers.

information, telling the stories of important plants from around the world that are used for a variety of purposes from medicine to construction.

⑪ 🖉 🛍

Palazzo della Ragione

🏛 Piazza delle Erbe (via the town hall) 📞 049 820 50 06
🕐 Feb-Oct: 9am-7pm Tue-Sun; Nov-Jan: 9am-6pm Tue-Sun 🚫 Mon and public hols

The "Palace of Reason", also known as the "Salone" by locals, was built to serve as Padua's law court and council chamber in 1218. The vast main hall was originally frescoed by the celebrated artist Giotto, but fire

---

THE BRENTA CANAL

The River Brenta, between Padua and the Venetian Lagoon, was canalized in the 16th century. Flowing for a total of 36 km (22 miles), its potential as a transport route was quickly realized, and fine villas were built along its length. Today, three of these elegant buildings open their doors to the public: the Villa Foscari at Malcontenta, the Villa Widmann-Foscari at Mira, and the Villa Pisani at Stra. They can be visited either on an eight- to nine-hour guided tour from Padua to Venice (or vice versa) along the river on a motor launch, or by bus, a cheaper and faster alternative. Booking is necessary through a local travel agent or online at www.ilburchiello.it. A ticket includes a bus between Padua and Stra, a boat tour and guide, and entrance to two villas.

↑ Walking through the lush gardens at the beautiful Orto Botanico

EAT

Belle Parti
A stellar fine dining restaurant, Belle Parti offers the best seasonal produce, impeccable wines and fault-less service.

⌂ Via Belle Parti 11
Ⓦristorantebelleparti.it

€€€

Dalla Zita
Loved by locals, this hole-in-the-wall joint has a cornucopia of sandwiches.

⌂ Via Gorizia 12
☏ 049 654 992 ◐ Sun

€€€

Pasticceria Graziati
Though ostensibly a cake shop, Graziati serves meals in its wine-cellar restaurant.

⌂ Piazza della Frutta 40
◐ Wed Ⓦ graziati.com

€€€

destroyed his work in 1420. The frescoes that survive today are by the relatively unknown Nicola Miretto, though their astrological theme is fascinating.

The Salone is impressive in its sheer size. It is Europe's biggest undivided medieval hall, 80 m (260 ft) long, 27 m (90 ft) wide and 27 m (90 ft) high. The scale is empha-sized by the wooden horse displayed at one end – a massive beast, copied from Donatello's Gattamelata statue *(p200)* in 1466 and originally made to be pulled in procession during Paduan festivities. It makes for an impressive photograph.

The walls are covered in Miretto's frescoes (1420–25), a total of 333 panels depicting the months of the year with appropriate gods, zodiacal signs and seasonal activities. Also within the palazzo is the Stone of Shame, on which bankrupts were exposed to ridicule before they were sent into exile.

---

⑫

Prato della Valle

The Prato (field) claims to be the largest public square in Italy, and its elliptical shape reflects the form of the Roman theatre that stood on the site. St Anthony of Padua used to

← Statue of Pope Alexander VIII in Prato della Valle

preach sermons to huge crowds here, but subsequent neglect saw the area turn into a malaria-ridden swamp. The land was drained in 1767 to create the canal that now encircles the Prato. Four stone bridges cross the picturesque channel, which is lined on both sides by statues of 78 eminent citizens of Padua. These depict a range of figures, from Pope Alexander VIII to Gustavus Adolphus of Sweden.

The green area is a popular spot for locals and visitors to relax, catch up and bask in the sun. On Saturdays there is a market, selling everything from footwear to plants and fruits and vegetables.

Giotto's frescoes
covering the walls of
the Scrovegni Chapel ↑

⑬ 🖊

CAPPELLA DEGLI SCROVEGNI, PADUA

📍Piazza Eremitani 8 (entrance Eremitani Museums) 🚌To Piazzale Boschetti
🕘9am–7pm daily (book ahead) 🚫Public hols 🌐cappelladegliscrovegni.it

Enrico Scrovegni built this chapel in 1303, hoping thereby to spare his dead father, a usurer, from the eternal damnation in hell described by the poet Dante in his *Inferno*. The interior of the chapel is covered with beautiful frescoes of scenes from the life of Christ, painted by Giotto between 1303 and 1305. As works of great narrative force, they exerted a powerful influence on the development of European art.

↑ The fine exterior of the Cappella degli Scrovegni

Giotto's Frescoes

The Florentine artist Giotto (1266–1337) is regarded as the father of the Renaissance, the great revival in the Classical traditions in Western art. His frescoes in this chapel – with their sense of pictorial space, naturalism and narrative drama – mark a decisive break with the Byzantine tradition of the preceding 1,000 years. In such scenes as *Lament over the Dead Christ* figures are naturalistic and three-dimensional, not stylized, and emotions are clearly expressed. He is the first Italian master whose name has passed into posterity, and, although Giotto was considered a great artist in his lifetime, few of the works attributed to him are fully documented. The famous frescoes inside the chapel, nonetheless, are rare exceptions where his authorship is in no doubt.

←

Giotto's *Mary is Presented at the Temple*

VISITING THE CHAPEL

It is compulsory to book your visit on the website in advance as there are strict limits on the number of visitors allowed into the chapel at any one time. Before entering, visitors must spend 15 minutes in a decontamination chamber, where an explanatory film on the chapel and its famous frescoes is provided. The visit itself is restricted to 15 minutes.

↑ Figures expressing grief in Giotto's *Lament over the Dead Christ*

A SHORT WALK

PADUA

Distance 1.5 km (1 mile) **Time** 20 minutes
Nearest Bus Piazza delle Erbe

The city centre of Padua (known as Padova in Italian) is one of the liveliest in northern Italy, thanks to a large student population and to the two street markets, one specializing in fruit and the other in vegetables. These take place every day except Sunday around the vast Palazzo della Ragione, the town's medieval law court and council chamber. The colonnades round the exterior of the palazzo shelter numerous bars, restaurants and shops selling meat, game, cheeses and wine.

Palazzo del Capitaniato, *built between 1599 and 1605 for the head of the city's militia, incorporates an astronomical clock made in 1344.*

Piazza dei Signori *is bordered by attractive arcades which house small speciality shops, interesting cafés and old-fashioned wine bars.*

START

PIAZZA CAPITANIATO

VIA SAN CLEMENTE

PIAZZA DEI SIGNORI

Palazzo Liviano, *a 14th-century arts faculty, contains frescoes and a rare portrait of Petrarch.*

Now used as a conference centre, the elegant **Loggia della Gran Guardia,** *dating from 1523, once housed the Council of Nobles.*

VIA MONTE DI PIETA

VIA MANIN

PIAZZA DEL DUOMO

VIA SONCIN

VIA VANDELLI

The **Palazzo del Monte di Pietà** *has 16th-century arcades and statues enclosing a medieval building.*

The 12th-century baptistery of the **Duomo** (p200) *contains one of the most complete medieval fresco cycles to survive in Italy, painted by Giusto de' Menabuoi in 1378 and now restored.*

← Winged lion and clock tower of Palazzo del Capitaniato

There are good views on to the **Piazza delle Erbe** *marketplace from Palladio's 16th-century loggia, which runs alongside the Palazzo della Ragione.*

Palazzi Comunale,
which houses the city's council offices, has a 13th-century defensive tower.

↑ The picturesque Piazza delle Erbe lit up at night

FINISH

PIAZZA CAVOUR

VIA GORIZIA

PIAZZA DEI FRUTTI

VIA OBERDAN

PTTA GARZERIA

PIAZZA DELLE ERBE

VIA 8 FEBBRAIO

VIA SAN CANZIANO

Built like a Classical temple, **Caffè Pedrocchi** *(p198) has been a famous meeting place for students and intellectuals since it opened in 1831.*

Founded in 1222, Padua University is the second-oldest university in Italy. The main building, **Palazzo del Bo** *(p199), dates from the 16th century.*

The **Palazzo della Ragione** (p202) was, in medieval times, the city court of justice. Its interior is covered with magnificent astrological frescoes.

0 metres   75   N
0 yards   75   ↑

Did You Know?

Padua was founded in 1183 BCE and claims to be the oldest city in northern Italy.

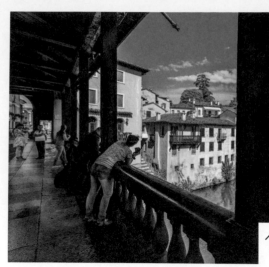

↑ Visitors looking out from the Ponte degli Alpini in Bassano del Grappa

EXPERIENCE MORE

❸

Bassano del Grappa

🚉🚌 **ℹ** Piazza Garibaldi 34; www.commune.bassano.vi.it

This town is synonymous with Italy's favourite after-dinner drink (*grappa* is not named after the town, but after *graspa*, the Italian term for the lees used to distil the liquor). Information on this and on the role played by Bassano during both world wars is given at the **Museo degli Alpini**, across the Ponte degli Alpini bridge. Designed in 1569 by Palladio, the current bridge dates from 1948: its timber allows it to flex when hit by spring meltwaters.

Bassano is also famous for the majolica wares at **Palazzo Sturm**. The works of locally born artist Jacopo Bassano (1510–92) and the sculptor Canova (1757–1822) are celebrated in the **Museo Civico**.

Museo degli Alpini

⊗😊👣 🏠 Via Angarano 2 📞 0424 50 36 62 🕐 9am–8pm Tue-Sun

Palazzo Sturm

⊗ 🏠 Via Schiavonetti 40 📞 0424 51 99 40 🕐 10am-7pm Wed-Mon

Museo Civico

⊗ 🏠 Piazza Garibaldi 🕐 10am-7pm Wed-Mon 🖥 museibassano.it

❹

Thiene

🚌 **ℹ** Piazzetta Rossi 17; 0445 80 48 37

Thiene is one of the area's many historic textile towns, manufacturing jeans and

---

GRAPPA DISTILLERIES

Grappa is a hugely popular drink in Italy, with around 40 million bottles produced every year. Essentially a hard liquor, it is made from almost every part of the grape left over after the initial pressing to make wine. Italians like it after dinner but will also add it to an espresso to produce the *caffè corretto* – an alcoholic pick-me-up (that is, hair of the dog). There are thousands of labels, but some of the best in Bassano are produced at distinguished distilleries such as Nardini (nardini.it) and De Poli (poligrappa.com), both of which offer fascinating tours and tastings.

sweatshirts for sale all over Europe. Two grand villas nearby are certainly worth a visit. Of these, the **Castello Porto-Colleoni** stood in open countryside at the time it was built. Its impressive defences were a precaution against bandits and raiders. Inside there are 16th-century frescoes by Giambattista Zelotti that add a lighter note, and many portraits of horses remind the visitor that the villa's owners, the Colleoni family, were employed by the Venetian cavalry.

Zelotti also frescoed the **Villa Godi Malinverni**, which was the first villa designed by Palladio (p195). The garden is charming and the frescoes are magnificent. Inside the villa are works by Italian Impressionists and a lovely portrait by Pietro Annigoni (1910–88) called *La Strega* (The Sorceress).

Castello Porto-Colleoni

⊗ ⊗ ⌂ Corso Garibaldi 2
🕙 10am–6pm Sat & Sun
🌐 castellodithiene.com

Villa Godi Malinverni

⊗ ⌂ Via Palladio 44
🕙 Times vary, check website 🌐 villagodi.com

⑤

Marostica

🚌 🛈 Piazza Castello 1; 0424 721 27

Marostica is an almost perfect medieval fortified town, with town walls built in 1370 by the Scaligeri (p233). The rampart walk from the **Castello Inferiore** (lower castle) to the Castello Superiore (upper castle) has fine views.

The lower castle exhibits costumes worn by participants in the town's human chess tournament, the Partita a Scacchi, which is held on a magnificent marble chessboard in the piazza every other September. Up to 650 people participate in this colourful re-enactment of a game first played here in 1454.

Castello Inferiore

⊗ ⌂ Piazza degli Scacchi
🕙 9am–1pm & 2:30–6:30pm daily 🚫 1 Jan, 25 Dec
🌐 marosticascacchi.it

Cyclists in the chequered piazza in Marostica

EAT

Antico Ristorante Cardellino
Enjoy seasonal fare here; the asparagus with tagliatelle is popular in spring.

⌂ Via Bellavitis 17, Bassano del Grappa
🕙 Thu 🌐 ristorant ecardellino.it

€ € €

Osteria Trinità
This restaurant offers delicious grilled meats and a great wine list.

⌂ Via Contrà San Giorgio 17, Bassano del Grappa
🕙 Tue & Wed 🌐 osteriatrinita bassano.it

€ € €

Ristorante Trevisani
Housed in a 14th-century building, this spot serves traditional dishes.

⌂ Piazzale Trento 13, Bassano del Grappa
🕙 Breakfast, Sat lunch 🌐 ristorantetrevisani.it

€ € €

6

Cittadella

FS 🚌 *i* Porte Bassanesi 2; 0499 40 44 85

This attractive town is the twin of Castelfranco. Both were fortified and Cittadella still preserves its 13th-century moated walls. These are interrupted by four gates and 16 towers. The Torre di Malta near the southern gate was used as a torture chamber by Ezzelino de Romano, who ruled in the mid-13th century. Far more pleasant is the *Supper at Emmaus* in the Duomo, a masterpiece by local Renaissance artist Bassano.

7

Valdobbiadene

🚌 *i* Piazza Marconi 1; 0423 97 69 75

Valdobbiadene, surrounded by vine-covered hills, is a centre for the sparkling white wine called Cartizze, a type of prosecco. To the east, the Strada del Vino Bianco (white wine route) stretches 34 km (21 miles) to the town of Conegliano (*p212*), passing vineyards offering wine to try and to buy.

About 10 km (8 miles) northeast of Valdobbiadene is the small town of Follina, known for its well-preserved Romanesque abbey.

8

Treviso

FS 🚌 *i* Piazza Borsa 4; www.visittreviso.it

Full of attractive balconied houses, Treviso is a rewarding city for visitors. Comparisons are often made with Venice, but Treviso has its own distinctive character. A good place to explore the architecture is the main street, Calmaggiore. The tradition of painting the exterior of the houses dates back to the medieval period, when this form of decoration compensated for the lack of suitable stone. The modern fish market also has medieval origins. It is held on an island in the middle of Treviso's River Sile so that the remains of the day's trading can be flushed away instantly.

Treviso's Duomo, founded in the 12th century, was reconstructed in the 15th, 16th and 18th centuries. Inside is Titian's *Annunciation* (1570), but it is upstaged by the *Adoration of the Magi* fresco (1520) of his arch rival, Il Pordenone. Other works of note are *The Adoration of the Shepherds* fresco by Paris Bordone and the monument to Bishop Zanetti (1501) by Pietro Lombardo and his sons.

Did You Know?

A fresco in Treviso's Church of San Nicolò contains the first ever depiction of someone wearing glasses.

The **Museo Civico** houses an archaeology collection and a picture gallery in the restored convent of Santa Caterina dei Servi. Lorenzo Lotto's *Portrait of a Dominican* (1526), Titian's *Portrait of Sperone Speroni* (1544) and Bassano's *Crucifixion* are highlights.

Near the 16th-century town wall is the Dominican church of San Nicolò, full of tombs and frescoes, including some by Lorenzo Lotto. There is a painting of St Christopher by Antonio da Treviso.

Museo Civico – Sede Santa Caterina
◎ 🏛 Piazzetta Mario Botter 1 🕐 10am-6pm Tue-Sun 🚫 Public hols
w museicivii treviso.it

↓ A winding road in the vineyards of the Prosecco Hills, Valdobbiadene

Lavish period interiors of Villa Barbaro, and *(inset)* the building's imposing façade

⑨
Castelfranco Veneto

🚉🚌 ℹ️ Via Riccati 14; 0423 49 50 00

Fortified in 1199 by rulers of Treviso, the historic core of this town lies within the well-preserved walls. **Casa di Giorgione**, the birthplace of artist Giorgione (1478–1511), houses a museum devoted to his life. He created such works as *The Tempest (p143)*. His *Virgin and Child with Saints Liberal and Francis* (1504) is displayed in the Duomo. Tuzio Costanza commissioned it to stand above the tomb of his son, Matteo, killed in battle in 1504.

At Fanzolo, northeast of Castelfranco, is Palladio's **Villa Emo**, designed in 1564. Here, Zelotti's frescoes show the love lives of Greek deities.

> **Valdobbiadene, surrounded by vine-covered hills, is a centre for the sparkling white wine called Cartizze, a type of prosecco.**

Casa di Giorgione

♿ 🏠 Piazza San Liberale 🕐 10am–1pm Tue–Thu, 10am–6pm Fri–Sun 🚫 1 Jan, Easter, 25 Dec 🌐 museocasagiorgione.it

Villa Emo

♿ 📷 🏠 Via Stazione 5, Fanzolo 🚉🚌 🕐 Apr–Sep: 10am–6pm Wed–Sun; Oct–Mar: 10am–5:30pm Thu–Sun 🌐 villaemo.org

---

⑩
Asolo

🚌 ℹ️ Piazza Garibaldi 73; www.asolo.it

Asolo is beautifully situated among the cypress-clad foothills of the Dolomites. Queen Caterina Cornaro (1454–1510) once ruled this tiny walled town, and the poet Cardinal Pietro Bembo coined the verb *asolare* to describe the bittersweet life of enforced idleness she endured. Others who have fallen in love with these narrow streets include poet Robert Browning, who named a volume of poems after the town, and travel writer Freya Stark, who lived here until her death in 1993.

Just east of Asolo is the Villa Barbaro at Masèr, while to the north is the village of Possagno, birthplace of Antonio Canova. His remains lie inside the church that he designed himself. Nearby is the family home, the **Casa di Canova**. The Gypsoteca here houses the plaster casts and clay models for many of Canova's sculptures.

Casa di Canova

♿ 🏠 Via Canova 74 🕐 9:30am–6pm Tue–Fri, 9:30am–7pm Sat, Sun & public hols 🚫 1 Jan, Easter, 25 Dec 🌐 museocanova.it

⑪ Caorle

📻 **ℹ** Rio Terrà 3; 0421 810 85 **w** caorle.eu/en

Like Venice, Caorle was built among the swamps of the Venetian Lagoon by refugees fleeing the Goths in the 5th century. Today it is a bustling fishing village perched on the edge of an expanse of purpose-built lagoons, carefully managed to encourage fish to enter and spawn. The young are then fed and farmed.

The area is also of great interest to naturalists for its abundant birdlife. The town's 11th-century Duomo is worth a visit for its Pala d'Oro, a gilded altarpiece made up of Byzantine panel reliefs.

⑫ Mestre

📻 **ℹ** Via Antonio Lazzari 32

Mestre, the industrial offspring of Venice, is often favoured by

> **Mestre, the industrial offspring of Venice, is often favoured by visitors as a relatively less expensive base for exploring the region than Venice or other towns.**

visitors as a relatively less expensive base than Venice or other towns for exploring the region.

Mestre's M9 museum is a highlight of the town itself. As well as interactive exhibits about the 20th century, the ultra-contemporary building houses exhibition space, an auditorium, and a hugely popular restaurant and bar.

⑬ Conegliano

📻📻 **ℹ** Via XX Settembre 132; 0438 21 230

Conegliano lies between the prosecco-producing vineyards and those that produce fine red wine. Winemakers from both areas learn their craft at Conegliano's renowned wine school. The town's winding

and arcaded main street, Via XX Settembre, is lined by 15th- to 18th-century palazzos, some decorated with external frescoes, some in Venetian Gothic style. The Duomo contains a gorgeous altarpiece by Cima da Conegliano (1460–1518) showing the *Virgin and Child with Saints* (1493).

Reproductions of Cima's paintings are displayed in the **Casa di Cima**, the artist's birthplace. His detailed landscapes were based on the hills around the town; they can still be seen from the gardens surrounding the **Castelvecchio** (old castle). A small museum of local history is housed in the castle.

Casa di Cima
⊘ 🅰 Via Cima 24 **☎** 347 105 53 10 🕐 Apr-Sep: 4-7pm Sat & Sun; Oct-Mar: 3-6pm Sat & Sun

Castelvecchio
⊘ 🅰 Piazzale S. Leonardo 7 **☎** 0438 228 71 🕐 Times vary, check website **w** visitconegliano.it/en

⑭ Euganean Hills

ℹ Via Euganea Treponti 98, Teolo; 049 859 50 02

The Euganean Hills rise abruptly out of the Veneto Plain and offer plenty of walking opportunities. Hot springs bubble up out of the ground at Abano Terme and Montegrotto Terme, where scores of establishments offer thermal treatments. These

← Walking through the steep, narrow streets of Caorle's Old Town

spa cures date back to Roman times, and visitors can see extensive remains of the Roman baths and theatre at Montegrotto.

Abbazia di Praglia, the Benedictine monastery at Praglia, 6 km (4 miles) west of Abano Terme, is a peaceful haven in the tree-clad hills. The monks have long been growing herbs commercially and there is a shop selling aromatic wares. They also lead guided tours of parts of the abbey and the Renaissance church (1490–1548), with its beautiful cloister.

The picturesque town of Arquà Petrarca, south of the Euganean Hills, was once simply Arquà. Its name changed in 1868 to honour the medieval poet Francesco Petrarca, or Petrarch (1303–74), who lived here in his old age in a house frescoed with scenes from his poems. **Casa di Petrarca** still contains the poet's desk, chair, bookshelves and mummified cat. His sarcophagus sits in the piazza in front of the church.

To the north of Arquà is the **Villa Barbarigo**, which is open to groups. The real attraction is its outstanding Baroque garden. Planted from 1669, it is full of variety, with fountains, statues and lakes.

Abbazia di Praglia
◈ ⬤ Via Abbazia di Praglia, Bresseo di Teolo ⬤ Times vary, check website
⬜ praglia.it

↑ Villa Barbarigo, a spectacular 17th century villa in the Euganean Hills

Casa di Petrarca
◈ ⬤ ⬤ Via Valleselle 4, Arquà Petrarca ☎ 0429 71 82 94 ⬤ 9am–12:30pm & 3–7pm Tue–Sun ⬤ 1 Jan, 25 & 26 Dec

Villa Barbarigo
◈ ⬤ ⬤ Valsanzibio
⬤ Times vary, check website
⬜ valsanzibiogiardino.it

15

Portogruaro

▦ ▦ 🚻 Piazza della Repubblica 1; 0421 27 72 11; https://comune. portogruaro.ve.it/it

Linking Venice to Trieste, Portogruaro is the medieval successor to the Roman town of Concordia Sagittaria. The town's **Museo Concordiese** display statues and mosaics. These were unearthed in the village of Concordia, 2 km (1 mile) to the

south, where the ruined Roman buildings can be seen around the church and baptistry.

Museo Concordiese
◈ ⬤ Via Seminario 26
⬤ Times vary, check website
⬜ polomusealeveneto. beniculturali.it/musei

LA STRADA DEL PROSECCO

Perched in the foothills of the Dolomites, the Strada del Prosecco (*www.prosecco.it*) connects Conegliano and Valdobbiadene *(p210)*. Meandering past farmhouses and quaint *cantinas*, this route passes by some of the area's best vineyards, and offers fabulous views of the surrounding landscape. Book a driver: not only is the narrow road not for the faint-hearted, it also means that you can stop and sample the wines.

← A striking statue on display in Portogruaro

⑯ Este

FS 🚌 *i* **Via Guido Negri 9; 0429 600 462**

Excavations at Este have uncovered impressive remains of the ancient Ateste people, who flourished from the 9th century BCE until they were annexed by the Romans in the 3rd century BCE. The archaeological finds, including funerary urns, bronze vases and jewellery, are on display in the excellent **Museo Nazionale Atestino**, set within the walls of the town's 14th-century castle. The museum also displays examples of Roman and medieval art, and pieces of local pottery, renowned since the Renaissance period, and still produced.

Museo Nazionale Atestino
⊘ 🏛 Via Guido Negri 9c
🕔 8:30am–7:30pm Tue–Sat, 2:30–7:30pm Sun 🌐 atestino. beniculturali.it

⑰ Montagnana

FS 🚌 *i* **Piazza Trieste 15; 0429 813 20**

Medieval brick walls encircle this town, pierced by four gateways and defended by 24 towers. Just inside the castellated Padua Gate is the town's archaeological museum. The Gothic-Renaissance Duomo contains Paolo Veronese's *Transfiguration* (1555). Outside the city walls is Palladio's Villa

INSIDER TIP
Chioggia by Boat

Rather than enduring the long drive from Venice to Chioggia, why not catch the ferry? The scenic boat journey from Venice Lido to the fishing port of Chioggia takes around 70 minutes.

Pisani (around 1560). Now rather neglected, its façade features the original owner's name (Francesco Pisani) in bold letters below the pediment.

⑱ Chioggia

FS 🚌 🚌 *i* **Lungomare Adriatico 101; www. lididichioggia.it**

Chioggia is the principal fishing port on the lagoon, and the bustling fish market is a good reason to come here early in the day (it's open every morning except Monday). Many visitors enjoy the gritty character of the port area, with its smells, its vibrantly coloured boats and the tangle of nets and tackle.

For those looking to museum-hop, the **Museo Civico della Laguna Sud** is a good place to start. It offers a solid introduction to the lagoon and has a large model boat collection. Art fans should head for the **Museo Diocesano**, where a large collection of religious art, including two Paolo Veneziano polyptychs, is housed.

The town also has many inexpensive restaurants that serve fresh fish; eel, crab and cuttlefish are the local specialities. There is a beach area at Sottomarina, and also worth seeking out is Carpaccio's *St Paul* (1520), the artist's last known work, which is housed in the church of San Domenico.

Museo Civico della Laguna Sud
⊘ 🕔 🏛 Campo Marconi 1
🕔 10am–1pm Tue–Thu & Sun, 6–10pm Fri & Sat 🌐 museo. chioggia.org

Museo Diocesano
⊘ 🏛 Via Rione Duomo
🕔 Times vary, check website
🌐 amei.biz/musei/museo-diocesano-darte-sacra-d-chioggia

⑲ Monselice

FS 🚌 *i* **Via del Santuario 2; 0429 78 30 26**

The town of Monselice stands at the foot of two hills, one of which has been quarried extensively for rich deposits of crystalline minerals. The other is topped by the ruined Castle

→ The towering walls of Castello do Monselice, and *(inset)* its gilded period interiors

Rocca, now a nature reserve. It's worth walking up the cobbled Via del Santuario as far as San Giorgio, to admire its exquisite inlaid marble work.

Other features on the way up are the 13th-century cathedral and the statue-filled Baroque gardens of the Villa Nani, which can be glimpsed through the gates. Nearby is **Castello di Monselice**, a 14th-century castle complete with period furnishings, suits of armour, frescoes and tapestries.

Castello di Monselice

⊗ ⊗ ⊗ ⧉ Via del Santuario
⊙ For guided tours only; times vary, check website
ⓦ castellodimonselice.it

---

⑳

Polesine and Rovigo

FS⊞ *i* Piazza Ciceruacchio 1, Porto Tolle; 042 68 11 50

Polesine is the flat expanse of fertile agricultural land, crisscrossed by canals and subject to flooding, between the River Adige and the Po. The Po Delta is now a national park and has a wealth of fascinating birdlife, including egrets, herons and bitterns.

The most scenic areas are around Scardovari and Porto Tolle, on the south side of the Po. Companies in Porto Tolle offer canoe and bicycle hire and half-day boat cruises.

The modern city of Rovigo has one outstanding monument: the splendid octagonal church called La Rotonda (1594–1602), decorated with paintings and statues in niches.

Adria, 22 km (14 miles) east of Rovigo, gave its name to the Adriatic Sea and was once a Greek and later an Etruscan port. A programme of silt deposition, undertaken to increase Adria's agricultural potential, left the city dry, apart from a 24-km (15-mile) canal. Among the exhibits on display in the **Museo Archeologico** is a complete

↑ Boats moored on a lake near the town of Polesine

iron chariot dating back to the 4th century BCE.

Museo Archeologico

⊗ ⧉ Via Badini 59, Adria
ⓒ 0426 216 12 ⊙ 8:30am–1:30pm Tue-Fri, 8:30am–7:30pm Sat, 2:30-7:30pm Sun

VERONA AND LAKE GARDA

Set within the curves of the Adige river, Verona has been a prosperous and cosmopolitan city since the Romans colonized it in 89 BCE. It stands astride two important trade routes – the East-West route, connecting the port cities of Venice and Genoa, and the Brenner Pass, used by commercial travellers crossing the Alps from northern Europe. This helps to explain the Germanic influence in Verona's magnificent San Zeno church and the realism of the paintings in the Castelvecchio museum, owing more to Dürer than to Raphael. Verona's passion and panache, however, are purely Italian. Stylish shops and cafés sit amid the impressive remains of Roman monuments. The massive Arena amphitheatre fills with music lovers, who are thrilled by opera beneath the stars.

Italy's largest lake, Lake Garda has been settled since the Bronze Age, but it was the Romans, who arrived in 225 BCE and began to develop the lake's southern towns. This lovely area, blessed with a benign microclimate is still popular today, attracting visitors to its charming lakeside promenades. Further north, the Monte Baldo mountain range rises up, getting steeper as the lake narrows towards the north. In its foothills, to the east, is the Monti Lessini plateau scoured by fertile river valleys which drain into the River Adige.

VERONA AND LAKE GARDA

Must Sees
1. Verona
2. Lake Garda

Experience More
3. Soave
4. Montecchio Maggiore
5. Valdagno
6. Grezzana
7. Sant'Anna d'Alfaedo
8. Solferino
9. Bolca
10. Bosco Chiesanuova
11. Giazza

THE VENETO PLAIN
p186

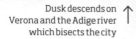

Dusk descends on
Verona and the Adige river
which bisects the city ↑

❶

VERONA

✈ Villafranca 14 km (9 miles) 🚆🚌 Piazzale 25 Aprile
ℹ Via degli Alpini 9; www.turismoverona.eu

Vibrant Verona is the second-largest city in the Veneto after Venice, and one of the most prosperous in northern Italy. A UNESCO World Heritage Site, its ancient centre has many Roman remains, second only to those of Rome itself, and palazzos, built of rosso di Verona, the local pink-tinged limestone. Verona has two main focal points: the massive 1st-century CE Arena and the Piazza delle Erbe with its colourful market, separated by a maze of narrow lanes lined with elegant boutiques.

① ⊘ 🛍

Castelvecchio

🏛 Corso Castelvecchio 2
🕐 10am–6pm Tue–Sun
🌐 museodicastelvecchio.comune.verona.it

This spectacular castle, built by Cangrande II between 1355 and 1375, has been transformed into one of the Veneto's finest art galleries. Various parts of the medieval structure have been linked together using aerial walkways and corridors, designed by Carlo Scarpa to give striking views of the building itself, as well as the exhibits contained within.

The first section contains a wealth of late Roman and early Christian material. The martyrdom scenes depicted on the marble sarcophagus of Saints Sergius and Bacchus (1179) are gruesomely realistic.

The following section, which is devoted to medieval and early Renaissance art, vividly demonstrates the infuence of Verona's Alpine neighbours. Here, instead of the serene saints and virgins of Tuscan art, the emphasis is on brutal realism. This is summed up in the 14th-century *Crucifixion with*

1301
Dante is welcomed to the Scaligeri court, and dedicates the final part of his epic *Divine Comedy* to the ruler Cangrande I.

1866
The Veneto is reunited with Italy.

1913
▽ First Arena di Verona Festival.

1263
△ The Scaligeri family begins their 124-year rule of Verona. They use ruthless tactics to rise to power but once established, the family brings peace to the city.

1387
Verona falls to the Visconti of Milan, and then a succession of outsiders - Venice, France and Austria - rule the city.

1597
△ Shakespeare sets *Romeo and Juliet* in "fair Verona".

Saints, depicting the tortured musculature of Christ and the racked faces of the mourners in painful detail. Far more lyrical is a 15th-century painting by Stefano da Verona called *The Madonna of the Rose Garden*.

After the armour room, take the walkway that leads out along the river flank of the castle, with its dizzying views of the fast-flowing waters of the River Adige and the Ponte Scaligero. Turn the corner to reveal Cangrande I, a 14th-century statue that

once graced Cangrande's tomb. Beyond lie some of the museum's celebrated paintings, notably Paolo Veronese's *Deposition* (1565) and a portrait attributed by some to Titian, by others to Lorenzo Lotto.

---

②

Ponte Scaligero

This medieval bridge was built by Cangrande II between 1354 and 1376. The people of Verona love to stroll across

it to ponder the River Adige in all its moods, or to admire summer sunsets and distant views of the Alps. Such is their affection for the bridge that it was rebuilt after the retreating Germans blew it up in 1945, an operation that involved dredging the river to salvage the irreplaceable medieval masonry. The bridge leads from Castelvecchio to the Arsenal on the north bank of the Adige, built by the Austrians between 1840 and 1861 and now fronted by serene public gardens.

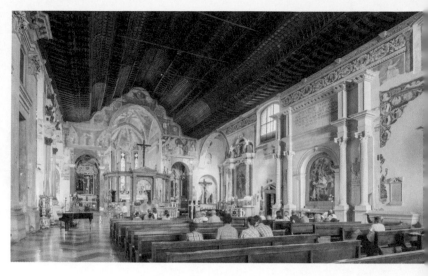

EAT

Enocibus
Close to the Arena lies this friendly restaurant serving no-frills dishes at bargain prices.

🏠 Vicolo Pomodoro 3
🌐 enocibus.com

€€€

Locanda 4 Cuochi
Inventive dishes and seasonal menus, plus fresh pasta made on the premises and an impressive wine cellar.

🏠 Via Alberto Mario 12
🌐 locanda4cuochi.it

€€€

Ristorante Torcolo
Hearty food in lovely surroundings. Dishes include the Veronese classic *bollito misto*.

🏠 Via Carlo Cattaneo 11
🌐 ristorantetorcolo.it

€€€

③

San Fermo Maggiore

🏠 Stradone San Fermo
🕐 10am–6pm Mon–Sat, 1–6pm Sun & public hols
🌐 chieseverona.it

San Fermo Maggiore consists of not one but two churches. This can best be appreciated from the outside, where the eastern end is a jumble of rounded Romanesque arches below with pointed Gothic arches rising above. The lower church, now rather dank due to frequent flooding, dates from 1065, but the upper church (1313) is more impressive. It has a splendid ship's-keel roof and medieval frescoes by Stefano de Zevico. They show the fate of four Franciscan missionaries who journeyed to India in the mid-14th century.

---

④

San Lorenzo

🏠 Corso Cavour 28
📞 045 805 00 00 🕐 10am–12:30pm & 3–5:30pm Sat
🕐 During Mass

San Lorenzo is one of Verona's lesser-known churches, but it is one of the city's most beautiful.

Built in 1117 on the remains of a Paleo-Christian basilica, the Romanesque exterior, with alternate strips of stone and bricks, is typical of Veronese churches. The bell tower dates from the 15th century and inside there are 13th-century frescoes. The church has two unusual cylindrical towers.

---

⑤

Arco dei Gavi and Corso Cavour

Dwarfed by the massive brick walls of Castelvecchio, the monumental scale of this Roman triumphal arch is now hard to appreciate. Originally the arch straddled the main Roman road into the city, today's Corso Cavour. But French troops who were occupying Castelvecchio in 1805 damaged the monument so much that a decision was made to move it to its present position just off the Corso in 1933.

Continue up Corso Cavour to see some fine medieval and Renaissance palaces (especially Nos. 10, 11 and 19) before reaching the Roman town gate, the Porta dei Borsari, which dates back to the 1st century BCE.

←

The decorative interior of the upper church at San Fermo Maggiore

INSIDER TIP
Arena Tickets

There are usually tickets available on the day, especially midweek. Cheap seats aren't numbered; arrive early for a good spot. Take a cushion for comfort and a waterproof for summer downpours.

Museo Lapidario Maffeiano

📍 Piazza Brà 28 🕐 2-6pm Tue & Wed, 10am-6pm Thu-Sun 🌐 museiverona.com

This "museum of stone" is home to all kinds of architectural fragments that hint at the last splendour of this Roman city. There are many intricately carved funerary monuments, and a large part of the collection consists of Greek inscriptions collected by the museum's 18th-century founder, Scipione Maffei.

The Arena

📍 Piazza Brà 🕐 Sep-Jun: 9am-7pm Tue-Sun (Jul & Aug: daily); closes early on performance days 🌐 arena.it

Dominating the eastern side of the piazza is the Roman Arena, Verona's most important monument, still in use today for operatic performances. Verona's amphitheatre, completed around 30 CE, is the third largest in the world, after Rome's Colosseum and the amphitheatre at Capua, near Naples. Originally, the Arena could hold almost the entire population of Roman Verona, and visitors came from across the Veneto to watch mock battles and gladiatorial combats. In the centuries that followed, the Arena was the setting for public executions, fairs, theatre performances and bullfighting. Today its opera productions are world renowned.

↑ Exterior walls of Verona's ancient Roman Arena

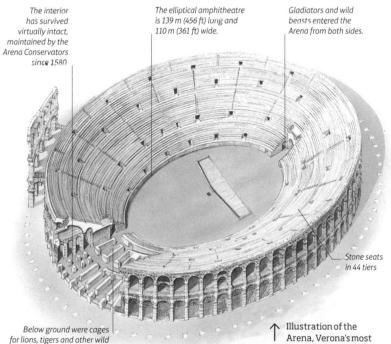

The interior has survived virtually intact, maintained by the Arena Conservators since 1580

The elliptical amphitheatre is 139 m (456 ft) long and 110 m (361 ft) wide.

Gladiators and wild beasts entered the Arena from both sides.

Stone seats in 44 tiers

Below ground were cages for lions, tigers and other wild beasts, and a maze of passages.

↑ Illustration of the Arena, Verona's most important monument

⑧
Duomo

📍 Piazza Duomo ⏰ Times vary, check website 🌐 chieseverona.it

Verona's cathedral was begun in 1139 and is fronted by a Romanesque portal carved by Nicolò, one of two master masons responsible for the façade of San Zeno Maggiore *(p228)*. The highlight of the interior is Titian's *Assumption* (1535–40). Outside is a cloister in which the excavated ruins of earlier churches are visible. The 8th-century baptistry San Giovanni in Fonte (St John of the Spring) was built from Roman masonry; the marble font was carved in 1220.

⑨
Santa Maria Antica and Scaligeri Tombs

This tiny Romanesque church is almost swamped by the bizarre Scaligeri tombs built up against its entrance wall. Because Santa Maria Antica

> In the centre of Piazza dei Signori is a 19th-century statue of Dante, who surveys the surrounding buildings.

was their parish church, the Scaligeri rulers of Verona chose to be buried here, and their tombs speak of their military prowess.

Over the entrance to the church is the tomb of Cangrande I, or Big Dog (d 1329), topped by his equestrian statue. This statue is a copy; the original is now in the Castelvecchio *(p220)*. The other Scaligeri tombs are next to the church, surrounded by a wrought-iron fence featuring the ladder motif of the family's original name (*della Scala*, or "of the steps"). Towering above the fence are the spire-topped tombs of Mastino II, or Mastiff (d 1351), and Cansignorio, meaning Noble Dog (d 1375). Adorned by Gothic pinnacles,

these tombs are a truly unique example of European funerary architecture.

⑩
Piazza dei Signori

In the centre of Piazza dei Signori is a 19th-century statue of Dante, who surveys the surrounding buildings. His gaze is fixed on the grim Palazzo del Capitaniato, built in the 14th century and home of Verona's military commander. Fine views of the Alps can be had by climbing the Torre dei Lamberti, which rises from the western side of the courtyard. Behind the statue of Dante is the pretty Renaissance Loggia del Consiglio, or council chamber, with its frescoed façade and statues of Roman worthies born in Verona, including Catullus the poet, Pliny the natural historian and Vitruvius the architectural theorist.

The piazza is linked to Piazza delle Erbe by the Arco della Costa, or the arch of the rib, whose name refers to the whale rib hung beneath it.

↑ Cobbled medieval streets near the Arche Scaligeri in central Verona

CASA DI GIULIETTA

Travellers love to visit Juliet's house at Via Cappello 23, though it was almost certainly a den of iniquity back in her day, and the balcony was added in 1928. But why quibble in the face of romance? Get your quill and parchment out with the letter-writing Juliet Club *(www. julietclub.com)* or grab tickets for the Estate Teatrale Veronese, a summer theatre festival inspired by the star-crossed lovers *(www.estateteatrale veronese.it).*

⑪
Galleria d'Arte Moderna Achille Forti

🅰 Palazzo Ragione, Cortile Mercato Vecchio 6 🕒 2-6pm Tue & Wed, 10am-6pm Thu-Sun 🌐 gam. comune.verona.it

On the first floor of the Palazzo della Ragione, the Palace of Reason (or law court), is Verona's excellent modern art gallery. The large and varied collection spans the period from 1840 to 1940 and includes wonderful pieces by Giorgio Morandi, Umberto Boccioni and Francesco Hayez. It's highlight is the vaulted Chapel of Notaries, covered in 17th and 18th-century frescoes.

⑫
Piazza delle Erbe

Once the site of the Roman forum, Piazza delle Erbe is named after the city's old herb market. Today's stalls, shaded by huge umbrellas, sell everything from vegetables and lunchtime snacks to clothes and souvenirs.

The Venetian lion on top of a column to the north of the square marks Verona's absorption in 1405 into the Venetian empire. The statue-topped building that completes the north end of Piazza delle Erbe is the Baroque Palazzo Maffei (1668), now converted to shops and luxury apartments.

The piazza's fountain features a statue at its centre that dates from Roman times, a gentle reminder that the piazza has been in almost continuous use as a marketplace for some 2,000 years.

⑬ 🚭
Sant'Anastasia

🅰 Piazza di Sant'Anastasia 📞 045 59 28 13 🕒 9:30am-6pm Mon-Sat, 1-6pm Sun 🌐 chieseverona.it

Sant'Anastasia was built in 1290 to hold the massive congregations which came to listen to the sermons preached by the fundamentalist Dominican Order. Most interesting is the Gothic portal, with its 15th-century frescoes and carved scenes from the life of St Peter Martyr. Inside, the two holy water stoups are

↑ The ornate interior of the enormous Basilica Sant'Anastasia

supported on realistic figures of beggars, known as *i gobbi*, the hunchbacks (the one on the left carved in 1495, the other a century later).

Off the north aisle is the sacristy, home to Antonio Pisanello's fresco, *St George and the Princess* (1433–8). Despite being damaged, the fresco still conveys the grace of the Princess of Trebizond as St George mounts his horse in pursuit of the dragon.

→ The winged Venetian lion of St Mark takes pride of place in Piazza Delle Erbe

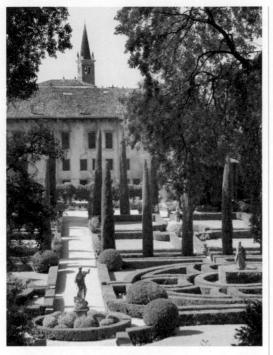

↑ Manicured lawns, elegant statues and clipped hedgerows at Giardino Giusti

⑯

San Giorgio in Braida

🏠 Lungadige San Giorgio 6

San Giorgio is a rare example in Verona of a domed Renaissance church. It was begun in 1477 by Michele Sanmicheli, an architect best known for his military works. Sanmicheli also designed the classically inspired altar, which is topped by Paolo Veronese's *Martyrdom of St George* (1566). This celebrated painting is out-shone by the calm and serene *Virgin Enthroned* between St Zeno and St Lawrence (1526) by Girolamo dai Libri.

⑭ 🎨

Giardino Giusti

🏠 Via Giardino Giusti 2
🕐 10am- 8pm daily 🚫 25 Dec
🌐 giardinogiusti.com

Hidden among the dusty façades of the Via Giardino Giusti is the entrance to one of Italy's finest Renaissance gardens, laid out in 1580. Artifice and nature are deliberately juxtaposed, as with other gardens of the same period, with the lower garden of clipped box hedges contrasting with the upper area of wild woodland.

Past visitors have included the English traveller Thomas Coryate, who, writing in 1611, called this garden "a second paradise". The diarist John Evelyn, visiting 50 years later, thought it the finest garden in Europe. Today the garden makes an excellent, pictur-esque spot for a quiet picnic.

⑮

Santo Stefano

🏠 Vicolo Santo Stefano 2
📞 045 834 85 29 🕐 10am-5:30pm Sat 🌐 verona minorhierusalem.it/santostefano

This is one of the city's oldest churches; the original, long-demolished building was built in the 6th century. It served as Verona's cathedral until the 12th century when the Duomo was built on the opposite bank of the Adige. Visitors can enjoy a striking view of the Duomo across the river, taking in the Romanesque apse and the bishop's palace. Santo Stefano was rebuilt by Lombard archi-tects and given its octagonal red-brick campanile, but the original apse survives.

Towering above the church to the east is Castel San Pietro, fronted by flame-shaped cypress trees.

⑰ 🎨 🏛️

Museo Civico di Storia Naturale

🏠 Lungadige Porta Vittoria 9 🕐 2-6pm Tue-Wed, 10am-6pm Thu-Sun 🚫 1 Jan, Easter, 1 May, 25 Dec 🌐 museodistoria naturale.comune.verona.it

Verona's natural history museum contains an outstanding collection of fossils. Whole fish, trees, fern leaves and dragonflies, found in rock in the foothills of the Little Dolomites, are captured in extraordinary detail.

Human prehistory is represented by finds from ancient settlements around Lake Garda, and there are reconstructions of original lake villages. On the upper floor, cases full of stuffed birds, animals and fish provide an extensive account of today's living world.

⑱ 🖉

Teatro Romano and Museo Archeologico

🅰 Rigaste Redentore 2
🕐 2-6pm Tue & Wed, 10am-6pm Thu-Sun 🅦 museoarcheologico.comune.verona.it

When this theatre was built, in the 1st century BCE, the plays performed would have included satirical dramas by such writers as Terence and Plautus. The tradition continues here with open-air performances at the annual summer Shakespeare festival.

The theatre is built into a bank high above the Adige river and the spectacular views over the city must have

> **The spectacular views over the city must have been as entrancing to Roman theatre-goers as the events on stage.**

been as entrancing to Roman theatre-goers as the events on stage. Certainly it is for the views that the theatre is best visited today, since little is left of the original stage (although the semicircular seating area remains largely intact).

A lift carries visitors from the Teatro Romano up through the cliffs to the monastery above, which has been converted into an archaeological museum. The first part of the museum displays well-restored mosaics, one of which depicts the kind of gory gladiatorial combat that once went on in Verona's amphitheatre (p223). Such performances, seen as a legitimate way of disposing of criminals and prisoners of war, came to an end in the early 5th century following a decree from the Christian emperor Honorius.

In the little monastic cells to the side of this room, visitors can see a bronze bust of the first Roman emperor, the young Augustus Caesar (63 BCE–14 CE), who succeeded in overcoming his opponents, including Mark Antony and Cleopatra, to become the sole ruler of the Roman world in 31 BCE.

STAY

What better place for a romantic getaway than fair Verona? Luxurious, full of charm and a short stroll from the city's main sights, these hotels will add a little romance to your trip.

Palazzo Monga Boutique Guesthouse
🅰 Corso Porta Borsari 36
🅦 palazzomonga.com

€€€

Il Relais
🅰 Corso Castelvecchio 23 🅦 ilrelais.com

€€€

Il Sogno di Giulietta
🅰 Via Cappello 23
🅦 sognodigiulietta.it

€€€

Verona's Teatro Romano and Castel San Pietro overlook the city ↑

SAN ZENO MAGGIORE

📍 Piazza San Zeno 🚌 31, 32, 33 from Castelvecchio
🕐 9am-6pm Mon-Sat, 1-6pm Sun & public hols
🌐 chieseverona.it

Worth visiting for Andrea Mantegna's glorious altarpiece alone, this magnificent church is brimming with trinkets, treasures and priceless artworks.

One of the most spectacular examples of Romanesque architecture in Italy, San Zeno Maggiore is also the most revered in Verona, housing the shrine of the city's patron saint, San Zeno. Built between 1120 and 1138, the façade is embellished with marble reliefs of biblical scenes, matched in vitality by bronze door panels showing the miracles of San Zeno. Beneath an impressive rose window, a graceful porch canopy rests on two slim columns. A brick campanile soars to the south, while a squat tower to the north is said to cover the tomb of King Pepin of Italy (777–810). The cloister, together with the tower, are all that remain of the Benedictine abbey that was demolished in the 19th century.

Did You Know?

Saint Zeno is the patron saint of anglers and is often depicted with fish or fishing rods.

The nave has a ship's-keel ceiling, so called because it resembles the inside of an upturned boat. It was constructed in 1386, when the apse was rebuilt.

Striped brickwork is typical of Romanesque buildings in Verona. Courses of local pink brick are alternated with ivory-coloured tufa.

Andrea Mantegna's three-part altarpiece (1457–59) depicts the Virgin and Child with various saints. The painting served as an inspiration to local artists.

BRONZE DOOR PANELS

The 48 bronze panels of the west doors are simple but effective in their depiction of stories and scenes from the life of San Zeno. Those on the left date from 1030; those on the right were made 100 years later. Huge staring eyes and Ottoman-style hats feature prominently, and the meaning of some scenes remains unknown - such as that of the woman suckling two crocodiles.

North of the church the fine, airy cloister (1293–1313) has rounded Romanesque arches on one side and pointed Gothic arches on the other.

↑ Illustration of the church and grounds of San Zeno Maggiore

↑ The three distinct structures of San Zeno Maggiore

The campanile, started in 1045, reached its present height of 72 m (236 ft) in 1173.

↑ Entrance to the vaulted crypt that contains the tomb of San Zeno

The sanctuary rood screen has marble statues of Christ and the Apostles, dating from 1250, ranged along it.

The nave of the church is modelled on an ancient Roman basilica, the Hall of Justice. The main altar is situated in the raised sanctuary where the judge's throne stood.

The rose window symbolizes the Wheel of Fortune: figures around the rim show the rise and fall of human fortunes.

Marble side panels, carved in 1140, depict events from the life of Christ to the left of the doors, and scenes from the Book of Genesis to the right.

The vaulted crypt contains the tomb of San Zeno, appointed eighth bishop of Verona in 362 CE, who died in 380 CE.

Each of the western wooden doors has 24 bronze plates joined by bronze masks, nailed onto the wood to look like solid metal. A bas-relief above the doors depicts San Zeno vanquishing the devil.

↑ Still waters of Lake Garda, viewed from Limone sul Garda

②

LAKE GARDA

🚆 Peschiera del Garda, Desenzano del Garda 🚌🚌 To all towns 🛈 Viale Marconi 8, Sirmione; www.visitgarda.com

Garda, the largest and easternmost of the Italian lakes, is a favourite summer playground for sports lovers. Strong winds make ideal conditions for windsurfing and sailing, there are numerous yacht harbours and artificial beaches, and luxury hotels offer tennis and horse-riding facilities. The less energetic can explore the lake and shore by boat, while the magnificent scenery of craggy peaks and spectacular sunsets will appeal to every visitor.

①

Garda

🚌 🛈 Mar-Oct Piazza Donatori di Sangue 1; www. lagodigardaveneto.com

This ancient fishing village is packed with visitors in the summer months. But it's still worth a lunch stop. Numerous pavement cafés brighten the streets around the central Palazzo dei Capitani, built in the 15th century for the use of the Venetian militia. Prehistoric rock engravings feature along the Strada dei Castei, an old route above the town. Stroll along shingle beaches, or head to the scenic Punta San Viglio, just 3km (2 miles) out of town.

②

Peschiera

🚆🚌 🛈 Piazzale Bettelone 15; www.tourismpes chiera.com

At Peschiera, the Mincio river flows out of Lake Garda to join the Po river. The main site of interest is a fortress built in the 19th century. Named Fortezza del Quadrilatero because of its square shape, it replaced a 15th-century stronghold. Just outside town is **Gardaland®**, a theme park with roller-coasters, carnival rides, a waterpark, a jungle safari and medieval shows.

Gardaland®

⊛ ⓨ 🏠 Via Derna 4 🕒 Apr-Sep: daily 🖥 gardaland.it

LAKE TRIPS

Lake Garda's two steamers and fleet of hydrofoils serve the major towns around the lake. All have jetties where visitors can buy tickets for a leisurely cruise. Gardens and villas that are otherwise hidden from view can be seen from the water. A trip from one end of the lake to the other takes around two hours 20 minutes by hydrofoil, and four hours by steamer. Catamarans also serve the southern end of the lake.

③
Salò

🚇 ℹ️ **Piazza Sant'Antonio; 0365 214 23**

Locals prefer to associate this elegant town with Gaspare da Salò (1540–1609), the inventor of the violin, rather than with Mussolini, the World War II dictator. Mussolini set up the so-called Salò Republic in 1943 and ruled northern Italy from here until 1945, when he was executed by the Italian resistance firing squad.

Salò has many fascinating buildings, including the cathedral with its unusual wooden altarpiece (1510) by Paolo Veneziano. The main appeal of the town derives from its pastel waterfront buildings, picturesque squares and alleyways, and a long pedestrian promenade with beautiful views of the lake. Salò marks the beginning of the Riviera Bresciana, where the shore is lined with lovely villas and grand hotels set in semi-tropical gardens.

---

④
Gardone Riviera

🚇 ℹ️ **Corso Repubblica; 0365 294 630**

Gardone's most appealing feature is the terraced public park that cascades down the hillside. Planted with all manner of noble trees, it is the perfect spot for a picnic. Equally impressive are the Mediterranean and African plants in the lush **Giardino Botanico Hruska**, founded in 1910, which benefit from the town's mild winters. Gardone has long been a popular resort – the magnificent 19th-century Villa Alba (now a congress centre) was built for the Austrian emperor to escape the bitter winters of his own country. However, the Art Deco Grand Hotel on the waterfront was built for

those seeking fun, frolics and fortune in this beautiful lakeside setting.

Above the town is the **Villa il Vittoriale** – poet Gabriele d'Annunzio's Art Deco villa. It has blacked-out windows (he professed to loathe the world) and is filled with curiosities.

Giardino Botanico Hruska

🌐 🅿️ **Via Roma 2** 🕐 **Mar-Oct: 9am-7pm daily** 🌐 **heller garden.com**

Villa il Vittoriale

🌐🌐🌐🅿️🅿️ **Via Vittoriale 12** 🕐 **Times vary, check website; ticket office closes 1 hour earlier** 🚫 **1 Jan, 24 & 25 Dec** 🌐 **vittoriale.it**

DRINK

Villa Calicantus
Bardolino has long been famous for its light red wine, and this little winery hidden away in the idyllic Bardolino hills produces some of the best in the region. Booking is essential.

🅿️ **Via Concordia 9, Bardolino** 🕐 **Sun** 🌐 **villacalicantus.it**

⑤

Riva del Garda

🚌 ℹ Largo Medaglie d'Oro;
www.gardatrentino.it

Riva's waterfront is overlooked by the moated **Rocca di Riva**, a former Scaligeri fortress. Inside is a museum with exhibits from the region's prehistoric lake villages, which were built by driving huge wooden piles into the lake bed to support platforms. This point on the lake is particularly popular with windsurfers, with equipment available for hire during the summer months. Lessons and guided tuition is also available.

Rocca di Riva

🏛 ♿ ⓐ Piazza Cesare
Battisti 3/a 🕐 10am–
6pm daily 🌐 museoalto
garda.it

📷 GREAT VIEW
Rocca Scaligera

On a clear day, the high central tower of the majestic Rocca Scaligera castle commands spectacular views over the castle, its grounds and the whole of Sirmione, as well as Lake Garda.

---

⑥

Malcesine

🚌 ℹ Via Gardesana 238

German visitors who come to Malcesine trace the journey taken by the poet Goethe in 1788. His travels were full of mishaps, and at Malcesine he was accused of spying and was locked up.

From Malcesine, visitors can take the rotating cable car up to the broad ridge of Monte Baldo (1,745 m/ 5,725 ft). The journey takes 15 minutes, and on a clear day it is possible to see the distant peaks of the Dolomites, including the Brenta range. Footpaths for walkers are signposted at the top. The lower slopes are designated nature reserves; a good place to see the local flora is the Riserva Naturale Integrale Gardesana Orientale, just to the north of Malcesine, on the western side of Monte Baldo.

Piazza Castello

Rocca Scaligera was built in the 13th century by the Scaligeri of Verona. It was designed to trap invading ships, leaving them vulnerable to missiles dropped from the castle walls.

The moat, originally a complex defence system, is today home to schools of carp.

A lakefront café with spectacular mountain views at Riva del Garda

⑦
Sirmione

🚇🚌 ℹ Viale Marconi 8; www.visitsirmione.com

A scenic peninsula extending into the southern end of the lake, Sirmione is connected to the mainland by a bridge. Visitors have waxed lyrical about this area since Roman times, when Catullus described it as a "gem". With its thermal spas, Roman ruins and breathtaking views, Sirmione remains a charming spot and is popular with tourists. The Roman poet Catullus (b 84 BCE) allegedly owned a villa here: the ruins of the **Grotte di Catullo** lie among ancient olive trees at the northern tip. The **Rocca Scaligera** castle stands guard at the base of the peninsula. The castle used to act as a fortress to protect the town against intruders. Beyond the Scaligera, the narrow, stone-paved streets of the village give way to peaceful lakeside walks and elegant spa hotels.

Grotte di Catullo
📞 030 91 61 57 🕐 Aug-Oct: 8:30am-7:30pm Tue-Sat, 9am-7:30pm Sun, 2-6pm Mon

Rocca Scaligera
♿ 📞 030 91 64 68
🕐 8:30am-7:30pm Tue-Sat, 8:30am-1:30pm Sun 🚫 1 Jan, 1 May, 25 Dec

---

THE SCALIGERI

The Rocca Scaligera is one of many castles built throughout the Veneto by the Scaligeri family. During the 13th and 14th centuries, powerful military rulers fought each other in pursuit of riches and power. Despite the autocratic nature of their rule, the Scaligeri brought a period of peace and prosperity to the region, fending off attacks by the predatory Viscontis who ruled Lombardy.

The main keep tower was used for bombarding attackers trapped below.

The inner harbour provided a haven for fishers during lake storms and an anchorage for the castle fleet.

The heavily fortified castle of Rocca Scaligera

The drawbridge is heavily fortified, linking the castle to the mainland and offering an escape route to the castle's inhabitants.

EXPERIENCE MORE

③

Soave

🚌 🛈 Piazza Foro Boario 1;
045 224 02 50

Soave is a heavily fortified town ringed by 14th-century walls, and it is known all over Europe because of the light and dry white wine produced here. The vineyards are located in the hills to the north and can be explored via the engaging Strada del Soave wine route (www.stradadel vinosoave.com). During harvest season, the town buzzes with activity as vintners bring their Garganega grapes for crushing at Soave's factories. Visitors can sample fine local vintages at cafés and wine cellars around the town centre.

Beyond its wine, Soave is also known for its historic buildings. The city walls rise up the hill to the best known of these, the dramatically sited **Rocca Scaligera**. An ancient castle that was enlarged by the Scaligeri rulers of Verona in the 14th century, it has been furnished in period style. The route to the castle makes for a scenic drive, or an exhilarating – though

steep – hike. From here, you can take in extraordinary views across the Veneto countryside.

Rocca Scaligera

🚹 🏠 Via Castello Scaligero
🅲 045 768 00 36 🕒 Mar-Sep: 9am–noon, 3–6pm Tue–Sun; Oct–mid-Feb: 9am–noon, 2–4pm Tue–Sun

---

④

Montecchio Maggiore

🚌 🛈 Via dei Trozi 2; 0444 69 65 46

Visitors to industrialized Montecchio Maggiore come principally to see the two 14th-century castles that stand guard on the hill above the town. Although these are known as the **Castello di Romeo** and the **Castello di Giulietta** (which includes a restaurant), there is no evidence that they belonged to Verona's rival Capulet and Montague families, but they look

53 million

The number of bottles of Soave produced here annually.

romantic and offer lovely views over the vineyard-clad hills to the north.

Castello di Romeo

🚹 🏠 Via Castelli 4 🕒 Feb–Oct: 3–6:30pm Sat, 10am–12:30pm & 3–6:30pm Sun

Castello di Giulietta

🏠 Via Castelli 4 🅲 0444 40 09 79 🕒 Wed–Sun

---

⑤

Valdagno

🚌 🖳 comune.valdagno.vi.it

A scenic drive of 20 km (12 miles) from Montecchio

←

The frescoed interiors of
Villa Allegri-Arvedi, located
just outside Grezzana

EAT

Locanda Lo Scudo
A great restaurant with
pleasant rooms, serving
up mouthwatering
dishes such as risotto
with scallops and
porcini mushrooms.

🏠 Via Covergnino 9
🕐 Breakfast, Sun & Mon
🌐 locandaloscudo.it

€€€

L'Osteria di Via Roma
With tables set in an
atmospheric wine cellar,
this spot offers delicious
and hearty meals.

🏠 Via Roma 21
🕐 Breakfast, Tue
🌐 losteriadiviaroma.com

€€€

DRINK

Cantina di Soave
This charming winery
combines traditional
techniques with
cutting-edge technology
to produce this award-
winning Soave.

🏠 Viale Vittoria 128,
Soave 🌐 cadis1898.it

Ca' Rugate Winery
Situated on dark
volcanic soil, Ca' Rugate
produces a concentrated,
prestigious Soave.
Regular vineyard tours
and tastings.

🏠 Via Pergola 36,
Montecchia di Crosara
🌐 carugate.wine

Maggiore leads to Valdagno,
a town of woollen mills and
18th-century houses. Just
northwest is the Montagna
Spaccata, its rocky bulk split
by a dramatic 100-m- (330-ft-)
deep gorge and waterfall.
The fissure is wreathed in
evocative local legends, and
is open to the public who can
take in great views from the
site's walkway platforms.

❻
Grezzana

In Grezzana itself, seek out
the 13th-century church of
Santa Maria, which (though
it was frequently rebuilt over
the years) retains its robustly
carved Romanesque font
and its beautifully coloured
campanile of pink, white
and gold limestone.

Grezzana is in the foothills
of the scenic Piccole Dolomiti
or Little Dolomites. Close
to the town, at nearby
Cuzzano, is the 17th-century
Baroque **Villa Allegri-Arvedi**,
which is decorated with
beautiful frescoes by
Ludovico Dorigny. To the
south, in Santa Maria in Stelle,
there is a striking Roman
nymphaeum (a shrine to the
nymphs who guard the
freshwater spring) next
to the church (nicknamed
the Pantheon).

Villa Allegri-Arvedi
♿ 🏠 Via Conti Allegri 🕐 For
private hire 🌐 villarvedi.it

←

Rolling, vineyard-lined hills
overlooking the fortified
town of Soave

❼
Sant'Anna d'Alfaedo

🚆 W visitlessinia.
eu/en/The-Lessi
nia/Municipalities

Distinctively Alpine in character, Sant'Anna d'Alfaedo is noted for the stone tiles used to roof local houses. The hamlet of Fosse, immediately to the north, is a popular base for walking excursions up the Corno d'Aquilio (1,546 m/5,070 ft), a mountain that has one of the world's deepest potholes: the Spluga della Preta, which plunges to 850 m (2,790 ft) deep.

Just south of Sant'Anna and more accessible is another natural wonder – the Ponte di Veia, a great stone arch bridging the valley. Prehistoric finds have been excavated from the caves at either end. This spectacular natural bridge is one of the largest of its kind in the world.

---

❽
Solferino

The allied armies of France and Sardinia under Napoleon III met the Austrian army at the small village of Solferino in 1859, as part of what was the wider battle for the unification of the Italian peninsula. The bloody Battle of Solferino left more than 6,000 dead and 40,000 wounded. All of them were completely abandoned without medical care or burial. Shocked by such neglect, a Swiss man named Henri Dunant began a campaign for better treatment. The result was the first Geneva Convention, signed in 1863, and the establishment of the International Red Cross. In 1901, Dunant was jointly awarded the first ever Nobel Peace Prize for his efforts.

In the town of Solferino there is a war museum and an ossuary chapel, lined with bones from the battlefield. There is also a memorial to Dunant built by the Red Cross with donations from member nations.

> ### Did You Know?
> The Ponte di Veia is the remains of a karst cave which collapsed between 80,000 and 120,000 years ago.

> ### THE BATTLE OF SOLFERINO
> The Battle of Solferino took place on 24 June 1859 and was a decisive episode in the struggle for Italian independence. It saw Emperor Franz Joseph's Austrian troops defeated by the Franco-Sardinian Alliance, which consisted of Napoleon III's French Army and Victor Emanuel II's Sardinian Army. It was the last time in history that armies were led onto the battlefield by their monarchs. Following the battle, the Treaty of Villafranca was signed, ending the war between France and Austria, and marking the beginning of Italy's unification and independence.

The Ponte di Veia, an impressive natural bridge near Sant'Anna d'Alfaedo

Pretty Bolca sits at the centre of the Monti Lessini plateau, looking down the valley of the River Alpone and encircled by fossil-bearing hills.

⑨ Bolca

📧 ℹ Via Villa Bolca; 045 656 00 13

Pretty Bolca sits at the centre of the Monti Lessini plateau, looking down the valley of the River Alpone and encircled by fossil-bearing hills. The most spectacular finds have been transferred to Verona's Museo Civico di Storia Naturale (*p226*), but the local **Museo di Fossili** still has an impressive collection of plants, reptiles and particularly fish perfectly preserved in the local basalt stone. The museum first opened in 1971, but interest in the region and the size of the collection increased, so much so that a new building was inaugurated in 1996. Most of the specimens are thought to be some 49 million years old. A circular tour just outside the town (details available from the museum) takes in the quarries where the fossils were found.

Museo di Fossili
🌐 🏠 Via San Giovanni Battista, Vestenanova
🕐 Mar-Oct: 9am-noon & 2-6:30pm daily; Nov-Feb: 10am-noon & 2-5pm daily
🌐 museodeifossili.it

⑩ Bosco Chiesanuova

📧 🌐 visitlessinia.eu/it/la-lessinia/icomuni/Bosco

One of the principal ski resorts of the region, Bosco Chiesanuova is well supplied with hotels, ski lifts and cross-country routes. In summer, there are a number of bicycle routes from which to explore the area. To the east, near Camposilvano, is the picturesque Valle delle Sfingi (Valley of the Sphinxes), so called because of its landscape of large and impressive rock formations.

---

⑪ Giazza

The small town of Giazza has an almost Alpine appearance. Its **Museo dei Cimbri** was inaugurated in the 1970s and covers the history of the Sette Comuni (Seven Municipalities). In reality there are far more than seven little hamlets dotted about the plateau, many of them settled by Bavarian farmers who migrated from the German side of the Alps in the 13th century. Cimbro, their unique, German-influenced dialect, has now almost completely disappeared, but other traditions survive, such as their huge mountain horns, known as *tromboni*, which still play an important part in the town's local festivities.

Museo dei Cimbri
🌐 🌐 🕐 🏠 Via dei Boschi 62
🕐 Jul & Aug: 4-6pm Thu-Sun
🌐 cimbri7comuni.it

↑ Pretty whitewashed buildings in the alpine town of Giazza

A DRIVING TOUR
VALPOLICELLA WINE TOUR

Length 45 km (28 miles) **Stopping Points** The main village of the Valpolicella region, San Pietro in Cariano, has numerous cafés and restaurants.

This circular tour takes in the undulating hills and remarkably varied scenery of the famous wine district that lies between Verona and Lake Garda. On the shores of Lake Garda itself, deep and fertile glacial soils provide sustenance for the grapes used to make Bardolino, a wine that is meant to be drunk young. Inland, the rolling foothills of the Lessini mountains shelter tiny, unassuming hamlets where lives and working rhythms are astutely atuned to the needs of the vines. These particular vines are grown to produce the equally famed Valpolicella, a distinctive red wine that varies from light and fruity to the famous full-bodied Amarone.

*The wine-producing village of **Affi** is surrounded by vineyards planted in the sheltered basin of the Adige Valley.*

*Famous for its light red wine of the same name, the town of **Bardolino** hosts a grape festival in September and has numerous cellars offering tastings.*

Costermano

Garda

Albarè

Caprino Veronese

Rivoli Veronese

Affi

Cavaion Veronese

Bardolino

Cisano

Calmasino

Sega

Lazise has long been the chief port of Garda's eastern shore, its picturesque harbour and medieval church guarded by a 14th-century castle.

Lazise

Pastrengo

Lake Garda

Colà

Pacengo

Sandrà

Castelnuovo del Garda

← Pastel-coloured buildings line the entrance to Lazise harbour on the banks of Lake Garda

↑ Vineyards line the hillsides surrounding
the town of Sant Ambrogio di Valpolicella

Locator Map
For more detail see p218

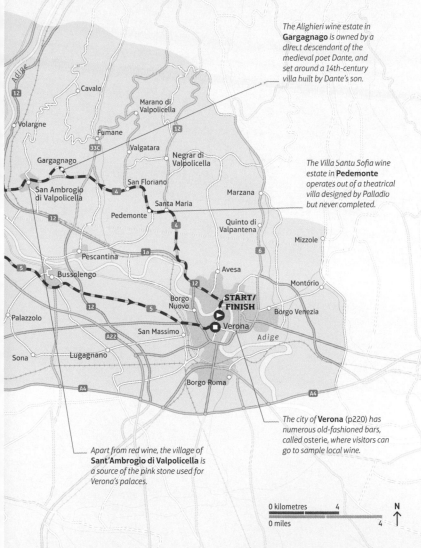

The Alighieri wine estate in
Gargagnago *is owned by a
direct descendant of the
medieval poet Dante, and
set around a 14th-century
villa built by Dante's son.*

The Villa Santa Sofia wine
estate in **Pedemonte**
*operates out of a theatrical
villa designed by Palladio
but never completed.*

The city of **Verona** (p220) *has
numerous old-fashioned bars,
called osterie, where visitors can
go to sample local wine.*

Apart from red wine, the village of
Sant'Ambrogio di Valpolicella *is
a source of the pink stone used for
Verona's palaces.*

0 kilometres 4
0 miles 4

N ↑

THE DOLOMITES

The name of the Dolomites conjures up a vision of spectacular mountains, as noble and awe-inspiring as the Alps. To the south of the region lie the cities of Feltre, Belluno and Vittorio Veneto. To the north is the renowned ski resort of Cortina d'Ampezzo. In between, travellers will encounter no more cities – just spectacular panoramas unfolding endlessly before them and pretty hamlets tucked into remarkably lush and sunny south-facing valleys.

The Dolomites cover a substantial portion of the Veneto's landmass, yet it is easy to forget when visiting the cities of the flat Veneto Plain that behind them lies this range of mountains rising to heights of more than 2,000 m (6,500 ft). Italian is the region's principal language, but in the northwest a German influence can sometimes be heard, reflecting the region's strong historic links with the Austrian Tyrol. Once ruled by the Habsburgs, certain areas of the region only became part of Italy in 1918, after the break-up of the Austro-Hungarian empire at the end of World War I. Some of that war's fiercest fighting took place in the Dolomites, as both sides tried to wrest control of the strategic valley passes linking Italy and Austria-Hungary. Striking war memorials in many villages and towns provide a sad reminder of that time.

THE DOLOMITES

Must See

1 The Dolomite Mountains

Experience More

2 Cortina d'Ampezzo
3 Misurina
4 Pieve di Cadore
5 Belluno
6 Val di Zoldo
7 Vittorio Veneto
8 Feltre

THE DOLOMITES

TRENTINO-ALTO ADIGE

Restalt

Piz de Sant Antone
2,655 m (8,710 ft)

Passo Giau

Corvara

Passo di
Falzarego

M. Averau
2,648 m (8,688 ft)

Arabba

Passo
Fedaia

Marmolada
3,343 m (10,968 ft)

Colle
S. Lucia

Canazei

Pozza di
Fassa

Sasso Vernale
3,058 m (10,032ft)

Alleghe

Laives

Nova
Levante

Falcade

Cencenighe
Agordino

Bronzolo

Moena

Monte S. Lucano
2,409 m (7,903 ft)

Predazzo

Monte Agner
2,872 m (9,422 ft)

Frassene

Molina di Fiemme

San Martino
di Castrozza

Gosaldo

Titelle

Fiera di Primiero

Centrale

Monte Valpiana
2,368 m (7,769 ft)

Mezzano

M. Pizocco
2,188 m (7,178 ft)

Monte Croce

M. Pavione
2,334 m (7,657 ft)

Cesiomaggiore

Bieno

Moline

Aune

Villabruna

Pullir

Borgo
Valsugana

Pedavena

Busche

Grigno

Arina

Cismon

Fonzaso

8 FELTRE

Tovio

Anzù

Arsiè

Seren del
Grappa

Carpen

Enego

Casere

Vas

Stoner

Alano di Piave

Valdobbiadene

Brenta

Pederobba

Col Moschin
1,278 m (4,193 ft)

Possagno

Castelcucco

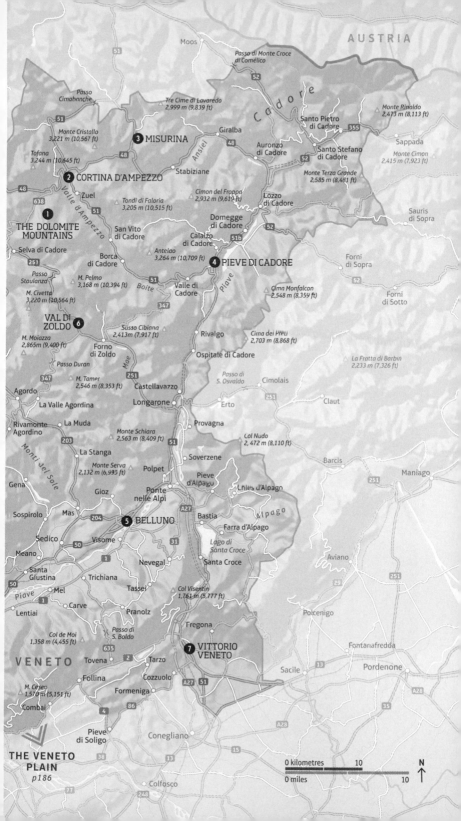

AUSTRIA

Moos

Passo di Monte Croce
di Comélico

Passo
Cimabanche

51

Tre Cime di Lavaredo
2,999 m (9,839 ft)

Monte Cristallo
3,221 m (10,567 ft)

3 MISURINA

Giralba

Ansiei

Cadore

52

Santo Pietro
di Cadore

Monte Rinaldo
2,473 m (8,113 ft)

355

Sappada

Tofana
3,244 m (10,645 ft)

48

2 CORTINA D'AMPEZZO

Zuel

Tondi di Faloria
3,205 m (10,515 ft)

Stabiziane

Auronzo
di Cadore

Santo Stefano
di Cadore

52

Monte Cimon
2,415 m (7,923 ft)

1

**THE DOLOMITE
MOUNTAINS**

638

48

Valle d'Ampezzo

51

San Vito
di Cadore

Cimon del Froppa
2,932 m (9,619 ft)

Monte Terza Grande
2,585 m (8,481 ft)

Lozzo
di Cadore

Sauris
di Sopra

Selva di Cadore

251

Passo
Staulanza

M. Civetta
3,220 m (10,564 ft)

Borca
di Cadore

M. Pelmo
3,168 m (10,394 ft)

Antelao
3,264 m (10,709 ft)

51

Boite

Domegge
di Cadore

Calalzo
di Cadore

51b

52

Forni
di Sopra

4 PIEVE DI CADORE

Valle di
Cadore

Piave

Cima Monfalcon
2,548 m (8,359 ft)

Forni
di Sotto

52

347

**VAL DI
ZOLDO 6**

Susso Cibiana
2,413m (7,917 ft)

Rivalgo

Cima dei Preti
2,703 m (8,868 ft)

La Fratta di Barbin
2,233 m (7,326 ft)

M. Moiazza
2,865m (9,400 ft)

Forno
di Zoldo

Mae

Ospitate di Cadore

Passo Duran

M. Tamer
2,546 m (8,353 ft)

251

Castellavazzo

347

Passo di
S. Osvaldo

Cimolais

251

Claut

Agordo

Longarone

Erto

La Valle Agordina

Provagna

Rivamonte
Agordino

La Muda

203

Monte Schiara
2,563 m (8,409 ft)

51

Col Nudo
2, 472 m (8,110 ft)

Barcis

Monti del Sole

La Stanga

Monte Serva
2,132 m (6,995 ft)

Polpet

Soverzene

Maniago

251

Gena

Gioz

Ponte
nelle Alpi

Pieve
d'Alpago

Chies d'Alpago

Alpago

Sospirolo

Mas

204

5 BELLUNO

A27

Bastia

Farra d'Alpago

Sedico

50

Visome

31

Lago di
Santa Croce

Aviano

251

Meano

1

Nevegal

Santa Croce

Santa
Giustina

Trichiana

Tassei

29

50

Mel

Piave

Col Visentin
1,761 m (5,777 ft)

Polcenigo

Fontanafredda

Pordenone

1

Carve

Pranolz

Fregona

Lentiai

Col de Moi
1,358 m (4,455 ft)

Passo di
S. Boldo

**7 VITTORIO
VENETO**

Sacile

13

A28

VENETO

Tovena

635

2

Tarzo

A27

51

M. Cesen
1,570 m (5,151 ft)

Follina

Cozzuolo

Formeniga

86

35

A28

Combai

4

Pieve
di Soligo

Coneglione

A28

**THE VENETO
PLAIN**
p186

38

13

15

Colfosco

248

0 kilometres   10

0 miles   10

N
↑

❶

THE DOLOMITE MOUNTAINS

ℹ️ Piazza Duomo 2, Belluno; www.visitdolomitibellunesi.com

A striking mountain range in northeastern Italy, the Dolomites are home to bubbling springs, thick tangles of forest, cool glacial lakes, swathes of lush green fields and sunny south-facing valleys. It's the perfect place for some adrenaline-pumping activities. Snow covers the peaks from October to May, and it is possible to ski all year round on Marmolada, the highest peak in the range. However, the solitude of these stunning mountains also appeals to those looking to escape and unwind in one of the areas many alpine spas or mountain retreats.

The Dolomites are the most distinctive and arguably most beautiful mountains in Italy. Unlike the glacier-eroded saddles and ridges of the main body of the Alps, they were shaped by the corrosive effects of ice, sun and rain, sculpting the cliffs, spires and "organ pipes" that we see today. The eastern section is the more dramatic, especially the Catinaccio (or Rosengarten) range, which famously turns rose-pink at sunset.

Outdoor activities in the area include skiing in winter, and walking and rambling along marked footpaths to picnic sites in summer. Chair lifts from the main resorts provide visitors with easy access up into the mountains themselves, transporting you to some breathtaking view points.

GREAT VIEW
Freccia nel Cielo

Take the cable car to the highest peak of Cortina: the imposing Tofana, where a platform affords 360-degree views of the surrounding landscape from this dizzying height.

1 An afternoon at Lake Misurina in the Tre Cime di Lavaredo Natural Park.

2 Alpine ibex roam freely on steep mountainsides.

3 A snowboarder, mid-jump, as they descend the snowy Dolomite slopes.

Did You Know?

Dolomite rocks are known for their cleansing properties, and are used in many toothpastes.

HIKING IN THE DOLOMITES

The Dolomites offer hiking for experienced and novice hikers alike. Whichever routes you plan to do, it is essential to check with the local tourist board that they are safe and accessible before you attempt to hike them. For the more difficult climbs and Via Ferrata, make sure you have insurance as mountain rescue is expensive. Plan the route ahead of time, hike with others if you can, bring appropriate gear and let someone know where you are going.

←

The village of Santa Maddalena sits below dramatic peaks

EXPERIENCE MORE

② Cortina d'Ampezzo

🚌 ℹ Corso Italia 81; www.dolomiti.org/en/cortina/

Italy's top ski resort (www.dolomitisuperski.com), much favoured by the smart set from Turin and Milan, is well supplied with restaurants and bars. The reason for its popularity is the dramatic scenery, which adds an extra dimension to the pleasure of speeding down the slopes. Guests are encircled by crags and spires, thrusting their weather-sculpted shapes above the trees.

As a consequence of hosting the 1956 Winter Olympics, Cortina has above-average sports facilities. There is a ski jump and a bobsleigh run, the Olympic ice stadium holds skating discos, and there are swimming pools, tennis courts and riding facilities. During the summer months, Cortina becomes an excellent base for walkers. Information on the many trails is available from the tourist office.

Visitors can also take the cable car Freccia nel Cielo (Arrow in the Sky), which ascends to a height of 3,243 m (10,639 ft) above sea level.

---

③ Misurina

🚌 ℹ Via Monte Piana 2; www.auronzomisurina.it

Smaller and quieter than Cortina, Misurina nestles by the exquisite Lake Misurina. The lake's mirror-like surface reflects the peaks of Monte Sorapiss and the Cadini group. Take the toll road that climbs northeast for 8 km (5 miles) to the Auronzo mountain refuge and to the base of the Tre Cime di Lavaredo peaks, which rise to 2,999 m (9,840 ft).

Did You Know?

Cortina d'Ampezzo stars as a glamorous location in the 1981 James Bond film For Your Eyes Only.

④ Pieve di Cadore

🚌 ⓦ comune.pievedicadore.bl.it

For centuries the Cadore forests supplied Venice with its timber. The main town of this vast mountainous region is Pieve di Cadore, primarily known as the birthplace of Titian. The humble **Casa di Tiziano** can be visited, and the nearby **Museo Archeologico Cadorino** has exhibits of finds from the pre-Roman era.

Principally, though, this is a base for touring the scenic delights of the region. North of Pieve the valley narrows to a dramatic ravine, and the road north to Comelica and Sesto is noted for its Alpine scenery and its traditional balconied houses. It also winds alongside the Piave river.

Casa di Tiziano

⊗ 🏠 Via Arsenale 4 📞 0435 322 62 🕐 Jun-Aug: 9:30am-12:30pm & 3-6pm daily

Museo Archeologico Cadorino

⊗ 🏠 Palazzo della Magnifica Comunità Cadorina, Piazza Tiziano 2 📞 0435 322 62 🕐 Jun-Aug: 9:30am-12:30pm & 3-6pm daily

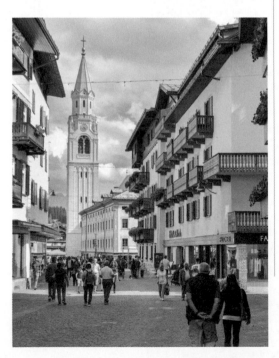

← Tourists walking along the main street in the ski town of Cortina d'Ampezzo

↑ Gorgeous autumn foliage framing an Alpine village near Belluno

5
Belluno

FS☒ *i* Piazza Duomo 2; www.visitdolomitibellunesi.com

Picturesque Belluno serves as a bridge between the two very different parts of the Veneto, with flat plains to the south and the Dolomite peaks to the north. Both are encapsulated in the picture-postcard vistas to be seen from the 12th-century Porta Rugo at the southern end of Via Mezzaterra. Even more spectacular are the panoramic views from the 16th-century Duomo, designed by Tullio Lombardo, but rebuilt twice due to damage by earthquakes.

The nearby baptistry contains a font cover carved by Andrea Brustolon (1662–1732). Close by is the 12th-century Torre Civica and the city's most elegant building, the Renaissance Palazzo dei Rettori (1491), once home to Belluno's Venetian rulers.

The **Museo Civico**, housed in the Baroque splendour of the Palazzo Fulcis, is worth visiting for the paintings by Bartolomeo Montagna (1450–1523) and Sebastiano Ricci (1659–1734). Beside it is the Piazza del Mercato, with arcaded Renaissance palaces and a fountain built in 1410.

South of the town are the ski resorts of the Alpe del Nevegal. It is worth taking the chair lift in the summer to the Rifugio Brigata Alpina Cadore,

←

A bronze statue of Titian that stands in Pieve di Cadore, the town of his birth

which has superb views and a botanical garden specializing in Alpine plants.

Museo Civico

⊘⊘⊘ 🏛 Via Roma 28
🕐 Times vary, check website
w mubel.comune.belluno.it

⑥
Val di Zoldo

🚌 From Longarone 🛈 Pecol; www.dolomiti.org/val-di-zoldo/

The wooded Zoldo Valley is a popular destination for walking holidays. Its main resort town is Forno di Zoldo and the surrounding villages are noted

for their Tyrolean-style Alpine chalets and haylofts. Examples built in wood on stone foundations can be seen at Fornesighe, 2 km (1 mile) northeast of Forno di Zoldo, and on the slopes of Monte Penna at Zoppe di Cadore, 8 km (5 miles) north.

If you have time, a circular tour is a good way to explore the area. Drive north on the S251, via Zoldo Alto to Selva di Cadore, then west via Colle di Santa Lucia (a favourite view-point for photographers). From here take the S203 south through the lakeside resort of Alleghe. The route passes through woodland scenery dotted with pretty mountain hamlets that complement the splendour of the rocky crags.

The southernmost town of the area is Agordo, nestling in the Cordevole Valley. From here, a spectacularly scenic route follows the S347 northeast to the Passo Duran, descending to Dont, close to the starting point of the tour. Wayside shrines mark the route and it is worth stopping to visit village shops selling local woodcarving. Take care when driving along this narrow and winding road.

VITTORIO VENETO AT WAR

Vittorio Veneto was the site of a significant battle at the tail end of World War I, ending on 3 November 1918 with the Italians defeating the Austro-Hungarian troops and effectively ending the war on the Italian front. Over 350,000 troops from across the empire were captured. The Veneto saw many battles and the area is strewn with cemeteries and monuments that bear witness to the fighting that took place in these peaceful surroundings.

Did You Know?

Not all of the Dolomites are composed of dolomite rock. Marmolada, the highest peak, is in fact limestone.

⑦
Vittorio Veneto

🚉🚌 🛈 Viale della Vittoria 110; 0438 572 43

Two separate towns, Ceneda and Serravalle, were merged and renamed Vittorio Veneto in 1866 to honour the unification of Italy under King Vittorio Emanuele II. The town later gave its name to the last decisive battle fought in Italy in World War I. The **Museo della Battaglia** in the Ceneda quarter commemorates this. Serravalle is much more picturesque, with many fine

→

Visitors strolling through colonnaded arcades in scenic Feltre

←

The lakeside town of Alleghe near Val di Zoldo, encircled by mountains

15th-century palazzos and pretty arcaded streets. Franco Zeffirelli shot scenes for his film *Romeo and Juliet* in this town, which sits at the base of the rocky Meschio gorge. To the east, via Anzano, the S422 climbs up to the Bosco del Cansiglio, a wooded plateau.

Museo della Battaglia
◈ ⑤ ⌂ Piazza Giovanni Paolo I ◷ 9:30am-12:30pm Tue-Fri; 10am-1pm, 3-6pm Sat & Sun ⊚ museivittorio veneto.it

⑧
Feltre

FS ▦ ⊚ comune.feltre.bl.it

The Holy Roman emperor Maximilian I sacked the town of Feltre twice, in 1509 and in 1510, at the outbreak of the war against Venice waged by the League of Cambrai *(p52)*. Despite the destruction wreaked, Feltre remained stoutly loyal to Venice, and in return Venice rebuilt the town after the war. Today the main street of the old town, Via Mezzaterra, is lined with arcaded early 16th-century houses. At the striking Piazza Maggiore it is possible to see the remains of Feltre's medieval castle, the church of San Rocco and a fountain by Tullio Lombardo (1520).

On the eastern side of the square is Via Lorenzo Luzzo, a lovely street lined with Renaissance palaces, one of which houses the **Museo Civico**. The museum displays a fresco by the local artist Lorenzo Luzzo, who was known as Il Morto da Feltre (The Dead Man of Feltre) due to the deathly pallor of his skin.

Museo Civico
◈ ⌂ Palazzo Villabruna, Via Luzzo 23 ◷ Times vary, check website ⌚ 1 Jan, 25 & 26 Dec ⊚ visitfeltre.info/luoghi/ museo-civico

NEED TO KNOW

Busy canal on the island of Murano

BEFORE
YOU GO

Things change, so plan ahead to make the most of your trip. Be prepared for all eventualities by considering the following points before you travel.

AT A GLANCE

CURRENCY
Euro (EUR)

AVERAGE DAILY SPEND

SAVE	SPEND	SPLURGE
€50	€100	€200+

COFFEE	BEER	DINNER FOR TWO
€1.50	€5.00	€60

ESSENTIAL PHRASES

Hello	Buon giorno
Thank you	Grazie
Please	Per favore
Goodbye	Arrivederci/Ciao
Do you speak English	Parla inglese?
I don't understand	Non capisco

ELECTRICITY SUPPLY

Power sockets are type F and L, fitting two- and three-pronged plugs. Standard voltage is 220–230v.

Passports and Visas

For entry requirements, including visas, consult your nearest Italian embassy or check the **ENIT** website. Citizens of the UK, US, Canada, Australia and New Zealand do not need a visa for stays of up to three months but, from 2024, must apply in advance for the European Travel Information and Authorization System (**ETIAS**). EU nationals do not need a visa or an ETIAS.
ENIT
w italia.it/en/home.html
ETIAS
w etiasvisa.com

Government Advice

Ensure that you consult both your and the Italian government before travelling. The **UK Foreign, Commonwealth & Development Office**, the **US State Department**, the **Australian Department of Foreign Affairs and Trade**, and Italy's **Ministero della Salute** offer the latest information on security, health and local laws.
Australian Department of Foreign Affairs and Trade
w smartraveller.gov.au
Ministero della Salute
w salute.gov.it
UK Foreign, Commonwealth & Development Office
w gov.uk/foreign-travel-advice
US State Department
w travel.state.gov

Customs Information

Laws relating to goods and currency taken in or out of Italy are on the ENIT website *(see above)*.

Insurance

Taking out an insurance policy covering theft, loss of belongings, medical care, cancellations and delays is advisable. EU and UK citizens are eligible for free emergency medical care in Italy with a valid European Health Insurance (**EHIC**) or UK Global Health Insurance Card (**GHIC**).

Australians should be registered to **Medicare** to receive this benefit. Other tourists are advised to arrange their own private medical insurance.
GHIC
W gov.uk/global-health-insurance-card
Medicare
W humanservices.gov.au/individuals/medicare

Vaccinations

For information regarding COVID-19 vaccination requirements, seek government advice. No other inoculations are needed for Italy.

Booking Accommodation

Book hotels in advance, especially during peak season (Carnival, Easter, June to September, and over Christmas and New Year).

Hotels in Italy charge overnight guests a small, variable tourist tax *(imposta di soggiorno)*. By law, hotels are required to register guests at police headquarters and issue a receipt *(ricevuta fiscale)*, which you must keep until you leave Italy.

Money

Most places accept major credit, debit and prepaid currency cards, with contactless payments increasingly common. Carry cash for small items and for *traghetti* fares. Exchange foreign currency at a *cambio* exchange booth or at banks (for better rates). Cash machines *(bancomat)* can be found in various locations around town. It is customary to tip hotel porters €1 per bag, housekeeping €1 per day and concierge staff €1–2.

Travellers with Specific Requirements

Seventy per cent of Venice is accessible to those with impaired mobility. Most sites are reachable by public transport. However, older buildings may not have wheelchair access or lifts. Most city museums are accessible and some offer induction loops and audio guides for the hearing impaired and partially sighted. Many bridges are fitted with low steps but no stair lifts, while all vaporetto stops are accessible for people with impaired mobility. The main routes 1 and 2 can carry up to four wheelchairs and a discounted disabled ticket costs €1.50, including a carer.

Beyond Venice, all buses of the Mestre urban network and some of the Lido buses have extendable platforms and a designated area within them for wheelchairs.

The **Comune di Venezia** website includes a map of accessible Venice, plus itineraries designed for disabled travellers. **Sage Traveling** is a great resource for more indepth information.
Comune di Venezia
W comune.venezia.it
Sage Traveling
W sagetraveling.com

Language

Italian is the official language, though many speak a Venetian dialect. English is widely spoken.

Opening Hours

> Situations can change quickly and unexpectedly. Always check before visiting attractions and hospitality venues for up-to-date opening hours and booking requirements.

Mondays Some restaurants and attractions close.
Sundays Many shops close early or for the day.
Public holidays Many shops, restaurants, museums and attractions close.

PUBLIC HOLIDAYS

1 Jan	New Year's Day
6 Jan	Epiphany
Mar/Apr	Easter
25 Apr	Liberation Day
1 May	Labour Day
2 Jun	Republic Day
15 Aug	Feast of the Assumption
1 Nov	All Saints' Day
8 Dec	Feast of the Immaculate Conception
25 Dec	Christmas Day
26 Dec	St Stephen's Day

GETTING
AROUND

With its canals and waterways, and no cars or buses within the city limits, Venice is unlike many destinations when it comes to transportation.

AT A GLANCE

TRAVEL COSTS

VAPORETTO

€9.50

One way; valid for 75 minutes

TRAGHETTO

€2

Single trip

GONDOLA

€80

Max six people for 30 minutes

SPEED LIMITS IN VENETO

MOTORWAY

130 km/h (80mph)

DUAL CARRIAGEWAYS

100 km/h (60mph)

NATIONAL ROADS

80 km/h (50mph)

URBAN AREAS

50 km/h (30mph)

Arriving by Air

The main international airport, Aeroporto di Venezia Marco Polo (Venice Marco Polo Airport), is situated 14 km (9 miles) from Venice on the shores of the Venetian Lagoon, just a short bus or boat ride away from the city. A secondary, much smaller airport, Aeroporto di Treviso Antonio Canova (Treviso Antonio Canova Airport), is located 40 km (25 miles) north of Venice. This airport is popular for charter flights and some European budget airlines, including Ryanair, which offers a convenient connecting coach service with Piazzale Roma, Venice's major bus terminal.

To transfer to the city from Marco Polo Airport, you can travel by bus, airport shuttle or taxi, or go by boat from the airport boathouse, in a vaporetto or water taxi. There is little point in hiring a car from the airport, as Venice is a totally car-free city.

For those visiting the Veneto, Valerio Catullo Airport in Verona receives direct flights from the UK, other European countries and Africa. A bus service connects to Verona city centre, and costs around €6 each way.

Train Travel

International Train Travel

Italy's train network is operated by **Trenitalia**. Regular high-speed trains connect the main towns and cities of the Veneto to the rest of Italy, Austria, Germany, France and Eastern Europe. Reservations for these services are essential.
Trenitalia
w trenitalia.com

Train Travel in Venice and the Veneto

The easiest and most convenient way to get around the Veneto is by rail. Trenitalia runs an extensive and efficient network throughout the region, and the cost of travel is very reasonable. Services range from the slow *regionale*, which stops at every station en route, through the various intercity trains to the high-speed Freccia and Eurostar, which link Venice with Verona Porta Nuova and beyond.

Direct lines serve **Venezia Santa Lucia** (Venice's main railway station) and **Venezia Mestre** from

GETTING TO AND FROM VENICE MARCO POLO AIRPORT

Public transport	Journey time	Fare
Airport Bus Express (ATVO)	35 mins	€8
Public Bus (ACTV)	21 mins	€8
Water bus (Alilaguna)	30 mins	€15
Taxi	20 mins	€40
Water Taxi	20 mins	€105-135

numerous northern Italian towns, including Milan, Florence and Verona. Both stations are very busy, with over 450 trains arriving in Venice daily.

Train tickets must be validated before boarding by stamping them in machines at the entrance to platforms. Heavy fines are levied if you are caught with an unvalidated ticket.

Venezia Mestre
W veneziamestre.it

Venezia Santa Lucia
W veneziasantalucia.it

Long-Distance Bus Travel

Eurolines offers international coach routes to Venice and other destinations throughout the Veneto from numerous European cities. Fares are very reasonable, with discounts available for students, children and seniors. **SITA Bus**, meanwhile, offers reasonably priced coach travel throughout Italy. You can buy tickets on board, and services usually depart from outside main railway stations or from the main piazza of smaller towns or cities. **FlixBus** is a low-cost intercity coach network with direct services to Venice from Milan, Florence, Naples, Rome and Turin, as well as from international destinations. Coaches into Venice arrive at the main bus terminus in Piazzale Roma.

Eurolines
W eurolines.eu

FlixBus
W flixbus.com

Sitabus
W sitabus.it

Cruise Travel

Venice is one of the busiest cruise ports in the Mediterranean, with around 500 ships per year and over 700,000 cruise passengers. If you do choose to arrive here by cruise ship, it's important to be aware of the issues that surround this popular mode of transport, and the detrimental effects it is having on the city and its lagoon.

Venetians have a complicated relationship with cruising vessels. Although they do provide local jobs, the average cruise liner pollutes as much as 14,000 cars, damages the already fragile lagoon environment and brings in an unmanageable number of visitors to this tiny city. While their plight was often overlooked by the Italian government, the No Grandi Navi (no big ships) campaign – which called for a ban on large cruise ships entering the lagoon – received support from UNESCO, who threatened to put Venice and its lagoon on their list of endangered heritage sites unless the ban went ahead. On 1 August 2021, an Italian government decree banned massive cruise ships (weighing over 25,000 tonnes) from entering the Giudecca Canal. It is still undecided where these larger ships will be allowed to dock in future, although a new harbour and port is slated to be built outside the lagoon on the Adriatic Sea. As a short-term solution, in April 2022, a temporary berthing facility was inaugurated at Marghera (an industrial zone on the mainland). Smaller cruise ships dock in one of two cruise basins: San Basilio (in Giudecca canal) and Santa Marta (near the mouth of the Giudecca canal), but are also allowed to dock at Marittima (near the main Santa Lucia railway station).

Santa Marta and San Basilio are served by vaporetto line 6, which terminates at the Lido. The Marittima is served by the automated People Mover, which takes passengers to the Piazzale Roma in the historic centre and the Tronchetto parking island. For ships that exceed the new limits and moor on the mainland, cruise lines will need to provide a shuttle bus or other transportation between the pier and the city centre.

Public Transport

Each city in the Veneto has its own public transport provider. Verona is served by **ATV**, Padua by **APS Holding**, Vicenza by **AIM Mobilità** and Belluno and the surrounding area by **Dolimiti Bus**. Safety and hygiene measures, timetables, ticket information, transport maps, and more can be obtained from all of their websites.

Venice has a unique transport system. No cars, buses or bicycles are allowed in the streets, and boats are the city's main mode of transportation. Venice's transit authority, the **ACTV**, operates three different types of water bus (*vaporetti, motoscafi* and *motonavi*) , plus a network of buses on the Lido and the mainland. Most services run between 5am and midnight. Some modes of transport also offer hourly night services.

Belluno: Dolimiti Bus
w dolomitibus.it
Padua: APS Holding
w apsholding.it
Venice: ACTV
w actv.avmspa.it
Verona: ATV
w atv.verona.it
Vicenza: AIM Mobilità
w aimmobilita.it

VAPORETTO ROUTES

Line 1
Zigzag leisurely down the Grand Canal, calling at 20 stops between Piazzale Roma and the Lido.

Line 2
Take a circular route from San Zaccaria (one stop on from Piazza San Marco) via the Giudecca Canal and Tronchetto, then back down the Grand Canal to Rialto or San Marco.

Line 4.1
Travel around Venice anti-clockwise on the outer side of the city, then to Murano and back via the Cannaregio Canal. (Line 4.2 does the same route clockwise.)

Line 12
From Fondamente Nuove, this line calls at a number of Venice's outlying islands, including Murano, Torcello and Burano.

Line N
This night service runs 11.30pm-4.30am daily from San Marco and San Zaccaria to the Lido via the Giudecca Canal and the Grand Canal. It is a cheap and spectacular way to see the city sights lit up at night.

Water Bus

Vaporettos are slow, single-storey water buses that chug along the major canals. They are flat-decked and fully accessible for wheelchairs, prams and buggies, with plenty of seating and standing room. The most popular routes are lines 1 and 2. Faster, more stream-lined *motoscafi* travel beyond the sheltered waters of the city to outlying islands, as do the large double-decker *motonavi* ferries.

Water bus stops are shown on most Venice maps and are clearly signposted around the city. Their yellow and white floating platforms are easy to spot. At stops with multiple platforms, check the boat number you require and the direction of travel. All the departure quays (*pontile*) have route maps and timetables.

Tickets are available from ACTV booths, from machines at larger stops and also at some newsstands and tobacconists. Validate your ticket at the white electronic ticket reader near the entrance to the platform prior to boarding. Note that green ticket readers are "read only" and will not validate your ticket. If the stop doesn't have a ticket machine, you can approach the conductor immediately after embarkation and ask for a *biglietto*. If you are caught travelling without a validated ticket, you may be fined.

Traghetti

These are large unadorned gondolas which cross the Grand Canal at seven points between San Marco and the railway station from early morning until around 7 or 8pm (although they are not all always in operation). They have no fixed timetable; simply wait on a *traghetto* pier for the boat to arrive. Pay cash (€2 per person) to the oarsman as you board or leave the gondola. It is customary to stand up for the crossing, but you can opt to sit if you prefer. (Note that these vessels are not suitable for wheelchair users. Instead, travel one stop on vaporetto Line 1 to cross, as it conveniently zigzags the length of the Grand Canal.)

Gondola

Venice's traditional hand-built wooden gondolas are undoubtedly the most romantic way to see the city, but also the most expensive, used almost exclusively by tourists. There are a number of gondola ranks along the Grand Canal, including beside the Palazzo Ducale and Rialto, and also at busy pedestrian crossings along secondary canals. Each location offers a different type of gondola experience – choose whether you would prefer to experience the hustle and bustle of the Grand Canal or a quieter backwater before you start. Official tariffs should be available at the dock. Expect to pay around €80 for the first 40 minutes, then €40 for additional 20-minute increments. After 7pm, prices are hiked to around €120, and €50 for an extra 20 minutes. However, do not assume you will automatically pay the going rate:

before boarding, agree a price with the gondolier to avoid being overcharged. Most gondoliers speak English and have a good knowledge of the main Venetian sights, art and history.

Water Taxi

Small, sleek motorboats, with polished wooden decking and stylish leather-upholstered cabins comprise Venice's water taxi fleet – an elite form of transport. Expect to pay around €50–70 for a short hop within the city; and between €105 and €135 to travel from the airport to a city centre abode. Water taxis can hold up to ten people, making it a viable option if you are splitting the fare with family or friends.

Bus

In Venice, buses serve the mainland and the Lido only. The main bus station in Venice is at Piazzale Roma near the main train station. On the Lido, route A serves the north of the island, while route B heads south.

City buses in the Veneto are cheap and regular. Tickets, which must be bought prior to travel, are available from newsstands, tobacconists and shops that display the relevant bus company logo in the window. A flat fee usually covers the city centre and suburbs. Tickets must be validated upon boarding.

People Mover

This high-tech elevated People Mover tramway, run by the ACTV, shuttles passengers cheaply and rapidly between the city's three main arrival points: Marittima cruise terminal, the Tronchetto parking island and Piazzale Roma. It runs 7am to 11pm Monday to Saturday, 8am to 10pm (9pm in winter) on Sundays and costs €1.50. Tickets are available at all three stations. You must scan your ticket to validate it at ground level before you can access the tramway.

Walking

Although it is very pleasant to sit on a vaporetto as you cruise down the Grand Canal or visit the outlying islands on one of the big *motonavi* ferries, Venice is a tiny city and all the main sights in the *centro storico* are accessible on foot within half-an-hour of each other, so remember to pack comfortable walking shoes. Beyond the main drag and the must-see sights, it is well worth taking time to explore the backwaters, with their hidden churches, monuments, squares and local bars and restaurants, for a taste of hidden Venice.

Many of the Veneto's other towns and cities are a delight to stroll through as well, including Verona and Padua. In addition, the Dolomites region in the north offers some excellent opportunities for walking and hiking amid stunning mountain scenery.

Bicycle Hire

Cycling is not allowed in Venice city centre, but bike hire is popular on the mainland and on some of the islands in the lagoon, including the Lido. The **BicinCittà** city bicycle scheme has a number of stations for bike hire in Marghera and Mestre, and three on the Lido (at Piazzale Santa Maria Elisabetta; Palazzo del Cinema/Via Candia; and Riva di Giovanni Diacono/Piazzale Malamocco). The first hour is free, the second hour costs €1, then €2 per hour thereafter. Beyond Venice, the city of Padova offers a bike-sharing service called **Goodbike Padova**, with a network of stations dotted across the city. A number of companies in the Dolomites rent road, mountain and e-bikes.

BicinCittà
🅦 bicincitta.com
Goodbike Padova
🅦 goodbikepadova.it

Driving

Car Rental

There are car rental offices at Marco Polo, Treviso Antonio Canova and Valerio Catullo airports and at Piazzale Roma, including Avis, Europcar and Hertz, for those wishing to explore the Veneto or further afield. Some of the smaller towns and scenic drives are only accessible by private vehicle.

To rent a car you must be over 21 and have held a valid driver's licence for at least a year. Driving licences issued by any of the EU member states are valid throughout the EU, including Italy. If visiting from outside the EU, you may need to apply for an International Driving Permit.

Avis
🅦 avis.com
Europcar
🅦 europcar.com
Hertz
🅦 hertz.com

Rules of the Road

Drive on the right, use the left lane only for passing, and yield to traffic from the right. Seat belts are required for all passengers, and heavy fines are levied for using a mobile phone while driving. A strict drink-drive limit (*p258*) is enforced. During the day dipped headlights are compulsory when you are driving on motorways, dual carriageways and on all out-of-town roads. A red warning triangle, spare tyre and fluorescent vests must be carried for use in an emergency. In the event of an accident or breakdown, switch on your hazard warning lights and place the warning triangle 50 m (55 yd) behind your vehicle. For breakdowns, call the ACI emergency number (116) or the emergency services. The ACI will tow any foreign-registered vehicle to the nearest ACI-affiliated garage free of charge.

PRACTICAL
INFORMATION

A little local know-how goes a long way in Venice and the Veneto. Here you can find all the essential information you will need during your stay.

AT A GLANCE

EMERGENCY NUMBERS

GENERAL EMERGENCY	AMBULANCE
113	**118**

FIRE SERVICE	POLICE
115	**112**

TIME ZONE
CET/CEST
Central European
Summer Time (CEST)
runs Mar–Oct

TAP WATER
Tap water in Venice is
safe to drink - water
fountains are dotted
throughout the city.

WEBSITES AND APPS

Venezia Unica
Tourist information for Venice (www.veneziaunica.it).

Veneto Inside
Tourist information across the Veneto (www.venetoinside.com).

CheBateo
Water bus route and schedule app.

iBacari
App listing popular bars in the vicinity.

Hi!Tide Venice
Tide times and heights, to plan your route if the city floods.

Personal Security

Venice is one of the safest cities in Europe. Serious crime is rare. Nevertheless, it is wise to take a few simple precautions, particularly against pickpockets. Leave valuables and any important documents in the hotel safe and carry only the minimum amount of money necessary for the day. After dark, stick to main thoroughfares rather than gloomy alleyways.

If you have anything stolen, report the crime as soon as possible at the nearest police station and take ID with you. Get a copy of the crime report (denuncia) to claim on your insurance. Contact your embassy or consulate if your passport is lost or stolen, or in the event of a serious crime or accident.

As a rule, citizens of Venice and the Veneto are accepting of all people, regardless of their race, gender or sexuality. Homosexuality was legalized in 1887 and in 1982, Italy became the third country to recognize the right to legally change your gender. Due to a rise in anti-immigrant sentiment, some people of colour may experience racism.

Health

Italy has a world-class healthcare system. Emergency medical care in Italy is free for all UK, EU and Australian citizens (p252). If you have an EHIC or GHIC, be sure to present this as soon as possible. You may have to pay for treatment upfront and then reclaim the money later on.

For other visitors, payment of medical expenses is entirely the patient's responsibility. It is therefore important to arrange comprehensive medical insurance prior to your visit.

Seek medicinal supplies and advice for minor ailments from pharmacies (farmacia). You can find details of the nearest 24-hour service on all pharmacy doors.

Smoking, Alcohol and Drugs

Smoking and vaping are banned in enclosed public places, and the possession of illegal drugs is strictly prohibited and could result in a prison sentence.

Italy has a strict limit of 0.05 per cent BAC (blood alcohol content) for drivers. This means that you cannot drink more than a small beer or a small glass of wine if you plan to drive afterwards. For newly qualified drivers who have less than three years' driving experience, the limit is 0.

ID

By law you must carry identification at all times in Italy. A photocopy of your passport photo page (and visa if applicable) should suffice.

Responsible Tourism

In response to the high volume of tourists visiting Venice, the **#EnjoyRespectVenezia** campaign was launched in 2017 to raise awareness of tourist impact and to encourage responsible tourism in the city. The campaign asks that visitors follow certain rules to lessen their impact: walk on the right, do not linger on busy bridges, do not cycle in the city or lead bikes by hand. The steps of churches, bridges, wells, monuments and canalbanks are not picnic areas, nor are busy squares or *campi*. Do not jump into the canals or attempt to swim in the lagoon, except at designated spots. Do not wear inappropriate clothing such as swimwear in the city. Don't drop litter or feed pigeons, and respect the privacy of local residents. Camping is also prohibited in the city, as is attaching padlocks to buildings or bridges, or buying fake goods from illegal street vendors.

In spring 2024 a new €5 tax on day trippers is due to be implemented to help manage visitor numbers from the mainland and provide funds for maintenance and waste management. The tax will apply to all visitors over the age of 14. .
#EnjoyRespectVenezia
🅦 comune.venezia.it/en/content/enjoyrespectvenezia

Visiting Sacred Sights

When entering religious buildings, strict and rigorous dress codes apply: cover your torso and upper arms, and ensure shorts and skirts cover your knees. Shoes must be worn.

Mobile Phones and Wi-Fi

Wi-Fi is generally widely available throughout Venice, and cafés and restaurants will usually give you the password for their Wi-Fi on the condition that you make a purchase. Much of the city has wireless hot spots.

Visitors travelling to Italy with EU tariffs are able to use their devices abroad without being affected by roaming charges. Users will be charged the same rates for data, SMS and voice calls as they would pay at home.

Post

Main post offices are found in the Rialto and on the Piazzale Roma. Stamps *(francobolli)* can be purchased from any tobacconist *(tabacchi)* displaying a black and white T sign.

Taxes and Refunds

VAT (called IVA in Italy) is usually 22 per cent, with a reduced rate of 4–10 per cent on some items. Non-EU citizens can claim an IVA rebate.

Discount Cards

Venice tourist office, **Venezia Unica**, offers a range of different discount cards to make visiting Venice easier on the purse strings. The silver, gold or platinum City Pass, which includes discounted museum, gallery and church entry, is available from €31.90 for children and seniors and €52.90 for adults. For young people aged 16-29 years, the €6 Rolling Venice pass and ACTV 3 Day Youth Pass provide a worthwhile travel discount (€22 for a three-day travel pass instead of €40) plus reduced entry to a number of city sights.

ACTV also offer a variety of discounted travel cards *(biglietti a tempo)*, valid on all ACTV water and land routes for 24 hours (€25), 48 hours (€35), 72 hours (€45) or seven days (€65). They can be purchased at ACTV ticket booths, tobacconists *(tabacchi)* or online. All discount passes can be purchased online from Venezia Unica.
Venezia Unica
🅦 veneziaunica.it

INDEX

PHRASE BOOK

IN EMERGENCY

Help!	Aiuto!	eye-*yoo*-toh
Stop!	Ferma!	*fair*-mah
Call a doctor	Chiama un medico	kee-*ah*-mah oon *meh*-dee-koh
Call an ambulance	Chiama un' ambulanza	kee-*ah*-mah oon am-boo-*lan*-tsa
Call the police	Chiama la polizia	kee-*ah*-mah lah pol-ee-*tsee*-ah
Call the fire brigade	Chiama i pompieri	kee-*ah*-mah ee pom-pee-*air*-ee
Where is the telephone?	Dov'è il telefono?	dov-*eheel* teh-*leh*-foh-noh?
The nearest hospital?	L'ospedale più vicino?	loss-peh-*dah*-leh pee-*oo*vee-*chee*-noh?

COMMUNICATION ESSENTIALS

Yes/No	Si/No	see/*noh*
Please	Per favore	pair fah-*vor*-eh
Thank you	Grazie	*grah*-tsee-eh
Excuse me	Mi scusi	mee *skoo*-zee
Hello/good morning	Buon giorno	bwon *jor*-noh
Goodbye	Arrivederci	ah-ree-veh-*dair*-chee
Good evening	Buona sera	*bwon* ah *sair*-ah
morning	la mattina	lah mah-*tee*-nah
afternoon	il pomeriggio	eel poh-meh-*ree*-joh
evening	la sera	lah *sair*-ah
yesterday	ieri	ee-*air*-ee
today	oggi	*oh*-jee
tomorrow	domani	doh-*mah*-nee
here	qui	*kwee*
there	la/li	*lah/lee*
What?	Quale?	*kwah*-leh?
When?	Quando?	*kwan*-doh?
Why?	Perchè?	pair-*keh*?
Where?	Dove?	*doh*-veh

USEFUL PHRASES

How are you?	Come sta?	*koh*-meh stah?
Very well, thank you.	Molto bene, grazie	*moll*-toh *beh*-neh *grah*-tsee-eh
Pleased to meet you.	Piacere di conoscerla.	pee-ah-*chair*-eh dee coh-*noh*-shair-lah
See you soon.	A più tardi.	ah pee-*oo* tar-dee
That's fine.	Va bene.	va *beh*-neh
Where is/are ...?	Dov'è/Dove sono ...?	dov-*eh/doveh* soh noh?
How long does it take to get to ...?	Quanto tempo ci vuole per andare a ...?	*kwan*-toh *tem*-poh chee voo-oh-leh pair an-*dar*-eh ah...?
How do I get to ...?	Come faccio per arrivare a ...?	*koh*-meh *fah*-choh pair arri-*var*-eh ah...?
Do you speak English?	Parla inglese?	par-lah een-*gleh*-zeh?
I don't understand.	Non capisco.	non ka-*pee*-skoh
Could you speak more slowly, please?	Può parlare più lentamente, per favore?	pwoh par-*lah*-reh pee-*oo* len-ta-*men*-teh pair fah-*vor*-eh?
I'm sorry.	Mi dispiace.	mee dee-spee-*ah*-cheh

USEFUL WORDS

big	grande	*gran*-deh
small	piccolo	*pee*-koh-loh
hot	caldo	*kal*-doh
cold	freddo	*fred*-doh
good	buono	*bwoh*-noh
bad	male	*mal*-eh
enough	basta	*bas*-tah
well	bene	*beh*-neh
open	aperto	ah-*pair*-toh
closed	chiuso	kee-*oo*-zoh
left	a sinistra	ah see-*nee*-strah
right	a destra	ah *dess*-trah
straight on	sempre dritto	*sem*-preh *dree*-toh
near	vicino	vee-*chee*-noh
far	lontano	lon-*tah*-noh
up	su	*soo*
down	giù	*joo*
early	presto	*press*-toh
late	tardi	*tar*-dee
entrance	entrata	en-*trah*-tah
exit	uscita	oo-*shee*-ta
toilet	il bagno	eel *ban*-yo
free, unoccupied	libero	*lee*-bair-oh
free, no charge	gratuito	grah-*too*-ee-toh

MAKING A TELEPHONE CALL

I'd like to place a long-distance call.	Vorrei fare una interurbana.	vor-*ray* far-eh oona in-tair-oor-*bah*-nah.
I'd like to make a reverse-charge call.	Vorrei fare una telefonata a carico del destinatario.	vor-*ray* far-eh oona teh-leh-fon-*ah*-tah ah kar-ee-koh dell dess-tee-nah-*tar*-ree-oh.
I'll try again later.	Ritelefono più tardi.	ree-teh-leh-foh-noh pee-oo tar-dee.
Can I leave a message?	Posso lasciare un messaggio?	*poss*-oh lash-ah-reh oon mess-*sah*-joh?
Hold on	Un attimo, per favore	oon ah-tee-moh, pair fah-*vor*-eh
Could you speak up a little please?	Può parlare più forte, per favore?	pwoh par-*lah*-reh pee-*oo* for-teh, pair fah-*vor*-eh?
local call	la telefonata locale	lah teh-leh-fon-*ah*-ta loh-*kah*-leh

SHOPPING

How much does this cost?	Quanto costa questo?	*kwan*-toh *cos*-stah *kweh*-stoh?
I would like ...	Vorrei ...	vor-*ray*...
Do you have ...?	Avete ...?	ah-*veh*-teh...?
I'm just looking.	Sto soltanto guardando	stoh sol-*tan*-toh gwar-*dan*-doh
Do you take credit cards?	Accettate carte di credito?	ah-*chet*-*tah*-teh *kar*-teh dee *creh*-dee-toh?
What time do you open/close?	A che ora apre/ chiude?	ah *keh* or-ah *ah*-preh/*kee*-oo-deh?
this one	questo	*kweh*-stoh
that one	quello	*kwell*-oh
expensive	caro	*kar*-oh
cheap	a buon prezzo	ah bwon *pret*-soh
size, clothes	la taglia	lah *tah*-lee-ah
size, shoes	il numero	eel *noo*-mair-oh
white	bianco	bee-*ang*-koh
black	nero	*neh*-roh
red	rosso	*ross*-oh
yellow	giallo	*jal*-loh
green	verde	*vair*-deh
blue	blu	*bloo*
brown	marrone	mar-*roh*-neh

TYPES OF SHOP

antique dealer	l'antiquario	lan-tee-*kwah*-ree-oh
bakery	la panetteria	lahpah-net-tair-*ree*-ah
bank	la banca	lah *bang*-kah
bookshop	la libreria	lah lee-breh-*ree*-ah
butcher's	la macelleria	lah mah-chell-eh-*ree*-ah
cake shop	la pasticceria	lahpas-tee-chair-*ee*-ah
chemist's	la farmacia	lah far-mah-*chee*-ah
department store	il grande magazzino	eel *gran*-deh mag-gad-*zee*-noh
delicatessen	la salumeria	lah sah-loo-meh-*ree*-ah
fishmonger's	la pescheria	lah pess-keh-*ree*-ah
florist	il fioraio	eel fee-or-*eye*-oh
greengrocer	il fruttivendolo	eel froo-tee-*ven*-doh-loh
grocery	alimentari	ah-lee-men-*tah*-ree
hairdresser	il parrucchiere	eel par-oo-kee-*air*-eh
ice cream parlour	la gelateria	lah jel-lah-tair-*ree*-ah
market	il mercato	eel mair-*kah*-toh
newsstand	l'edicola	leh-*dee*-koh-lah
post office	l'ufficio postale	loo-*fee*-choh pos-*tah*-leh
shoe shop	il negozio di scarpe	eel neh-*goh*-tsioh dee *skar*-peh
supermarket	il supermercato	eel su-pair-mair-*kah*-toh
tobacconist	il tabaccaio	eel tah-bak-*eye*-oh
travel agency	l'agenzia di viaggi	lah-jen-*tsee*-ah dee vee-*ad*-jee

SIGHTSEEING

art gallery	la pinacoteca	lahpeena-koh-*teh*-kah
bus stop	la fermata dell'autobus	lah fair-*mah*-tah dell *ow*-toh-booss
church	la chiesa	lah kee-*eh*-zah
	la basilica	lah bah-*seel*-i-kah
garden	il giardino	eel jar-*dee*-no
library	la biblioteca	lah beeb-lee-oh-*teh*-kah
museum	il museo	eel moo-*zeh*-oh
railway station	la stazione	lah stah-tsee-*oh*-neh

| tourist information | l'ufficio turistico | loo-fee-choh too-ree-stee-koh |
| closed for the public holiday | chiuso per la festa | kee-oo-zoh pair lah fess-tah |

STAYING IN A HOTEL

Do you have any vacant rooms?	Avete camere libere?	ah-veh-teh kah-mair -eh lee-bair-eh?
double room	una camera doppia	oona kah-mair-ah doh-pee-ah
with double bed	con letto matrimoniale	kon let-toh mah-tree-moh-nee-ah-leh
twin room	una camera con due letti	oona kah-mair-ah kon doo-eh let-tee
single room	una camera singola	oona kah-mair-ah sing-goh-lah
room with a bath, shower	una camera con bagno, con doccia	oona kah-mair-ah kon ban-yoh, kon dot-chah
porter	il facchino	eel fah-kee-noh
key	la chiave	lah kee-ah-veh
I have a reservation.	Ho fatto una prenotazione.	oh fat-toh oona preh-noh-tah-tsee-oh-neh

EATING OUT

Have you got a table for ...?	Avete un tavolo per ... ?	ah-veh-teh oon tah-voh-loh pair ...?
I'd like to reserve a table.	Vorrei riservare un tavolo.	vor-ray ree-sair-vah-reh oon tah-voh-loh
breakfast	colazione	koh-lah-tsee-oh-neh
lunch	pranzo	pran-tsoh
dinner	cena	cheh-nah
The bill, please.	Il conto, per favore.	eel kon-toh pair fah-vor-eh
I am a vegetarian.	Sono vegetariano/a.	soh-noh veh-jeh-tar ee-ah-noh/nah
waitress	cameriera	kah-mair-ee-air-ah
waiter	cameriere	kah-mair-ee-air-eh
fixed price menu	il menù a prezzo fisso	eel meh-noo ah pret-soh fee-soh
dish of the day	piatto del giorno	pee-ah-toh dell jor-no
starter	antipasto	an-tee-pass-toh
first course	il primo	eel pree-moh
main course	il secondo	eel seh-kon-doh
vegetables	il contorno	eel kon-tor-noh
dessert	il dolce	eel doll-che
cover charge	il coperto	eel koh-pair-toh
wine list	la lista dei vini	lah lee-stah day vee-nee
rare	al sangue	al sang-gweh
medium	a puntino	a poon-tee-noh
well done	ben cotto	ben kot-toh
glass	il bicchiere	eel bee-kee-air-eh
bottle	la bottiglia	lah bot-teel-yah
knife	il coltello	eel kol-tell-oh
fork	la forchetta	lah for-ket-tah
spoon	il cucchiaio	eel koo-kee-eye-oh

MENU DECODER

apple	la mela	lah meh-lah
artichoke	il carciofo	eel kar-choff-oh
aubergine	la melanzana	lah meh-lan-tsah-nah
baked	al forno	al for-noh
beans	i fagioli	ee fah-joh-lee
beef	il manzo	eel man-tsoh
beer	la birra	lah beer-rah
boiled	lesso	less-oh
bread	il pane	eel pah-neh
broth	il brodo	eel broh-doh
butter	il burro	eel boor-oh
cake	la torta	lah tor-tah
cheese	il formaggio	eel for-mad-joh
chicken	il pollo	eel poll-oh
chips	patatine fritte	pah-tah-teen-eh free-teh
baby clams	le vongole	leh von-goh-leh
coffee	il caffè	eel kah-feh
courgettes	gli zucchini	lyee dzoo-kee-nee
dry	secco	sek-koh
duck	l'anatra	lah-nah-trah
egg	l'uovo	loo-oh-voh
fish	il pesce	eel pesh-eh
fresh fruit	frutta fresca	froo-tah fress-kah
garlic	l'aglio	lahl-yoh
grapes	l'uva	loo-vah
grilled	alla griglia	ah-lah greel-yah
ham	il prosciutto	eel pro-shoo-toh
cooked/cured	cotto/crudo	kot-toh/kroo-doh
ice cream	il gelato	eel jel-lah-toh
lamb	agnello	la-gnel-lo

lobster	l'aragosta	lah-rah-goss-tah
meat	la carne	la kar-neh
milk	il latte	eel laht-teh
mineral water sparkling/still	l'acqua minerale gassata/naturale	lah-kwah mee-nair-ah-leh gah-zah-tah/ nah-too-rah-leh
mushrooms	i funghi	ee foon-gee
oil	l'olio	loll-yoh
olive	l'oliva	loh-lee-vah
onion	la cipolla	lah chee-poll-ah
orange	l'arancia	lah-ran-chah
orange/lemon juice	succo d'arancia/ di limone	soo-kohdah-ran-chah/ dee lee-moh-neh
peach	la pesca	lah pess-kah
pepper	il pepe	eel peh-peh
pork	carne di maiale	kar-neh dee mah-yah-leh
potatoes	le patate	leh pah-tah-teh
prawns	i gamberi	ee gam-bair-ee
rice	il riso	eel ree-zoh
roast	arrosto	ar-ross-toh
roll	il panino	eel pah-nee-noh
salad	l'insalata	leen-sah-lah-tah
salt	il sale	eel sah-leh
sausage	la salsiccia	lah sal-see-chah
seafood	frutti di mare	froo-tee dee mah-reh
soup	la zuppa, la minestra	lah tsoo-pah, lah mee-ness-trah
steak	la bistecca	lah bee-stek-kah
strawberries	le fragole	leh frah-goh-leh
sugar	lo zucchero	loh zoo-kair-oh
tea	il tè	eel teh
herb tea	la tisana	lah tee-zah-nah
tomato	il pomodoro	eel poh-moh-dor-oh
tuna	il tonno	eel ton-noh
veal	il vitello	eel vee-tell-oh
vegetables	le verdure	leh vair-du-rah
vinegar	l'aceto	lah-chen-toh
water	l'acqua	lah-kwah
red wine	vino rosso	vee-noh ross-oh
white wine	vino bianco	vee-noh bee-ang-koh

NUMBERS

1	uno	oo-noh
2	due	doo-eh
3	tre	treh
4	quattro	kwat-roh
5	cinque	ching-kweh
6	sei	say-ee
7	sette	set-teh
8	otto	ot-toh
9	nove	noh-veh
10	dieci	dee-eh-chee
11	undici	oon-dee-chee
12	dodici	doh-dee-chee
13	tredici	treh-dee-chee
14	quattordici	kwat-tor-dee-chee
15	quindici	kwin-dee-chee
16	sedici	say-dee-chee
17	diciassette	dee-chah-set-teh
18	diciotto	dee-chot-toh
19	diciannove	dee-chah-noh-veh
20	venti	ven-tee
30	trenta	tren-tah
40	quaranta	kwah-ran-tah
50	cinquanta	ching-kwan-tah
60	sessanta	sess-an-tah
70	settanta	set-tan-tah
80	ottanta	ot-tan-tah
90	novanta	noh-van-tah
100	cento	chen-toh
1,000	mille	mee-leh
2,000	duemila	doo-eh mee-lah
5,000	cinquemila	ching-kweh mee-lah
1,000,000	un milione	oon meel-yoh-neh

TIME

one minute	un minuto	oon mee-noo-toh
one hour	un'ora	oon or-ah
half an hour	mezz'ora	medz-or-ah
a day	un giorno	oon jor-noh
a week	una settimana	oona set-tee-mah-nah
Monday	lunedì	loo-neh-dee
Tuesday	martedì	mar-teh-dee
Wednesday	mercoledì	mair-koh-leh-dee
Thursday	giovedì	joh-veh-dee
Friday	venerdì	ven-air-dee
Saturday	sabato	sah-bah-toh
Sunday	domenica	doh-meh-nee-kah

ACKNOWLEDGMENTS

DK would like to thank the following for their contribution to the previous edition: Jo-Ann Titmarsh, Toni de Bella, Susie Bolton, Christopher Catling, Gillian Price, Sally Roy

The publisher would like to thank the following for their kind permission to reproduce their photographs:

Key: a-above; b-below/bottom; c-centre; f-far; l-left; r-right; t-top

123RF.com: efired 108bl; fesus 19cb; Valentyn Volkov 47cla.

4Corners: Stefano Amantini 110-1t; Guido Baviera 148tl, 164t, 185b, 192b; Massimo Borchi 200b; Franco Cogoli 105c, 160-1t, 198t; Olimpio Fantuz 180-1t; Nicolò Miana 164-5b; Aldo Pavan 249b; Maurizio Rellini 13cr; Stefano Scatà 122t.

akg-images: De Agostini Picture Lib. / A. Dagli Orti 159br.

Alamy Stock Photo: AA World Travel Library 177cla; age fotostock / Andre Lebrun 121clb, / Carlo Morucchio 126tl, / Aldo Pavan 31cl; AGF Srl / Lorenzo De Simone 201tr; Duncan Anderson 192cr; Art Collection 2 141tc; Awakening Photo Agency 185tr, / Xianpix / Simone Padovani 47br; Azoor Photo Collection 141tr; B.O'Kane 81cr; Roman Babakin 229tr; Bailey-Cooper Photography 96bl, 125tl; Peter Barritt 112-3b; Bernard Bialorucki 225tr; FREESPACE / Riccardo Bianchini / *Bamboo Stalactite, 2018, installation bamboo 16. Mostra Internazionale di Architettura - La Biennale di Venezia* by Vo Trong Nghia Architects & Inexhibit 27br; Frank Bienewald 10c; Piere Bonbon 149clb, 181bl; Ceri Breeze 238bl; Eden Breitz 88-9t; Dalibor Brlek 207tl; John Burnikell 133br; John Cairns 135tr; Chronicle 51tl; Mary Clarke 49clb; ClickAlps Srls / Moreno Geremetta 245tr; Silvia Cozzi 215tr; Ian Dagnall 232t; Matteo Del Grosso 129br; Peter Delius 147t; FineArt 61tr; Kirk Fisher 184tl; Lois GoBe 97br; GoneWithTheWind 17bl, 116-7; Thierry GRUN - Aero 44-5b; Hackenberg-Photo-Cologne 214cr; hemis.fr / Gregory Gerault 140-1b, / Sylvain Sonnet 60clb; Heritage Image Partnership Ltd / Fine Art Images 58br, 141ca; Kate Hockenhull 90-1t; Peter Horree 141tl; imageBROKER / Barbara Boensch 127t, / Stefan Espenhahn 166cla; Independent Photo Agency Srl 48crb; Brian Jannsen 77clb; Jon Arnold Images Ltd 122cr; David Keith Jones 44tl; Andrew King 197cra; Art Kowalsky 27tr; Joana Kruse 248-9tl; Lebrecht Music & Arts / ColouriserAL 52br; Angel Manzano 159cla; Martin Thomas Photography 204; MB_Photo 193tr; Henk Meijer 66-7t; Hercules Milas 50t, 81bl, 92b, 103tr, 159cra; Mira 166t; Roberto Moiola 247t; Tim Moore 24clb; Russell Mountford 120-1t; Theo Moye 32-3t; nagelestock.com 43tr; North Wind Picture Archives 168tc; Samantha Ohlsen 202-3t; peizais 114clb; peterforsberg 182clb; Pictorial Press Ltd 41br; The Picture Art Collection 105cla, 105cra, 121crb, 142cr; Prisma Archivo 53clb, 78fcrb; Prisma by Dukas Presseagentur GmbH / Van der Meer Rene 124b; Stefano Ravera 169br; Realy Easy Star / Maurizio Sartoretto 208t, / Toni Spagone 213bl, 214-5b, 224b;

robertharding 131tl, / Nico Tondini 239tl; Stuart Robertson 171tl; Riccardo Sala 195tr; Scattolin 108-9t; Scenics & Science 226tl; Matthias Scholz 28cra, 177tr, 182b; Marco Secchi 170bl; Rastislav Sedlak 230t; Gordon Sinclair 48cl; Alan Skyrme 95br; Andrea Spinelli 46b; Slawek Staszczuk 57br,167bl; P Tomlins 43br; TRAVELSCAPES 45cb, 67cra, 87br, 104-5b, 109cla, 133tl,134bl,141br, / © Fondazione Musei Civici di Venezia 179crb; Jorge Tutor 229cra; Viennaslide 103br, 146bl, 150-1b; Richard Wayman 65crb; WENN Rights Ltd 49crb; Scott Wilson 94-5t; James Talalay 161bl; Jan Wlodarczyk 13br, 106-07t.

AWL Images: Alessia Bortolameotti 21, 240-1; Matteo Colombo 115br; Andrea Comi 45br; Francesco Iacobelli 10-1b, 70-1, 190-1t; Ken Scicluna 16c, 72-3.

Bridgeman Images: Cameraphoto Arte Venezia / Santi Giovanni e Paolo, Venice, Italy 121bc; De Agostini Picture Library 51cra, / A. Dagli Orti 51crb, 52-3t, / Veneranda Biblioteca Ambrosiana, Milan, Italy 29tr; Isabella Stewart Gardner Museum, Boston, MA, USA 53tr; Palazzo Ducale, Venice, Italy / *The Taking of Constantinople* Palma Il Giovane (Jacopo Negretti) 51bl; Private Collection 50bl; Luisa Ricciarini 142bl.

Da Fiore: 32bl.

Depositphotos Inc: Iakov 2-3; Isaac74 234-5b; Ody1988 221tc; Xantana 145br.

Dorling Kindersley: Roger Moss 247bl.

Dreamstime.com: Albmex 20tl, 186-7; Anton Aleksenko 56-7t, 65b, 151tr; Kuznetsov Andrey 159tr; Anyaivanova 103tl; Ivan Vander Biesen 60b; Brasilnut 179crb; Mauro Carli 203bl; Anna Chaplygina 48cra; Christophefaugere 153tl; Chun Ju Wu 168-69b; Paul Cowan 162br; Crisfotolux 126bc; Robert Crum 162cra; Daliu80 245tl; Svetlana Day 90bl; Dimabl 178; Emicristea 8clb, 80b; Enzodebe 205cl; Erickn 11br; Fedecandoniphoto 53br; Giovanni Gagliardi 38-9t; Janos Gaspar 244-5b; Giuseppemasci 208-9b; GoranJakus 36br; Zbigniew Guzowski 46-7t; Anna Hristova 45tr; Mihail Ivanov 144cr; Javarman 8cla; Keko64 149b; Jan Kranendonk 86br; Lucianbolca 42b; Olga Lupol 250-1; Makasanaphoto 43cb; Marcorubino 130-1b; Alberto Masnovo 225br; Milosk50 111b; Minnystock 11crb, 17t, 98-9, 128-9t; Monysasi 195tl; NatashaBreen 33cl; Neirfy 54; Njarvis5 31tr; Nullplus 6-7; Andrey Omelyanchuk 83t, 83cra; Ralph Paprzycki 221tl; William Perry 78crb; Photogolfer 19tl, 154-5, 162-3b; Enrico Della Pietra 123br; Pro777 42tl; Rndmst 196clb; Fesus Robert 172-3; Rosshelen 30-1b, 34-5b, 59t, 223tr; Rudi1976 8cl, 220t; Scaliger 84-5b, 158-9b; Jozef Sedmak 103cr; Ihor Serdyukov 53cra; Shunga_Shanga 68t; Michal Stipek 246bl; Toldiu74 11t, 20cb, 216-7; Vvoevale 206bl; Natalia Zakharova 12clb; александр макаренко 236t.

Fondazione Musei Civici di Venezia: 84cla, 85tr, 88bl, 112cr.

Fondazione Teatro La Fenice: Michele Crosera 40-1b.